PRAISE FOR PATHS LESS TRAVELLED

"In his memoir, Hon Lee ta[...] fascinating and inspiring. I [...] from Chinatown, to Vietnam, [...] Acupuncture Clinic where martial arts and Chinese medicine come together to provide healing. It is inspiring because we experience Hon's total dedication to follow a path less travelled as he takes us along to become the Scholar Warrior, The Spy, the Teacher, and the Healer. A good read!"

> – Lieutenant General Ron Christmas, USMC (Retired), Former President & CEO of the Marine Corps Heritage Foundation

"This is contemporary American history at its finest. Hon Lee's world as a young boy is five small blocks in NY Chinatown surrounded by wise guys. He fights as a Marine officer in Vietnam then serves in the senior ranks of the CIA. His lifelong dedication to martial arts saves him not from an outside enemy, but from within, leading him to discover his true calling in medicine. Well written. Enlightening."

> – Ernest Spencer, former commander of D company, 1st Battalion, 26th Marine Regiment; author of "Welcome to Vietnam Macho Man: Reflections of a Khe Sanh Vet"

"An authentic and fascinating memoir from the melting pot, affirming that anything is possible in America for those with the courage to take the paths less travelled. I knew the author during his time in the CIA. He was one of our best, using his leadership and team-building skills, his technical know-how, and his foreign language expertise, to make major contributions to the Agency's mission and to advance to its senior ranks."

> – Jack Downing, former CIA Deputy Director for Operations

"During Hon's career, he was directly involved in almost every aspect of the CIA: human operations, technical operations, analysis, requirements, and budget. This breadth of experience was instrumental in helping with the formation of the Clandestine Information Technology Office and in building a world-class operational organization.

— Jim Gosler, former Director of the Clandestine Information Technology Office, Retired Fellow — Sandia National Laboratories

"Hon is man we can all be proud of and that the CIA sought and still needs: intelligent, curious, with genuine ethical and moral standards. This candid memoir gives insight not only into a great American, but a man that has always sought to enrich his life and the lives of others."

— Jim Simon, former Assistant Director of Central Intelligence

"The term "Renaissance Man" is more often an ideal than a reality. But Hon Lee is indeed a real Renaissance Man - one who not only found depth and success in a wide variety of fields, but also did so with the pervasive soul of a proud warrior. The real-life journey of an urban-American that reads like high cinema, best characterizes the story of Hon Lee. With warriorship and honor as his unyielding spirit, Hon went on to experience all that life has to offer. And for me, his story is so inspiring, that I strongly urge anyone whose dreams feel under threat or whose confidence is weakened by the challenges of life and happiness, to consume his story and drink some of the warrior spirit that we all need and that Hon Lee continues to have in abundance."

— Stephan Berwick, Founder, True Tai Chi™

"A wonderful in-depth account of my good friend and fellow Kung Fu practitioner. Hon embodies the true meaning of Scholar (Mind), Warrior (Body) and Monk (Spirit) of Chinese martial art ethics. I have strived to impart this important philosophy to my own students. It has been an honor to have travelled this path with Hon through all our years of friendship."

— Grandmaster Norman Chin, Jook Lum Gee Tong Long Pai, Southern Mantis Kung Fu

"Hon is a quiet and modest man. To meet him, one might never know the range and depth of his experiences. Indeed, I shared a classroom with him for over two years and did not know this story. With a simple, calm voice, he paints vivid pictures of his remarkable life story. Readers will enjoy his dramatic and visual tale. I am honored to be even a small part of his exceptional journey."

> – Cara O Frank, L. OM, President of Six Fishes Healing Arts; Director of the Chinese Herb Department, Won Institute of Graduate Studies

"Hon epitomizes the classic highly skilled Kung Fu master – calm, centered, respectful - combined with power and grace. His story flows from his modest upbringing in New York, continuing with Marine training and a tour in Vietnam, to being a jet-set CIA operative and finally training in Traditional Chinese Medicine to be a healer in his community. Fast-paced and gripping, Hon's memoir will keep you on the edge of your seat."

> – Bill Reddy, L.Ac, Dipl.Ac, Director of the Integrative Healthcare Policy Consortium, President Emeritus of the Acupuncture Society of Virginia

PATHS LESS TRAVELLED

OF A SCHOLAR WARRIOR *(Spy)* TEACHER HEALER

A personal memoir

BY HON K. LEE

ISBN: 1494756250
ISBN 13: 9781494756253

Library of Congress Control Number: 2013923506
CreateSpace Independent Publishing Platform
North Charleston, South Carolina

DEDICATION

To my wife, daughters, parents, and brothers
To my brotherhood of Marine Corp warriors
To the men and women of the CIA
To all the teachers, masters, and mentors in my life
To all my siblings, students, and friends in the martial arts
To all my colleagues, students, and patients in the healing arts

CONTENTS

FOURTH PATH   HEALER

ACKNOWLEDGMENTS

Thanks to my martial arts brother Henry Hsiang for finding my life interesting and getting me to write about it. Special thanks to Judith Mudd-Krijgelmans, my writing instructor at the Reston Community Center, for her artful guidance, and to my memoir-writing classmates for sharing their stories and encouraging me to share mine.

This book wouldn't have been possible without the editorial assistance of E. S. Dempsey and Jerry Mason. Thanks to Andy Vaart and Michael Joseph Walsh for reviewing my manuscript and offering invaluable advice on how to improve it.

Any mistakes contained herein are mine alone. I apologize for any errors of fact or judgment.

CIA DISCLAIMER

Note

All proceeds from the sale of this book will go to charitable organizations that benefit wounded warriors and their families.

Foreword

Hon Lee writes a poignant and informative memoir in *Paths Less Travelled*. Growing up as "a scrawny kid" from New York City's Chinatown, he goes on to become a combat Marine and CIA operations officer and "returns home" to become a martial arts teacher and Chinese healer. He captures, with enthusiasm, the richness of growing up in the 1950s, and his unique and untraditional journey as a Chinese American. His humor is heartwarming and entertaining as he points to the irony in our lives, especially when our behaviors misalign with our true selves. His stories evoke the reader to reminisce with him on a journey that is not unlike Homer's Odyssey, or better yet, that of the classical Chinese novel of the Monkey King in *Journey to the West*. This book is an eminently readable memoir for all to learn and remember not only our physical journey through life, but also our psychological and emotional transformation in our journey to Nirvana.

Paths Less Travelled also adds to the collection of the New York City Chinatown Oral History Project, intended to capture the stories and lives of those growing up during the 1940s-1960s in New York City's Chinatown. As described on the Project website, "Today, many have had successful lives and productive careers despite the discrimination and poverty that surrounded us, and the limited opportunities and access to the mainstream. Our Chinese value system and Chinatown community kept us strong.... Each of us has had some life altering experience; each has had some fond memory that sustained us.... together we made extraordinary strides as a community. We formed the connections, bonds, and support that have lasted a lifetime." Hon Lee does just that in writing his memoir and capturing the nuanced interplay between his Chinese cultural values and early

Chinatown experiences with his career and his later entry into U.S. mainstream institutions.

Jean Lau Chin, EdD, ABPP
Professor of Psychology, Adelphi University
Former Dean at Adelphi and Alliant International Universities
Chair of the New York City Chinatown Oral History Project

Preface

No love, no friendship, can cross the path of our destiny with-
out leaving some mark on it forever.

— Francois Mauriac

I'm in a happy place. This book is about how I got here. It's about my journey as a Chinese-American boy raised on the streets of New York, who went to war in Vietnam, reached the senior ranks of the CIA, and became a martial arts teacher and Chinese medicine practitioner. It's not an autobiography. To keep the book from being too long, I've left out many events, places, and individuals that are meaningful to me but may be less so to the average reader.

Names of people and places in the stories have been changed where necessary to protect the innocent as well as the guilty. I've arranged these stories thematically rather than strictly chronologically, so I apologize for any confusion the reader may have as a result. Included are episodes I hope will entertain as well as honor those who have enriched my life, inspired me, and sustained my journey.

There are several reasons I decided to write this book. First and foremost, it's meant as a valentine to all the people (whether mentioned in this book or not), whose paths have intersected mine—and delivered with unconditional love, a touch of humor, and profound gratitude.

Second, I hope this book can contribute, in some small way, to the "New York Chinatown Oral History Project" led by Dr. Jean Lau Chin, a project "to capture the valuable memories and stories of survival and success for our children, ourselves, and for history. Despite many oral histories of Chinese in America, there have been few of those from NYC Chinatown."

Last, but far from least, I want to answer questions that I often get, even from people I've known for years. Questions like: "How could you go from being a combat Marine to a qigong teacher, and from being a clandestine operations officer to an acupuncturist? How did you switch roles, and what's one got to do with the other?"

"Hon, I can't believe you were a Marine; you just don't fit the image," my qigong student once remarked. "You say you worked undercover for the CIA? And now you practice Chinese medicine. How'd you go from being a 'trained killer' to preaching love, kindness, and forgiveness?" she asked, only half-jokingly.

I hope this memoir will answer those questions by tying together these seemingly paradoxical paths and showing that they're interconnected and mutually supportive. The starting point is New York's Chinatown where I, growing up as a scrawny kid, and yearning to be like the kung fu heroes I saw at Sun Sing Theater on East Broadway, took up the martial arts. Forever trying to prove myself, I joined the Marines to show I had what it took to wear the eagle, globe, and anchor. Military service whetted my appetite for overseas travel, foreign cultures, and new experiences. The CIA offered a logical progression after active duty, opening the door to a life of challenge, excitement, and adventure, while enabling me to explore my Asian heritage. And who could resist playing James Bond? While living and traveling throughout Asia, whenever I wasn't working, I took every opportunity to befriend experts in what would become my life's greatest passions: Chinese martial arts and Chinese medicine. These life paths sometimes crossed, often converged, but ultimately led back to my cultural roots. Along the way I discovered my life purpose.

CHINESE ROOTS
AND AMERICAN BRANCHES

CHAPTER 1

FROM CRANE MOUNTAIN

Though we travel the world over to find the beautiful, we must carry it with us or find it not.

—RALPH WALDO EMERSON

My parents named me Hon Kwong Lee. I hated it. Unlike many Chinese -Americans, my parents never gave me an Anglo name. Thinking my name was too short, I begged my parents to change it to Alexander—wanting to be like Alexander the Great, to ride an elephant across the Alps, and carry a big sword, slaying bad guys along the way.

In Chinese, Hon is a word synonymous with the Chinese people. Kwong means bright or shining. All third-generation male descendants in my family have Kwong as their middle name. Lee is a common Chinese surname, like Smith or Jones. I was born in Brooklyn on October 10, 1943. Chinese communities across the world celebrate Double Ten to commemorate the October 10, 1911, revolution against the Manchu-controlled Qing Dynasty and the establishment of a republic. My parents thought it was auspicious that I was born on a Chinese holiday. Did they see the rebellious streak in me then? The one that predisposed me to life paths different from those they would have chosen for me? But I'm getting ahead of the story.

Three years before I came into this world, my mother, Soo Ying, and brothers Bork and Yun left their native China to join my father in America. They set sail from the southern port of Guangzhou, waving good-bye to friends and relatives at the pier. Gum Jie, the boys' beloved nanny, standing on the dock and likely sensing this might be the last time she'd ever see them, wiped away the tears flowing down her chubby cheeks.

It had taken a whole day for them to get from Crane Mountain, their ancestral home, to the ship. They hadn't eaten since breakfast. Bork and his younger brother Yun, unsteadily holding onto the handrails as they walked down the cargo ship's steel gray passageway, stumbled into a crewmember. The sailor, in a foul mood, growled at them. The ship's captain had denied the crew shore leave in Guangzhou due to a smallpox outbreak. The sailor was the first white man the boys had ever encountered. His shaggy red beard, hooked nose, and bushy eyebrows looked menacing.

Bork drew up enough courage to blurt out, "Baah led, baah led!" The sailor took a step back, afraid of getting too close to the younger lad, the one with the pockmarked face. "What? Speak up, ya dam Chai nee!" he shouted. "Baah led," Bork said, this time louder. The sailor shrugged his shoulders. Bork opened his left palm, brushed it back and forth with his right, then raised both hands to his mouth and pretended to chew. "Oh, I get it. You want something to eat," the sailor said as he led the boys to the galley and ladled out two cups of hot soup. On the counter, Yun spotted what he knew Mama would like: a loaf of white bread and a jar of orange marmalade.

Mama smiled when they returned, glad they had gotten what she wanted. Bread was the first Western food she'd ever tasted and the only English word she knew. She made Bork repeat the word "baah...led" until satisfied he could pronounce it the way she thought it should sound. The boys had been seasick, unable to stomach the Western lunch served aboard. She hoped they'd be able to keep some bread down.

SALT FISH FOR SALE

Mama, born in 1908 on the outskirts of Guangzhou to a poor family, met my father (Baba) through a classmate. Baba, the son of a Chinese immigrant from New York, was attending Pui Jing Academy in Guangzhou, an exclusive boarding school. Baba was there to find his roots and improve his Chinese language skills.

After their marriage, Mama moved to her in-laws' family compound, enjoying creature comforts for the first time. With servants to take care of the kids and do housework, she had time to learn how to play the pipa and piano. Her in-laws introduced her to things that others thought mundane but she found exciting. To her, eating toast with jam and butter was an exotic treat.

My parents in the 1940s

Once Baba completed his studies in China, he returned to America but couldn't bring Mama and my brothers with him because of the Chinese

Exclusion Act.[1] When they finally landed in America, after waiting over ten years, Mama discovered that life in Gum San (or "Gold Mountain," as America was known to the Chinese then) was not what she'd expected. Leaving the protected environment of her in-laws' household and starting a new life in a strange land with two young boys was challenging.

Her transition was made easier when Baba rented an apartment in New York's Chinatown, an ethnic enclave populated with others from the towns and villages of Guangdong Province in southern China. She could shop for food and everyday items without uttering a word of English.

Their first apartment was a one-bedroom along the Bowery, right above a bar. At night, curtains couldn't block out the flashing neon sign that hung just outside their bedroom window. The sound of drunken laughter and the crash of beer bottles made sleeping difficult. The bar's jukebox blared out songs with lyrics she couldn't decipher. "Smoke Gets in Your Eyes," with its haunting melody, became Mama's favorite tune. Since she couldn't figure out the words, she made up her own refrain. It came out "Mai Haam Yuu Lieh!" which, in Cantonese, means, "salt fish for sale!"

Mama in the 1940s

---

1   The Chinese Exclusion Act was a US federal law enacted in the 1880s that allowed the United States to suspend Chinese immigration, a ban that was intended to last ten years. This law was repealed by the Magnuson Act on December 17, 1943. (From: http://ocp.hul.harvard.edu/immigration/exclusion.html)

FINDING HER PASSION

Once I was old enough to stay home alone or with a neighbor after school, Mama had time to pursue her own interests and went to school to become a beautician, studying hard to pass her licensing exams. It gave her a steady income and newfound independence. This was important since she always felt the need to stash away an emergency fund. Growing up poor, she would be forever frugal no matter what measure of financial security she achieved later in life. She worked at a friend's beauty parlor in Chinatown and then at the Abraham & Strauss department store's beauty salon in downtown Brooklyn. She enjoyed the chance to meet people outside the Chinese community. Mama's dream, to own her own shop, never materialized.

A GOOD AND GENTLE MAN

Baba, known to his American friends as Jimmy, was born in New York City on November 27, 1908. He was tall by Chinese standards, around six feet. Mama thought he was handsome and reminded her of Victor Mature, a popular movie star of that era.

Baba visited his new family in China as often as he could, but it was expensive, and each trip took a long time. He worked hard to save money, managing the family business during the day and working at a Chinese restaurant in the evening. Through the good offices of a sympathetic New York congressman, he was able to bring Mama and my brothers to America three years before the Chinese Exclusion Act was repealed.

Grandfather started two businesses in Chinatown: Yat Ga Min Chinese Noodle Factory and Lee & Lee's. Uncle Young, son of grandfather's first wife, managed Yat Ga Min. It was the first business to manufacture and distribute fresh egg noodles to Chinese restaurants throughout the New York metropolitan area. Baba ran Lee & Lee's, which made almond cookies and peanut candy. When I was small, I loved visiting the cookie factory, which was about a ten-minute walk from our house. I can still smell the sweet aroma of freshly baked cookies and candy coming out of their oven.

KEEPING COOL

"Your father's a murderer. He killed my grandpa!" screamed Mini Tang over and over. I cringed as her shrill voice echoed in the school hallway. If there was one superpower I wanted then, it was invisibility. As I ducked down the stairwell, she hounded me with her taunting refrain.

We were grade-schoolers and, like many Chinatown kids, attended an afterschool program at the Wah Kue Hok Hao (Overseas Chinese School) on Mott Street to learn how to read and write the language of our immigrant parents.

Every time she spotted me, Mini would start spewing lies about Baba. After a while it got so routine that nobody paid attention. But it embarrassed me nonetheless. I suppressed the urge to shake the venom from her, realizing that she didn't know any better, that she was merely parroting what her grandma Bertha was saying had caused the death of her husband, Cecil Tang. The portly Mr. Tang had died of a heart attack, most likely from eating too many greasy egg rolls from the kitchen of his own restaurant. But Bertha said the heart attack was caused by the stress he had suffered when his restaurant went under. She blamed it all on Baba.

Up until then, Baba enjoyed working at Tang's, enjoyed greeting stage and screen celebrities dining at the restaurant just off Broadway and near the theater district. But Mama disliked her husband hobnobbing with flirty actresses.

Extremely jealous, regularly searching my father's pockets for telltale signs of philandering, she once found a telephone number on the back of a matchbook that was scribbled, she suspected, by a woman's delicate hand. The fireworks began before Baba had a chance to close the front door that evening. Mama yelled and cried, accusing Baba of seeing another woman. My brother Yun tried to calm Mama down, telling her women were not throwing themselves at Baba, and that it was all in her mind.

"Look Ma, you gotta be nuts. He's just a poor 'Chinaman' to them. Why would they want to have anything to do with him?" Yun could be brutally honest.

"You jus dong know, I tell you! They think he got money!" Mama shot back.

Baba in front of Tang's Restaurant

Baba, starting as a waiter in Tang's Chinatown restaurant, had worked his way up to general manager for Tang's uptown branch just as the once-thriving business went sour. Old Man Tang defended Baba even as his wife, Bertha, turned against him. Adding insult to injury, although Baba hadn't been on the board of directors, creditors went after him and anyone else they could get to pay the bills. Because of this, Baba was himself forced to declare bankruptcy. A gentle man and a gentleman, I admired the way Baba took Bertha's criticism without losing his temper. When I asked how he was able remain so unflappable in the face of all his problems, he handed me a folded piece of paper from his wallet. Unfolding the sheet, yellowed by age, I found a poem by Rudyard Kipling, one I was too young then to appreciate. But as I grew older, and as I weathered life's inevitable storms, it would help me stay on course.

IF

If you can keep your head when all about you
Are losing theirs and blaming it on you,
If you can trust yourself when all men doubt you,
But make allowance for their doubting too;
If you can wait and not be tired by waiting,
Or being lied about, don't deal in lies,
Or being hated, don't give way to hating,
And yet don't look too good, nor talk too wise:

If you can dream—and not make dreams your master;
If you can think—and not make thoughts your aim;
If you can meet with Triumph and Disaster
And treat those two impostors just the same;
If you can bear to hear the truth you've spoken
Twisted by knaves to make a trap for fools,
Or watch the things you gave your life to, broken,
And stoop and build 'em up with worn-out tools:

If you can make one heap of all your winnings
And risk it on one turn of pitch-and-toss,
And lose, and start again at your beginnings
And never breathe a word about your loss;
If you can force your heart and nerve and sinew
To serve your turn long after they are gone,
And so hold on when there is nothing in you
Except the Will which says to them: 'Hold on!'

If you can talk with crowds and keep your virtue,
Or walk with Kings—nor lose the common touch,
If neither foes nor loving friends can hurt you,
If all men count with you, but none too much;
If you can fill the unforgiving minute
With sixty seconds' worth of distance run,
Yours is the Earth and everything that's in it,
And—which is more—you'll be a Man, my son!

Because of his generosity, easygoing personality, and genial manner, Baba made friends easily, coming into contact with people from all walks of life because of his work. From the cooks and drivers who worked for him to the bosses and customers he served, he treated everyone with dignity, respect, and courtesy. He seldom turned down a request from his workers for time off or an advance on salary. He remembered the names and birthdays of his staff. If you sat at the dinner table with him, he'd make sure you were served first and that your plate would always be full. He told me "everyone wants to feel appreciated" and said this was his secret to getting along with others.

While he was a good people-person, Baba wasn't much of a businessman. After the demise of Tang's Restaurant, he and a Jewish partner started a company called Me Too that manufactured kosher chicken chow mein from an unappetizing assortment of dehydrated ingredients I helped stuff into tiny cellophane bags after school. After a while Baba had a falling out with his partner and sold his share. His last job before retiring was managing a popular Chinese restaurant on Long Island owned by a former Chinese general from Taiwan. He enjoyed working for the owner and his wife because they treated him well.

It was probably good for him to work for someone else rather than manage his own business because of his one addiction: he loved to bet on the ponies. Mama said he would have gambled away the family's savings had she not religiously squirreled away money she was able to keep from him. She scolded him endlessly—but to no avail—to stop going to the track.

But eventually she resigned herself to allowing her husband his only diver-
sion. After all, she reasoned, he worked night and day holding down two or
three jobs. Why not let him have a little fun?

The sport of kings, Baba liked to say, was his favorite pastime. He and
Uncle Henry set off for the racetrack on their rare days off, sometimes dragging Mama and me along for the ride. At first I didn't mind it when we
detoured to the track on our way to the Jersey Shore for a week or weekend.
We'd stop for a couple of hours while Baba and Uncle Henry had a good
time. Anxiously awaiting their return so we could head off again, I was
bored sitting outside the track throughout all the races, kicking gravel in
the hot and dusty parking lot, listening to the roar from the stands, unable
to see what was happening, unable to go in because I was too young. Game
Boys and iPods hadn't been invented yet, and only the promise of a triple
dip chocolate chip cone if I was patient would placate me, but just barely.
The experience did have one lasting effect: it turned me off to gambling—
that is, if you don't count the purchase of an occasional Powerball ticket.

Baba and me

Although not a calligrapher himself, Baba admired good Chinese calligraphy, the flow of black ink on a white paper, and the calligrapher's artistic motions. At gatherings, when invited to express the art through pantomime, he'd stand up with focused attention to recreate the physical and emotional intensity of a famous master calligrapher by picking up a large imaginary brush, slowly dipping it into imaginary ink, and drawing a giant character on imaginary rice paper. After five minutes of this play-acting, beads of sweat dripped down his forehead. He also practiced an ancient Chinese exercise where you tense different parts of your body to strengthen your muscles, ligaments, and tendons. This was Yi Jin Jing, a form of qigong from the Shaolin Temple—one I'd have a chance to study many years later.

He did a few other things I thought odd at the time, like the way he'd drink a glass of milk, actually chewing each liquid mouthful two or three times before swallowing. I've since learned that chewing activates salivary enzymes to promote good digestion. Baba was in good physical shape but probably drank too much milk. That and his love for pork chops ultimately led to his downfall. Pork chops was the last meal Mama served him the night he died from a heart attack. He was only seventy-two years old.

BROTHERLY RECOLLECTIONS

My brothers Bork and Yun, respectively fifteen and ten years older than me, were my childhood heroes—except when Bork embarrassed me by telling my friends he used to change my diapers and when Yun acted as my disciplinarian. With Baba busy working several jobs and Mama employed as well, my brothers provided me the guidance parents normally doled out. Their personalities were polar opposites. Bork was an extrovert with an active social life. Yun was an introvert who didn't go out much. Both were intelligent in different ways. When they were kids, Mama got a kick out of Yun telling her, "Bork may be smart, but I'm shrewd, and shrewd is smarter than smart."

Mr. Popularity

Even as a youngster, Bork always seemed to know what to say. For example, he responded to a tricky question posed by an immigration officer who asked him, "If China and America went to war, which side would you fight on?" After a few moments of contemplation, the twelve-year-old Bork answered confidently, "I wouldn't fight!" The immigration officer chuckled, patted him on the head, and said Bork would have a bright future.

Like my father, Bork had a knack for making others feel important. When introducing one person to another, Bork would enumerate each one's accomplishments. He was generous; it was impossible to pick up the check if he was around. He got along well with others, always showing them the utmost respect, no matter if they were older or younger. And, like Baba, he seldom lost his temper.

When neighborhood bullies beat me up, Baba told me to emulate Bork by taking up kung fu. Bork's practice of Chinese martial arts at a local Chinatown club planted a seed that sprouted into my own lifelong interest. He was a gifted musician, played piano, was in the Army band, and, when I was seven years old, taught me how to play a ukulele.

My brothers influenced my eventual career choices. It was Bork who suggested I major in electrical engineering in college, believing a technical field would offer an Asian more opportunity for career advancement. When I left active duty and was recruited by a well-known firm to be a systems engineer, Bork knew people who had been dissatisfied with the firm and told me to think twice before taking the job. His advice was a factor that led me to enter government service instead.

Bork graduated summa cum laude from Columbia University as a math major and was head of the computer department for a large insurance firm. After leaving that job, he started a second career as a caseworker for New York City's Human Resources Administration. It wasn't an easy job and required driving to different parts of the city—mostly to poorer sections of town—to look after his clients on welfare. I found his willingness to help people in need admirable.

Bork, his wife Lang, and kids Stevie and Bevie circa 1964

THE PERFECTIONIST

Yun was born on December 26 and felt deprived because he only got one present for his birthday and Christmas. He saw himself as an ugly duckling compared to his older brother. His darker complexion and pockmarked face made him extremely self-conscious even though the blemishes were hardly visible. "Ma, you sure I'm not adopted?" he would ask in all seriousness. He told me he felt neglected as a child because, in his mind, the family nanny, and not my mother, had raised him. When you feel you're second best, you try harder. Perhaps that's why Yun was a perfectionist.

Yun often came to my rescue when I got bullied in grade school. One summer evening, when two school chums and I were walking through a neighborhood park, a big Italian kid named Ralphie threatened to beat us up if we didn't give him some money. While I diverted the bully's attention, I told my friends to run to my house to get my brother. Our apartment was only five minutes away, so I kept talking and stalling for time. When my brother appeared on the scene, Ralphie quickly turned from wolf to lamb.

On another occasion, Yun accompanied me to the apartment of another neighborhood tough who had extorted twenty-five cents from me for lunch money. We got the money back from the boy's apologetic mother. Probably tired of having to come to the rescue all the time, Yun taught me rudimentary boxing skills so that I could defend myself. We watched newsreel clips of famous fighters so that he could point out what made them champs. One of his favorites was Kid Gavilan, a welterweight boxer with an unstoppable "bolo punch" uppercut that his opponents couldn't see coming. Yun had me throwing bolo punches—hundreds of them—into the air, into a pillow, against imaginary attackers, until my arms seemed like they would fall off. Left, right, left, right.

Brother Yun

Visiting Yun during his basic training at Fort Dix, New Jersey, I thought he really looked sharp in uniform and hoped that someday I'd have the chance to join too. Yun enjoyed his military service, had a chance to see Europe, and made staff sergeant in just two years. When his men sought his advice, he said he'd always take a step back to think about it first, even if it meant ducking into the men's room for a quick smoke.

He told me that if I ever went into the military, I should do it as an officer, but I should avoid the Army. "Too many chicken-shit officers!" he warned. Worried that I was getting into too many fights and turning into a juvenile delinquent, he convinced my parents to send me to a prep school.

He loved telling me about his experiences, and I loved hearing about the interesting things he did and the places he visited while in the Army. After leaving the service, Yun attended New York University on the GI Bill, graduated with a business degree, and worked as an accountant. When the pressures of corporate life burned him out, he went to school to become a barber. After marrying Cindy, a hairdresser who had worked with Mama, they moved to San Francisco and opened a beauty salon.

THE SPOILED BRAT

My parents and brothers had unique personalities that were quite different from each other. Where Baba was calm, Mama was excitable. Where Bork was gregarious, Yun was shy. I don't know whom I resemble most, having picked up character traits from each of them. Being at least ten years younger than my brothers, I grew up almost as an only child, getting my own way most of the time until someone felt the need to rein me in.

After I was born, we moved to an apartment in a 1920s-era tenement in the heart of New York's Chinatown, a six-story brick building with a rusty metal fire escape that ran up the front. Aside from its emergency value, the fire escape landing served as a poor man's balcony. On hot summer nights you could open the window and climb outside your apartment for some fresh air and enjoy the breeze. In the winter, you could keep leftovers fresh if you didn't have a freezer.

My parents occupied one bedroom; my brothers and I shared the other. Steam heat kept us warm in the winter. Red linoleum tile covering our apartment floor offered a smooth surface on which I could slide, bike, and roller-skate. It's a wonder the tenants below us never complained as I zipped around crashing and careening off tables and chairs. I was a brat.

Whenever Mama got fed up with my naughty behavior, she spanked my bottom until it was red. I said I was sorry and swore never again to do whatever it was that got her angry. And I gave her ample opportunity to be upset.

PLAY IT AGAIN, SAM!

A Steinway upright piano occupied a prominent place in our living room and in our lives. Mama could play Chinese tunes, but I dreamed of being able to play as well as Bork, the musician in the family. One of my happiest childhood memories was sitting at the keys beside Snow, a teenager and family friend whose radiant smile warmed my heart. I was self-conscious that my head seemed to grow faster than the rest of my body. My odd-looking haircut didn't help, the result of Mama putting a rice bowl on my head to trim my hair.

Me with Mama and Snow

CHICKEN LITTLE

Mama brought home a live chicken one afternoon to prepare for our evening meal—this was the age before packaged foods. When she wasn't watching, I lunged at the bird. It screeched, flapping its wings as it ran around the kitchen table with me in hot pursuit, chasing it around and around until I grabbed hold of its neck, squeezing harder and harder until Mama yanked the poor creature from my clutches.

Mama never tired of telling others that I was spoiled because I was the youngest child. It's true. I knew I could get away with devilish deeds, playing pranks on unsuspecting visitors, sometimes sneaking up from behind and punching them in the back of their knees, making their legs buckle. If they were seated, I'd yank their earlobes.

Fashionably attired gentlemen, smelling of Old Spice cologne, were prime targets. They would be doubly sorry if they came to our house wearing fedoras, the kind Humphrey Bogart wore in Casablanca. At the end of their visits, when they went to retrieve their hats, they would find them crushed out of shape, as if someone had sat on them. I took these liberties, secure in the knowledge that most guests wouldn't dare lay a finger on me even if they were fast enough to catch me. I was wrong twice over.

The first to thwart my mischievous antics was Uncle Ed. While he wasn't my real uncle, as a show of respect Chinese youngsters are supposed to address their elders as "uncle" or "auntie." Like almost anyone old enough to smoke then, Uncle Ed enjoyed the habit, puffing away as I approached him from behind. Just as I was about to twist his earlobe, he ever so casually flicked the ash from his cigarette in my direction. I screamed in pain as some of the ash landed in my eye. Mama put my head under a faucet to flush my eyes with cold water. Uncle Ed claimed it was an accident, but his half-hearted apology and the smirk on his face said otherwise. In hindsight, I have to thank him for turning me off to smoking.

The second guy who beat me to the punch—literally—was Vincent, my brother Bork's friend. They were chatting one day when I tried to get their attention. When they ignored me, I got mad and tried to punch Vincent in the stomach, but he straight-armed me as I flailed away. Taking several steps back to gather momentum, I charged at him again. This time he twisted my arm behind my back, applying just enough pressure to make me wince, letting me know that he was in total control and able to really hurt me if he wanted. My brother complimented Vincent on his kung fu, thus increasing my desire to learn more.

UP ON THE ROOF

When I was around five years old, I woke up one night gasping, unable to see or breathe through the dark haze of smoke filling our apartment and billowing up from the floors below. With eyes burning and heart pounding, I was petrified as Mama took me by the hand and led me up the stairs to our roof, figuring we could hop over to an adjoining building and find a safe exit. Minutes later we heard the sound of fire engine sirens. A fireman came up, telling us it was OK to return to our apartment, saying a kerosene fire had started in the basement boiler room. For the longest time after that night, I had a hard time going to sleep, the smell of burning kerosene lingering in my nasal passages.

The roof was my refuge, my safe haven, not only from fire but also from the noisy street life below. The lyrics to the Drifters song "Up on the Roof" captured how I felt when I went up there: *I went to a peaceful place where the air smelled fresh and the world below couldn't bother me*. I used to sit up there silently, taking it all in, at night gazing at the stars, in the afternoons watching flocks of pigeons as they soared overhead. I envied the pigeons' owner, an Italian boy on a distant rooftop who got them to fly around in giant circles by waving a stick in the air, much like a conductor leading an orchestra.

One day a pigeon landed on my roof hurt and unable to fly. Maybe it wasn't the boy's and I could keep it, I hoped. It took me a day or so to put a Band-Aid on its leg and nurse the pigeon back to health. Just as I was about to see if it was strong enough to fly, the Italian boy hollered at me,

"Hey, that's my bird!" Thinking I had somehow trapped it, he cursed and threatened me if I didn't release it. I let the bird take flight and return to its owner, happy it could fly again but sad to see it go. My parents said no when I asked if I could raise pigeons. But, as a consolation prize, they bought me a pet parakeet that I let zoom around the apartment when no one was home.

SLINGSHOT SHENANIGANS

One of my most unpardonable childhood antics happened when I tested a slingshot crafted with a wire coat hanger and rubber bands. For target practice I went up on the roof to shoot at soda cans, but soon I wanted to see if I could hit something on the street from my third-floor bedroom window. Maybe a signpost. I waited for the cover of darkness to avoid the prying eyes of the fat lady across the street, who usually sat by her windowsill, perched from morning to night, taking in all that came into her view. She knew everything that happened on our block: when people went to school or work and when they came home.

I shut off the lights so I wouldn't be seen if someone looked up. I crouched below my window ledge with head raised just high enough to peer down at the street below. Just then a neighborhood bully and his gang sauntering down the street making a racket caught my attention. Loading a tiny black bean into the sling, drawing back the rubber bands until taut, I fired a foot ahead of my unsuspecting prey.

"Oww!" The bully began shouting, "Dammit, you m-----f-----! If I find you, I'm gonna kill you!" I was astonished, ashamed, and frightened in the same instant. Astonished since I'd never hit a distant, much less moving, target. Ashamed as I realized I could have taken out an eye. And frightened because these guys were the sons of Mafiosi from Little Italy, the neighborhood abutting Chinatown. Fortunately, while the bean stung my victim, he walked away unhurt. Unfortunately, the fat lady across the street, having seen everything that had transpired, leaned out the window, wagged her finger at me and shouted, "Shame on you! I'm going to tell your mother!"

DREAM JOBS

The fat lady wasn't the only one who enjoyed looking out the window, which was a favorite pastime for many tenement dwellers before TV. Our windows provided an unobstructed view of the daily pattern of friends, neighbors, and strangers. During hot weather—and before air conditioning—we'd climb out on the fire escape landing to enjoy the cooler night air. On holidays we'd watch marching bands, colorful floats, and beauty queens go by. What I witnessed from my window proved entertaining and provided images of what I wanted to do when I grew up.

Each morning a big garbage truck would stop in front of every apartment building to pick up trash. I admired the way the men, dressed in gray overalls, sleeves rolled up to reveal taut, sinewy forearms, jumped off and dashed in and out of buildings to collect the trash, heaving large metal containers like feathers, dumping the contents into the back of the truck, where it would be churned up and swallowed. I wanted to be one of them, to be like Superman: strong enough to toss around heavy cans, hanging onto the back of a truck with just one hand as it rumbled down the street.

If not a garbage man, my next choice was to be a fishmonger. Directly across the street from our building was a fish market with a picture window. From my observation post, I could see the day's live catch swimming around a large tank. I was impressed with the deft way the fishmonger did his job, with one fluid movement scooping up a fish from the tank with a net and plopping it into a customer's open container. He was like Spider-Man. If only I could do things with the same effortless grace!

Some parents want their kids to become doctors or lawyers. When I told my parents I wanted to be either a garbage man or fishmonger, they laughed, having no idea that my future career choices would be, at least to them, just as offbeat.

SINK OR SWIM

When I was about seven years old, I told Mama I wanted to learn how to swim, thinking it might add muscle to my scrawny frame. She was happy to channel my youthful exuberance into a healthy activity, but the only problem was that she herself couldn't swim a stroke. Undeterred, we sojourned to Coney Island, an hour's subway ride from our Chinatown apartment, during a sweltering New York summer's day. Coney Island was Disneyland before Disneyland, with roller coasters, boardwalk arcades, and a white sandy beach.

Mama thought the fastest way to teach me was to throw me in deep water. Leading me by the hand, she walked deeper and deeper out into the ocean to where she could stand with her chin just above water. She coaxed me to float, first on my back and then on my stomach, supporting me all the while with her arms. As I gained confidence, she let go and encouraged me to dog paddle toward her as she stepped backward toward shore. When she spotted a kid who appeared to be a good swimmer, she invited him to give me pointers.

Once I got the hang of it, we went swimming at Bradley Beach on the New Jersey shore, which remains a popular vacation spot for many Chinatown families fleeing the city during hot weather. We rented a house there in the summer. Baba joined us on weekends. We walked along the shore to Asbury Park and played boardwalk games that enticed us to test our skills. I can still hear the skill-ball barker on the boardwalk shouting, "Roll 'em, roll 'em, roll 'em...everybody wins!" This game was a combination of bingo and pinball and played with a rubber ball that you rolled down a long board; at the end of the board were twenty-five holes arranged in a square pattern. The first player to land the ball in five holes in a straight line won.

After a day at the beach, we went to the Purple Cow Ice Cream Parlor, so named because they served frothy, velvety, purple-colored milkshakes made with grape juice. If I was being bratty, which was most of the time, my parents knew that the promise of a Purple Cow would almost always make me behave.

HUSKY

My parents didn't mind my having Purple Cows or anything else that would fatten me up because I was, in their eyes, too skinny. Aside from a few favorite foods, I was a picky eater. "Eat! You gotta eat!" Mama would implore me, insisting that I have just one more bite of dinner. Finally tired of being a scrawny weakling, I made a conscious effort to put on weight, consuming steaks, pork chops, chicken, and eating whatever it took to add extra pounds to my rail-thin frame. It worked. By sixth grade I had ballooned out, forced to shop for clothes in the "husky section" of the boy's department. When a girl at school told me I was fat, my feelings were hurt, but it made me I realize I'd gone too far and needed to become more fit, a desire that's stayed with me ever since.

DO THE RIGHT THING

Mama taught me about integrity when I looked for a summer job during school. I came across a help wanted ad that guaranteed employment to anyone who paid a twenty-five-dollar fee. I went for an interview with the employment agency, located in a dilapidated building near Times Square. The office manager, without assessing my interests, sent me to interview at Schrafft's, a chain restaurant that dispatched coffee and pastry carts to feed hungry office workers in midtown Manhattan. The Schrafft's supervisor didn't know anything about the employment agency, but since turnover was high, he hired me on the spot.

I talked myself into believing the agency didn't deserve a finder's fee for a job I could have gotten on my own had I gone to the trouble of reading the Schrafft's help wanted ad in the newspaper myself. But when I told Mama I wasn't going to pay, she got mad and lectured me on the importance of doing the right thing. However, she said it was my decision. I returned to the agency that afternoon and paid them their due.

Mama stayed healthy until she turned eighty, when her health deteriorated due to a home accident. A fractured hip a few years later led to decline, hospitalization, and eventually a nursing home. In seeking medical treatments for her, I grew frustrated with the inadequacy of our healthcare system. My desire to find more effective solutions fueled my interest in pursuing a career in Traditional Chinese Medicine. It was her parting gift to me.

MY PLAYGROUND

It was fun growing up in New York's Chinatown, a self-contained community occupying about five square blocks in lower Manhattan. Many of my relatives never bothered learning English beyond a few simple phrases; they didn't need to. You could work, marry, and raise a family there without ever leaving its borders. When I grew up there in the 1950s and '60s, it was smaller and less crowded, before the relaxation of immigration laws enabled a huge influx of newer immigrants from Asia.

I lived on Bayard, an east-west cross street. Half a block east was Mott Street, Chinatown's north-south spine. Half a block west was Mulberry Street, Little Italy's main thoroughfare. Next door was Rocky's Hardware, which sold equipment for my favorite team sports: Spaldeens, broomsticks, and basketballs. Happiness was smacking a Spaldeen[2] with a broomstick over the municipal court building. Even though the balls were too soft to break windows, a passing patrolman would chase us away. But we'd return to our concrete playground as soon as he walked out of sight. In the spring and summer, we played stickball, punch ball, stoopball, and Chinese handball (unlike regular handball, which requires a bigger court, the ball is hit against the pavement before it bounces off the wall). Those were sports that were familiar to kids growing up on the streets of New York.

---

2 (From Wikipedia: http://en.wikipedia.org/wiki/Spaldeen, accessed January 25, 2014.) Spalding Hi-Bounce Ball, often called a Spaldeen (with the accent on the second syllable), is a small, pink rubber ball, somewhat similar to a racquetball, supposedly made from the defective core of a tennis ball without the felt. Spaldeens were available from 1949 to 1979 to city kids. In urban areas sparse in grass, Spaldeens became integral to many street games due to their bounciness and light weight.

Columbus Park

When the weather was nice, we played in Columbus Park, an oasis that was to Chinatown what Central Park was to the rest of Manhattan. Within the black iron-fenced perimeter were a basketball court, an area for softball or stickball, a pavilion, and small patches of green.

I attended Sunday services at True Light Lutheran Church. According to the church website, Miss Mary E. Banta, a missionary, founded the True Light Mission and Sunday school in 1935 and passed away in 1975. I remember Miss Banta as a short and wiry woman with a caring personality who treated everyone in Chinatown as part of her flock. She would organize outings to places like Palisades Amusement Park in New Jersey for us Chinatown kids. When my parents invited Miss Banta for a lobster dinner, we were impressed that she ate the meal with such heartfelt gratitude, thanking my parents, thanking the Lord for giving her the opportunity to have such a delicious dinner, taking her time with each morsel, and savoring each piece as if it was the tastiest thing she'd ever put in her mouth. Every time I eat lobster, I think of Miss Banta.

SAUSAGES, ZEPPOLES, AND TUTTI FRUTTI

The Chinese and Italian communities were intertwined by proximity yet separated by culture. Two parallel worlds, often in harmony but sometimes in conflict. Straddling both, I enjoyed the best of each, especially the food.

The neighborhood was a culinary paradise, with Chinese noodle shops and Italian pizzerias within a five-minute walk.

I always looked forward to the Feast of San Gennaro, an annual event sponsored by the Italian community in honor of the patron saint of Naples. Hundreds of vendors lined both sides of Mulberry Street. My friends Robert, Quan, and I joined the throngs of locals and out-of-towners inching their way along the jam-packed street.

We sampled Italian delicacies, played carnival games, and ogled shapely girls in tight sweaters. The spicy aroma of Italian sausages sizzling on the grill tempted us. Nothing was better than biting into a fat, juicy sausage served on a crusty roll and piled with sautéed onions, tomatoes, and bell peppers. My stomach always had room for zeppoles, deep-fat fried small dough balls that puffed up and turned golden brown. Sprinkled with powdered sugar and cinnamon, they resembled donut holes, only lighter and fluffier. Tutti Frutti gelato, a velvety blend of ice, fruits and nuts, was another favorite. I preferred it to ice cream, and I loved ice cream, once dreaming of driving a Good Humor truck.

Italian sausage stand

By midevening a church procession carrying a statue of Saint Gennaro marched through the neighborhood, giving people a chance to donate. Some said the festival was Mafia-run, generating cash for the "social clubs" along Mulberry Street. Gaudily clad singers belted out Italian opera over tinny loudspeakers on a stage a block from my apartment, keeping me up at night during the weeklong celebration, making me groggy for school the next morning. But it was a small price to pay for a chance to enjoy one of my two favorite street celebrations. The other was a month later, on October 10th.

ROAST PORK BUNS AND SOY SAUCE CHICKEN

Double Ten is not only my birthday but also a Chinese holiday that engages the whole community. It's like Chinatown throwing a giant birthday party for me every year. Cherry red banners with Chinese calligraphy adorn storefronts. Floats, marching bands, and school kids waving tiny American and Republic of China flags paraded past my window. Out-of-town friends came to celebrate and shop. We'd enjoy noodle dishes at Hong Fat's, buy soy sauce chicken and crispy roast pig from Leung's Chinese grocery, and order freshly baked roast pork buns from coffee shops on Mott Street. All the coffee shops in Chinatown served Chinese-style pastries except for Lonnie's, an American-style soda fountain and popular hangout for us.

Chinatown lion dance

Lion dancers in bright silk and satin costumes prance around the neighborhood. With one performer under the head and another under the tail, the lion, made of papier-mâché, bamboo, and silk, is designed to look ferocious. With a single horn on top, wing-shaped ears, and a long, multicolored tail, this mythical creature jumps around wanting to be appeased. The musical accompaniment of drums, gongs and cymbals lets everyone know it's getting closer. *DUK, DONG, CHANG! DUK, DONG, CHANG!*

Good fortune follows if the lion is satisfied with gifts in the form of lettuce and money. Shop owners dangle lettuce and red envelopes containing cash near their entrances to entice the lion to usher in good luck. People throw firecrackers in front of the lion's path to ward off evil spirits. The crack and bang of exploding fireworks fills the air with a smoky, lung-burning, and eye-reddening haze.

The thunderous drumming and powerful staccato rhythm reminded me of a subway train roaring down a tunnel. When I pleaded with my brother to teach me how to play, he presented me with a set of drumsticks and a rubber practice pad. Bork was no dummy and didn't need his kid brother banging away on a real drum, at least not while he and the rest of the family wanted any peace and quiet. Although I never reached the level of being considered a talented drummer, those early lessons did enable me to join the drum and bugle corps in college.

CHAPTER 2

YOUTHFUL EXPLORATION

*There's always one moment in childhood when the door opens
and lets the future in.*

—DEEPAK CHOPRA

I lived across the street from Public School (P.S.) 23, a five-story structure
with a reddish-gray stone façade. My least favorite teacher there was Mrs.
Reardon, who taught fourth grade. She was volatile and would blow up at
the slightest infraction of her rules. Not lining up promptly or not finishing
your milk and cookies were just a few examples. When she got angry she'd
hit, slap, or bang heads against the nearest hard surface. She whacked my
head once so hard that it left a mark on our classroom wall—I wouldn't be
surprised if it's still visible. Today she'd be sued for child abuse, but back
then her methods were tolerated.

I'll never forget the time she grabbed my friend Anthony by the hair
and smashed his head repeatedly against a solid oak desktop. *THUNK!*
THUNK! THUNK! I cringed at the sickening sound of skull on wood.
Mrs. Reardon usually stopped once she saw tears. But Anthony, who was a
streetwise Italian kid, didn't flinch. Failing to get the response she wanted,

Mrs. Reardon's face got redder and redder, and her body began trembling. I thought her head was going to erupt like a volcano, but she started sobbing instead. "You're as dense as this wood!" she cried as she released her grip. Anthony showed me that no matter how bad things got, you could survive just by hanging tough.

P.S. 23

My favorite teacher was Mrs. Brown, who taught sixth grade. She had a stern manner and didn't suffer unruly kids gladly. When asked if she was ever afraid of getting mugged, she said if anyone ever tried to assault her she'd go after him with a lead pipe so they'd never be able to hurt her or anyone again. Despite her tough talk, she also showed a soft side. When one of my classmates tried to fondle her breasts, she merely slapped his hand away without losing her composure, recognizing that the lad's behavior was hormonally driven.

She appointed me captain of the school safety squad after two other kids she had chosen didn't pass muster. Everyone thought it was cool to be on the squad as we strutted around wearing white canvas belts with shiny badges on our chests. Our job was to help youngsters cross the street and maintain order. Things got out of hand one snowy winter's day during a brief lull in traffic. Three of my squad members started pelting each other with snowballs. I felt obligated to include the incident in my weekly report, but glossed over the details, left out the names of those involved, and took responsibility for what happened because I was afraid my buddies would lose their positions. However, Mrs. Brown, having already heard what happened, wouldn't let me off the hook and demanded their names. When she kicked them off the squad, I felt awful. To my surprise, my classmates didn't hold it against me.

There were pluses and minuses to growing up in Chinatown. One advantage was that for the most formative years of our lives—from kindergarten to sixth grade—we didn't feel like minorities, because we weren't. Our teachers had names like Rosenberg, Reardon, and Brown, but the students of P.S. 23 were mostly Chins, Wongs, and Moys with a sprinkling of Busettis, Albanos, and Spiritos in the mix. People who looked just like us ran the churches we attended, the restaurants we frequented, and the shops we patronized. They—or their parents—came from southern China, either from the same or a neighboring village. One disadvantage was that it was like growing up in any small town, where everyone knows everyone else's business. Jealousy, clan rivalry, gossip, and slander incubate in confined spaces. Even as an eleven-year old, I was more than anxious to experience the world beyond Chinatown.

BLACKBOARD JUNGLE

My classmates Donald, Kenny, and I got our chance to venture out when our sixth grade teacher, Mrs. Brown, thought we should go to Junior High School 71. It was a newly built school located in an ethnically diverse Lower East Side neighborhood. She thought it was better for us than P.S. 130, the one just to the north and within walking distance of Chinatown, where the majority of students went for seventh and eight grades. She said we'd have to ride a city bus for about thirty minutes each way, but we viewed that as an enticement rather than a deterrent.

Each morning, before catching the bus to school, we met at the Chinatown Fair coffee counter on the southern end of Mott Street, a popular neighborhood hangout filled with pinball machines, a shooting gallery, and other arcade games. The elderly Chinese attendants yelled at us to "keep off the machines!" when we nudged the pinball machine to get extra points so we could win a prize. Kenny's father owned the food concession, which occupied a section of the premises.

The bus ride gave us a chance to swap stories about classmates, "hot chicks," a new rock idol named Elvis, and what was cool and what wasn't. We spent as much time preening as the girls in our class did, using pomade to slick back our hair into ducktails, trying to act tough to fit in with the leather jacket-wearing "in-crowd," smoking cigarettes and pipes to look cool. Fortunately for us, drugs were not yet part of the street scene. Street gangs and schoolyard fights were, however, and they were our main diversions from the drudgery of classes led by teachers who, with one or two exceptions, didn't care if we learned anything or not. They were preoccupied with keeping order while we were focused on experimentation.

One June morning, a week before the end of our seventh grade school year, we decided to break routine. Even at 7:30 am, we could tell it would be a scorching-hot day as we walked to the bus stop near Chatham Square. I don't recall who came up with the idea, but it didn't take long for the three of us to agree that it would be a great day to spend at the beach instead of in the classroom. We made a quick U-turn, hurrying toward the Canal Street subway station, hoping no one we knew would catch us hopping on the train to Coney Island.

PLAYING HOOKY

Coney Island, an hour's subway ride from Manhattan, was home to the Cyclone roller coaster, the Parachute Jump, the giant Wonder Ferris Wheel, and Nathan's Famous hot dogs. To many New Yorkers, it was a noisy, crowded, slowly deteriorating amusement center that had seen better days. To us it was paradise, an oasis of sand and sea in a city of concrete and asphalt. We spent the whole day swimming, building sandcastles, and gawking at young couples making out under the boardwalk. Running through the surf while our poor classmates were stuck in the classroom, I felt as free as the wind blowing across the ocean. Around two o'clock we showered, returned our rented swim trunks, and stopped at a few boardwalk eateries for refreshments. We left with just enough change for a subway token and spent the rest of our money on cokes, hot dogs, buttered corn, and cherry cheese knishes. After a long day in the sun, our bellies unable to hold another hot dog, and with no money left, we were more than ready to head home.

Coney Island

We got on the return train and waited...and waited. Coney Island was the last stop for the train before returning to Manhattan, so it wasn't unusual for it to be in the station for some time while crews changed. However, it seemed to take much longer than usual, and we were anxious to get home so our parents wouldn't be suspicious. Then we heard a message on the station loudspeaker that made our hearts skip a beat: "Attention, passengers! Please get off this train. There will not be any service from this platform!" We went looking for someone who could tell us more. It wasn't good news: the subway workers union had just called a strike!

We'd have to make our way home on foot, a fourteen-mile trek in the hot sun, with no money in our pockets. If you Google for directions today, it's about a four-hour walk from Coney Island to one of the bridges that crosses over to Manhattan and into Chinatown. But there was no Google back then, and our journey was delayed as we stopped at stores, groceries, and soda fountains to ask for directions and water. We pleaded, begged, and groveled for a drink without success. We even tried to trade our watches for a couple of cold drinks. No takers. Shopkeepers shooed us away. We eventually found a gas station with a water hose on the side of the garage. As we turned on the faucet, the attendant came out and shouted, "Why ain't yous in school? Get the hell outta heah before I call da cops!" I love New Yorkers, but they can be obnoxious.

Every billboard we passed seemed to mock us. When I looked up from the hot asphalt, all I noticed were pictures of people sipping ice-cold beers or Cokes from frosty mugs. Exhausted, thirsty, and frustrated, we shuffled along in silence, placing one foot in front of the other. "A thousand-mile journey begins with the first step," I muttered. Sometimes fortune cookie homilies come in handy. It took us almost six hours before we walked across the Brooklyn Bridge to Chinatown, perhaps good training for the Marine Corps.

Mama was fuming when I got home around nine o'clock. She calmed down when I told her I had to stay at school to finish a class project, but she gave me a puzzled look as I started gulping down glass after glass of tap water, exclaiming it to be the most delicious drink in the world.

To the consternation of my parents, that wasn't the only time I played hooky. When I felt adventurous, I'd explore various parts of the city near and far, strolling through Central Park, walking along Park Avenue or Wall Street, or visiting the city's many museums, including the Cloisters, well known for its medieval structure. One of the many reasons I loved

New York—and still do—is because of its rich cultural diversity. Within walking distance from home was a tremendous number of great eateries, not just Chinese, but Italian and Jewish as well. I could have dim sum for breakfast, a kosher hot pastrami sandwich for lunch, and Italian seafood pasta for dinner. When the psychological boundaries of the Lower East Side became too confining, I simply hopped on a subway and was quickly transported to another world.

The one time Baba ever got mad at me was when I played hooky from junior high once too often. I was embarrassed he had to accompany me for an interview with a school truancy officer. He was more disappointed than angry but realized he had to discipline me. Probably at Mama's urging, he whipped me on the butt with his belt. I let out a big yelp with every stroke, but the anguished look on his face told me the beating hurt him far more than it did me.

EDITH

I was in eighth grade when Edith, a Chinatown girl, started classes at J.H.S. 71. Her seventh-grade homeroom was across from mine. Our classroom doors had narrow windows you could look through. One afternoon I glanced up, and there was Edith with her face pressed against the windowpane staring at me. It wasn't the first time. My friends ribbed me about it. A preteen girl, even a cute one, was more annoyance than love interest then.

"Edith, leave me alone!" I shouted as we got off the bus on our way home that afternoon. When I felt words wouldn't persuade her, I grabbed her arm with one hand while I punched her on the shoulder with the other. Not hard enough to bruise but just enough to let her know I wasn't joking around. "Are you gonna stop now, Edith?"

"No!" she shook her head.

I hit her on the arm again, this time harder. I expected her to cry or at least whimper. Instead, she stood motionless, neither pulling away nor pushing back. Suddenly, out of the corner of my eye, I saw something coming at me. It was Edith's friend Margaret coming to her rescue. She swung her book bag at my head, missing by inches as I ducked.

"You f----! Why'd you do that?" Margaret cursed at me as she took Edith by the hand and escorted her home. As they walked away, Edith turned around to stare at me with a forlorn look.

Feeling guilty about my crude behavior, I tried repeatedly without success over the years to find her so that I could apologize. Some five decades later, I was finally able to locate her through Norman Chin, a mutual friend (more on Norman later in the martial arts chapters). To my relief Edith had no recollection of the incident...or of me.

Edith and me reenacting a scene from fifty years earlier

Miss Moreno

In junior high school, few classes held my attention. Either the teacher or the subject was boring. One exception was eighth-grade science class. Watching Mr. Wizard on TV every week, I developed an early fascination with science, watching him demonstrate simple experiments that viewers could do at home. For example, he piled dishes on top of a table and yanked the tablecloth underneath; the plates remained stationary, illustrating the law of inertia. I tried it at home when Mama wasn't watching. It worked! Mr. Wizard always closed the show by telling viewers, "Remember, boys and girls, the most important meal of the day is breakfast! And fruit, cereal, milk, bread, and butter are the elements of a good breakfast." For years that was exactly what I ate every morning.

Eighth-grade science was also my favorite class because of the teacher, Miss Moreno. Every guy in the school, myself included, had a crush on her. Smart and beautiful, Hilda Moreno was in her early twenties, with a radiant olive complexion and dark-brown hair. She was also an excellent teacher, one who knew her material and cared about her students.

On a warm spring day after school, Donald, Kenny, and I boarded the bus to go home when we spotted Miss Moreno leaving the school running in our direction. To our delight, she hopped on our bus and sat near the driver. She didn't see us seated in the back. "Where's she's going?" I wondered. Curiosity got the best of us, so we decided to follow her.

We would normally have gotten off in Chinatown but stayed on the bus until Miss Moreno got off two stops farther, near City Hall. We jumped off just after she did while trying to avoid getting too close. Neither Kenny nor Donald had been in her classes, so she probably wouldn't have recognized them even if she had run smack into them. Just to be safe, however, Kenny placed himself at a discreet distance, perhaps twenty feet behind her. His pace matched hers. I was farther back on the opposite side of the street with Donald trailing. We hopscotched positions whenever Miss Moreno stopped or turned a corner, trying to keep her in sight but avoiding being detected.

Miss Moreno strode along as if deep in thought while we darted across traffic and around cars, hoping she wouldn't turn around and spot us. She hurried past the municipal court until she reached the Department of Motor Vehicles. Aha! So that was why she seemed in such a hurry: she had to get to the DMV before it closed.

We huddled around the corner, asking ourselves if we should continue to see where she went next but decided to quit while we were ahead. It was close to dinnertime, and hunger pangs trumped pubescent hormones. We punched each other playfully as we walked back to Chinatown. To follow Miss Moreno without getting caught had been exciting. It foreshadowed what I'd be doing, and what would be done to me, many years later.

Decades later a woman came to my clinic in Virginia for acupuncture. I was amazed to learn that she was from New York, went to the same junior high school, and also had Miss Moreno as her homeroom teacher. This was just another of many examples convincing me that we're all connected.

STREET BRAWL

As an adult, I've always tried to control my temper even when provoked, but during my early teens it was all too easy to lose control and get physical. It could happen as fast as tripping down a flight of steps, which is exactly what occurred one spring day as I was leaving school.

In junior high, whenever the bell sounded to mark the end of each school day, everyone would rush to leave the building all at once. As I raced down the stairs so I wouldn't miss the bus, someone pushed me from behind. I instinctively shoved back. "Never let anyone push you around," was an unwritten rule in our blackboard jungle. I don't remember who threw the first punch, but our fists started flying. We began in the stairwell and continued trading blows as we stumbled out the door and onto the street. The other guy was throwing and landing more blows, mostly to my midsection. We kept going for several minutes until we heard someone shout, "Cops!"

We immediately disengaged. It was Friday, so we agreed to settle things after the weekend. My antagonist was a wiry, tough-looking Puerto Rican named Hermano. His equally tough-looking friends stood by him. I was heartened when Jose, my classmate and a Boys Club boxing champ, volunteered to be my corner man. He was a year or two older than the rest of us, having had to repeat grades. What he lacked intellectually he made up for physically. He never said much, but when he spoke, everyone listened.

Both sides agreed on the ground rules: it was to be one-on-one with just fists. No brass knuckles, chains, or knives. The good news was that I had three days to get in shape. The bad news was that I had three days to ruminate about what people were saying: that my opponent was an experienced street fighter. My classmates tried to pump me up and nicknamed me

"Chino," which I liked better than the pejorative "Chinito" that Hermano's friends were calling me.

Jose gave me pointers. "OK, Chino, you gotta get in da first shot. He gonna go down real fast, man!" To be on the safe side, I dusted off *The Manly Art of Self-Defense* home study course I'd ordered years earlier. I had cut out an ad from the back of a Superman comic book, which said former heavyweight boxing champ Joe Louis had endorsed it. It consisted of an illustrated manual with conditioning exercises, self-defense tips, and boxing drills.

It cost more than seventy dollars, a fortune for someone on a twenty-five-cents weekly allowance. It was the first thing I ever bought on my own, scrimping together money from my piggybank, collecting bottle deposits, and doing odd jobs for tips. I was drawn to the course because the kid who demonstrated the drills in the manual looked even more out of shape than I did. According to the ad, he turned from a flabby wimp into a well-muscled fighting machine after only three months.

I practiced boxing combinations by imagining Hermano standing in front of me. Jab, cross, hook, uppercut. One, two, three, four. Shuffle in, shuffle out, shuffle left, shuffle right. Given how little time I had to prepare, I felt I was as ready as I would ever be. Although I had developed a pretty good right cross, my secret weapon was Novocain. My dentist had given me a shot the morning of the fight before extracting my impacted wisdom tooth. I hoped it would numb any type of jaw pain, whether inflicted by a dentist's drill or Hermano's fist.

Both sides met as scheduled. Hermano's corner man patted me down for hidden weapons and inspected my hands to ensure they weren't wrapped around a roll of quarters, which was a favorite trick to add weight to your punch. My corner man, Jose, did the same to Hermano. We squared off, surrounded by a large crowd egging us on. Word spread around the school quickly about the fight. Everybody loved a good fight.

Pumped with adrenalin, I charged forward, landing a combination of shots to his head. It was just as I had imagined, having practiced hundreds of jabs, crosses, hooks, and uppercuts against an imaginary Hermano three days in a row. *BOP, WAP, BAP!* My punches found his chin with surprising accuracy.

But I was even more surprised, if not discouraged, when he didn't crumble like Jose had predicted. As I started tiring from throwing a continuous barrage, he started aiming uppercuts—big, looping ones—at my solar plexus. I should have been better prepared because he had used the same technique on me during our initial encounter. Only then I hadn't had time to take off my peacoat jacket, so I had been well insulated against his blows. Unfortunately, this time around we were in shirtsleeves and my gut was exposed. What was probably only a few seconds of pounding turned into an eternity as my stomach started cramping up.

My mind seemed to detach from my physical body as though someone had pressed the slow-play button on the video of our fight. My mind's eye watched Hermano wind up like a softball pitcher as if moving in slow motion. I could see his fist coming toward my stomach but couldn't move out of the way fast enough since I was physically in the same slow-motion time warp. My mind had enough time, however, to admire the efficacy of Hermano's technique, recognizing it was the bolo punch, the same technique my brother had taught me years earlier. *Why did I discard it in favor of perfecting my right cross?* I scolded myself.

When my brain finally registered the physical pain in my gut, I gasped for breath and was about to double over in agony. Just then a pair of giant hands yanked us apart. It was the neighborhood patrolman. Dispersing the crowd and dragging us into the school stairwell, he asked us why we were fighting. With the patrolman's prodding, we each told our side of the story, realized we had both overreacted, shook hands, and apologized. As we walked out of the building, we had a new respect for each other and parted as friends.

By the time we left, everyone had disappeared except Jose. Rushing up with a big smile on his face and pumping my hand with both of his, he exclaimed, "You won, Hon! You won!" as he raised my hand up in the air triumphantly. I was happy Jose thought I had done well. Earning his respect meant a great deal to me. The next day the rest of my classmates patted me on the back and congratulated me. "Hey, man, you acted like his punches were nothing!"

In my heart, however, I knew I hadn't really won the fight. Indeed, I was lucky Hermano had aimed at my belly instead of my face. To bystanders, I had scored the most punishing blows and seemed unmoved by anything Hermano had done to me. But what they didn't know was that if the fight had lasted just one second longer I would have passed out. Perhaps it was because my face had the same frozen expression throughout the contest. So I guess my secret weapon, the shot of Novocain, worked after all!

McBurney School

My parents were so worried about my schoolyard fisticuffs and juvenile delinquent behavior that they decided to send me to McBurney, a private school for boys on the Upper West Side. I didn't want to go to McBurney. I wanted to try out for one of the city's better high schools, the ones that required an entrance exam. But Yun, who had been tutoring me for the exam, dissuaded me from trying. And that discouraged me greatly, even more than going to a school where I didn't know anyone.

Prep school was a cultural shock. My junior high classmates were from poor working class families, about 50 percent of them eating subsidized lunches. You were ostracized if you showed up in class looking neat and clean. My McBurney classmates, on the other hand, were the sons of doctors and lawyers from privileged backgrounds and spent summers abroad. You had to wear coats and ties to class.

I invited Baba to a father-son night but was unduly concerned he might feel out of place with the other dads of a different social class. I should have known better. He got along well with everyone he met and did so by making them feel like they were the center of the universe. I was always proud to be my father's son but even more so that evening.

McBurney was a YMCA-affiliated school with excellent athletic facilities, including an Olympic-size pool and an indoor track. We had physical education classes five days a week and a variety of activities that kept us in good physical condition. I was on the wrestling team and enjoyed learning some basic moves but was disappointed we never competed against other schools.

One of my teammates, Denny Matshushita, introduced me to Shotokan karate, a style I was drawn to because it emphasized clean, crisp techniques done with speed and power. I joined a class and devoured every book I could find on karate. Many years later I would earn a black belt at the Shotokan Karate Headquarters in Tokyo under world-class instructors who were featured in the books I had studied as a teenager.

My favorite team sport in high school was basketball. When I didn't make the varsity, I spent countless hours trying to improve my ball-handling skills and jump shot. I was happy when my friend Matt Pon invited me to join a team he had formed. We called ourselves the Courtiers and were one of a dozen teams that competed in a league sponsored by True Light Lutheran Church, a community hub for Chinatown youth. On the team was Kam Yuen. I didn't know it then, but Kam's eventual career trajectory would be one I would try to follow: from engineer to kung fu master to medical professional. More on Kam later.

BOYS AND GIRLS TOGETHER

In my junior year at McBurney, I enrolled in a ballroom dance class taught by an instructor who called himself "Broadway Killer Joe." Every week he invited girls from a sister school over so we could practice with a partner. I wanted to show my girlfriend Bonnie my latest moves and invited her to a dance in Chinatown.

Someone with a collection of 45s typically hosted Saturday night dances there. Most of the younger teens came without dates, with the boys sitting on one side of the room, girls sitting on the other, getting up to dance when a song started, then separating again when it ended. I felt awkward the first time I went to one of these events, afraid of being turned down or stepping on my partner's foot.

Bonnie stood five foot six, had fashion model good looks, and was two years older than me. Heads turned as we moved across the dance floor slowly, holding each other closely, swaying to a ballad. The following day my friend Matt, pulling me aside, said, "Hon, you should go with someone in your own league. She looks a bit too mature for you." Well maybe we should have gone to a movie instead, but I was in love for the very first time and didn't care what anyone thought.

Bonnie, a fashion design student visiting New York for a year, hailed from the West Indies and was staying with a close family friend of ours. Mama frowned when I mentioned going out with Bonnie. "Don't wind up having to get married. College comes first!" she reminded me. I chaffed at her admonition, telling myself it would be the last time I'd tell Mama about who I was dating. It didn't take long for Bonnie's alluring smile and sweet-as-nectar kisses to capture my heart. It was an innocent romance, made more exciting because we kept it hidden from our families, knowing they wouldn't approve of our blossoming relationship.

I grew sadder as the end of her stay drew closer, acknowledging I'd have to let her go, perhaps forever, and knowing she'd be ready to settle down long before me. A decade later, Bonnie visited the United States again, this time with her childhood sweetheart and now husband. I liked him immediately, happy she had reunited with him.

TAIWAN GIRLS

In my senior year of high school, I dated Jodie. Fluent in several Chinese dialects, she poked fun at my heavily New York-accented Chinese, making me wish I had a better command of the language. A college student from Taiwan, she and her sisters worked at the same Chinese restaurant I did on weekends. Jodie's older sister Marsha wanted a date for a dinner dance and asked me to fix her up. I thought my cousin Jim would be a good match. He was intelligent, adventurous and, most importantly, had a car. To make it worthwhile for him to drive from his home in Philadelphia to New York, I described Marsha glowingly. "Very sexy! Just your type, Jim."

We circled the girls' apartment for over an hour until we found a parking spot. By the time we knocked on their door, we urgently needed to use the one and only bathroom the sisters were using to dress and put on makeup. "Be patient," they said sweetly. "We can't hold it much longer," we pleaded, but they ignored us. We left the apartment in search of a gas station. No luck. Unwilling to risk being fined for urinating in public, we dashed back into their apartment. "We'll be out in ten minutes," they cooed from behind the still-closed door. "That's what you said ninety minutes ago!" we groaned. We had no choice but to relieve ourselves under the stairwell of their apartment, experiencing one of those guilty moments of pleasure, a moment when you feel so good and so bad at the same time.

The rest of the evening didn't get much better. Jim wasn't Marsha's type, and she wasn't subtle about letting us know. She didn't speak to him the whole evening. I was thankful Jim had a strong enough ego that he simply shrugged it off. "Her loss!" he said.

St. George Hotel Dance, 1961
Front row from left: Matt, Joan, Marsha, Jim; back row from left: Al, Joan, me, Jodie

A month later Marsha and her sisters threw a dance party at their apartment and asked me to bring some male friends. I wasn't keen on playing matchmaker again, but she said I owed her for setting her up with someone she didn't like. When I saw her snuggling in a corner with my friend Gene, whom I'd brought to the party, I congratulated myself.

It was premature. Marsha called me the following week, asking why Gene hadn't called her. I contacted him for an explanation. "She's too hot for me," he said sheepishly. Gene said he preferred less-aggressive women. Since I was still dating her sister Jodie, I wanted to stay on her good side. I told Marsha that as much as Gene liked her, he was simply too preoccupied with work and school to date anyone. I didn't have the guts to point out that after treating my cousin so poorly, it was just her turn to be straight-armed.

After that, growing tired of the dating scene, I turned my attention from girls to academics. My grades were suffering, my mind had lost focus, and my first priority had to be on college. After my parents had sacrificed so much to send me to a private school in the face of their own financial problems, I couldn't let them down. But even though I pulled my grade point average up by my senior year, I couldn't make up for months of missed classes my freshman year. What had started as a case of mononucleosis developed into a more serious condition that required hospitalization (and the start of my search for alternative solutions that Western medicine had failed to provide).

A meeting with my school guidance counselor to discuss college applications was not encouraging. "Hon, you've got to be realistic. With your grade point average, you can forget about applying to any of the Ivy League schools. But I have a friend on the admissions board of a good public university, one I think would be an excellent choice for you."

THE IRON CHEF

Before heading off to college, I worked for Uncle Henry as a waiter, cashier, and takeout order boy at his Golden Phoenix Chinese Restaurant on Flatbush Avenue in Brooklyn. I didn't like working for a relative, but he was shorthanded, and I needed money for college. I should have known something was screwy when, on my first day there, Uncle Henry told me not to press the buzzer under the cash register. "It locks the front door when customers refuse to pay and sets off an alarm alerting the kitchen staff to run out with cleavers," he explained.

The dining room that could seat two hundred was mostly empty on a Friday night, with no more than four or five booths occupied. I looked out the windows onto the street and saw boarded-up storefronts that once housed mom-and-pop groceries and delis owned by middle-class Irish and Jewish immigrants. It was a neighborhood in decay. Muggings were so common that one waiter carried a butcher knife wrapped in newspaper to and from work.

One night the cook, who lived in a nearby building with a fire escape that went up to his apartment, woke up to the sound of someone climbing in through an open window. He opened his eyes and saw three intruders. Unfortunately for them, the cook was a kung fu master. He yanked one through the window, slammed him to the floor, and, with a bloodcurdling yell, knocked the burglar senseless with an iron skillet. The other two fled, deciding they didn't want to tangle with a frying pan-swinging Chinaman. Ironically, ten years later I would find myself in an identical predicament. Three armed men climbed through my open apartment window in the middle of the night and threatened me at knifepoint. I didn't acquit myself as well as the cook did, and I blamed Uncle Henry.

Before I could ask the cook-cum-kung fu master to teach me the how-to-thwart-midnight-intruders technique, Uncle Henry had fired him. I gagged when I heard the reason: Uncle Henry caught the cook soaking bean sprouts in the same bucket he used to mop the kitchen floor. Not that Uncle Henry was a paragon of hygienic virtue. Among things that wouldn't have passed health inspection was the flypaper he kept on the kitchen windowsill, not to keep flies out but rather to collect them. Every day he'd take his daily catch, mash the flies between his palms and vigorously massage them into his scalp. He claimed the flies nourished his scalp and kept his hair from turning white.

Uncle Henry had other folk remedies, and always had on hand a five-gallon jug of trauma liniment called Dit Da Jow, which literally means, "hit and fall wine." Made with over twenty kinds of raw Chinese herbs decocted in rice wine, it miraculously healed sprains, bruises, and broken bones. I regret not learning his secret Dit Da Jow recipe. Although I brew my own now, I've not been able to duplicate the potency of his magic formula.

Uncle Henry bragged that he knew kung fu and, when I was in grade school, tried to teach me some basics by making me stand in a half-squatting position called a horse stance for up to ten minutes while throwing punches. I liked how it strengthened my arms and chest and made my thigh muscles bulge, but I didn't think he knew real kung fu since he didn't look like my celluloid martial heroes.

KUMQUATS

Our relatives nicknamed Uncle Henry "Gabby" because he talked nonstop and was extremely opinionated, often peppering his speech with colorful expletives, frequently appalling customers when they heard his earthy language, but even more so when they heard his six-year-old son running around the restaurant shouting four-letter cuss words in English. Some people were amused by the boy, believing he had no idea what he was saying and that he was merely mimicking his father. I, on the other hand, had to put up with the brat all day and wanted to tape his foul mouth shut. When I met him twenty years later, I was pleased to see that he had grown into a soft-spoken, intelligent young man.

Uncle Henry never hesitated to argue with customers. When he overheard someone complaining that a meat dish was too chewy, he rushed into the walk-in freezer and lugged out a slab of beef. Slapping the meat and shoving the Grade A stamp inches away from the customer's face, he yelled, "See, I only use best grade, only best!" Of course, Uncle Henry didn't bother to mention how long the Grade A slab had sat in the freezer.

That Uncle Henry didn't believe in the adage that *the customer is always right* was obvious when a silver-haired couple—she in a red satin dress, he in coat and tie—came for dinner to celebrate their wedding anniversary. After finishing their main course, their waiter served them dessert: vanilla ice cream topped with preserved kumquats.

They seemed to be enjoying themselves until the woman bolted for the ladies room. The sound of retching could be heard even before the door closed behind her. When she emerged, her face ashen, her husband asked, "What happened?" as he eased her back into a chair.

"There was a roach in my dessert! It looked like a kumquat," she cried. Her husband tried to calm her as she wiped off yellow splotches that stained her dress and shoes. "Who's the manager? I'm gonna sue!" his wife demanded.

I watched as Uncle Henry sauntered over to their table, expecting him to make amends, to placate the irate couple, to offer them a free dinner. Maybe even pay to dry clean the dress. Instead, he nonchalantly said, "Don't worry madam, you don't have to pay for the kumquats."

Years later, Uncle Henry's restaurant burned down—something about a fire in the kitchen. Was it a disgruntled former employee or an angry customer? I'd hate to think it was Uncle Henry who torched the place himself.

The last time I saw him, Uncle Henry was a chef in a Chinatown restaurant, happy, back to his boisterous self. He was in his sixties, without a gray hair in sight. I was afraid to ask if he was still rubbing flies into his scalp. But, after saying farewell and shaking hands, I washed mine.

FIRST PATH

SCHOLAR WARRIOR

CHAPTER 3

GO WEST, YOUNG MAN

Education: the path from cocky ignorance to miserable uncertainty.

—MARK TWAIN

In the summer of 1961, I was on a Greyhound bound for the University of Oklahoma (OU) when the girl sitting next to me leaned into the aisle and vomited. Edging past her, trying to avoid stepping on her puddle, and hoping I wouldn't get carsick myself, I needed to use the toilet at the back of the bus. But it was locked, out of service, and it would be another hour before the next rest stop, and still twenty more before we reached Norman, Oklahoma.

I looked forward to life in a small college town. As we zipped past cars and trucks, drivers smiled and waved. People in the American heartland seemed friendlier than those back home. If you waved at someone on a New York roadway, you'd more than likely get the middle finger.

Aside from a desire to experience another part of the country, I chose OU for several reasons. It was inexpensive, had a Naval Reserve Officer Training Corps (NROTC) unit, and had a good engineering school. But above all, I could get in. Norman sat in the middle of the state, with OU comprising half of its 40,000 population. It had "the largest airport in the world used solely for educational purposes" and a couple of working oil wells. As our bus drove across campus, it looked like the colored brochures I had received, giving me a warm and welcoming feeling...until I checked into my dorm.

KINGFISHER HOUSE

My jaw dropped when I opened the door to my eight-by-twelve-foot room. Furnished with two pressboard desks and chairs and a steel bunk bed, it could have passed for a jail cell, except the windows had pull-down shades instead of iron bars. The room, in a two-story building that had once been a stable converted into a barracks for returning World War II veterans, left no doubt as to why it was the lowest-cost housing on campus.

My first time away from home, loneliness washed over me as the counselor handed me the key and shut the door behind him. I sat on the bunk bed wondering why I'd ever left New York. That evening, not wanting to be alone, I called up a McBurney classmate, also a newly arrived freshman, and visited his dorm on the newer side of campus. I envied his more luxurious room with real curtains and not pull-down shades, a real bed and not metal bunks, and soft carpets and not linoleum tile. I had settled for cheaper accommodations to save money because I didn't want to burden my parents any more than necessary.

My assigned roommate Mike arrived from Arkansas the next day. At five foot eight, with short brown hair, and a Southern drawl, he was smart, funny, and lovesick. My homesickness vanished as I tried to cheer him up. He spent every moment planning how he would reunite with Sarah, his high school sweetheart, who was at Mills College in California. After freshman year, Mike transferred to Stanford to be near her.

During freshman year I worked in the school library shelving books, a boring job but one that helped me earn extra spending money. School cafeteria food—nutritious, filling, if not always tasty—enabled me to eat things I'd never tried before and gave me an appreciation for pecan pie, collard greens, and creamed chipped beef on toast. At night, an enterprising student came through the dorms selling overpriced sandwiches, pastries, and drinks. Frugality goes out the window when you're hungry. One of my favorite snacks was "fried pies," a deep fat-fried turnover with a fruit filling.

Ruf Neks

There were three other New Yorkers in my dorm, guys kind enough to give me rides back home on holidays, including John Veccia, a high school track star and former Marine with a charismatic presence. When he spoke, people paid attention, possibly because his booming voice and thick Bronx accent rattled your eardrums.

John and five other Kingfisher residents were members of the Ruf Neks, a colorful if somewhat rowdy group. They invited me to a smoker to recruit new members. Organized in 1915, the Ruf Neks is OU's oldest men's pep club, appearing at football games and pep rallies to "assist the cheerleaders in enlivening school spirit and to protect the campus in cases of interschool rivalry." During games, Ruf Neks formed an arch with red-and-white paddles to greet the team as they ran onto the field, fired shotguns (loaded with blanks) when the team scored a touchdown, and recited a secret incantation at the beginning of each game.

Feendit feendit feendit fa!
Sooners Sooners rah rah rah!

I joined for the camaraderie, free entrance to the games, and the chance to meet other people. But I dreaded Hell Week, the final phase of initiation when, as pledges, we had to wear outlandish outfits while going around campus doing silly stuff, such as getting female students to sign their names with a pencil attached to a string that emerged from the tops of our shirts. It was obvious from their giggles and vigorous tugs that most figured out where the strings were attached.

Hazing was part of the Ruf Nek initiation ritual. During the final night of Hell Week, we were blindfolded and taken out to the middle of the woods, miles from campus. Around a campfire, we had to gulp down a mixture of laxative, hot sauce, and other vile-tasting ingredients. Stripped to our underwear, we were tied together and had to make it back to campus on our own.

Later, as club vice president, I tried to end hazing's more abusive aspects. Some members resisted, arguing that if they had to endure hell, others would too. Just when I thought I'd gotten everyone's agreement to stop excessive practices, the member in charge of pledge training went too far. Several pledges showed me black-and-blue marks on their legs and red welts on their buttocks where he had smacked them with a solid oak paddle. I blamed myself for letting things get out of control, for not being specific enough about what was allowed and what was not, and volunteered to take over pledge training myself. The red-and-white paddles were Ruf Nek symbols, ones that members were allowed to use playfully to slap pledges on the butt but not to inflict injury. I was glad when the overzealous pledge trainer wasn't reelected.

The club earned money by selling sun visors at games—just enough for us to go to out-of-town events and to visit other schools in the Big Eight Conference, a chance I wouldn't have gotten otherwise. Two alumni donated the Sooner Schooner, a red-and-white-covered wagon drawn by two white Shetland ponies, which our club looked after during its public appearances.

Me seated at left, holding the shotgun

An annual club highlight was the crowning of Ruf Nek Queen during the halftime ceremonies. You'd think the process of interviewing young and beautiful women would be a snap, but it wasn't that easy due to the large number of candidates vying for the title. Since the finalists were all gorgeous, and as unlikely as this may sound to some, in the end we usually voted for the one who seemed the most intelligent and articulate—someone who could be a good representative for not only the club, but also the school.

NROTC

Sitting in the student union auditorium with other freshman, listening to Reserve Officers Training Corps (ROTC) representatives trying to persuade us to select their program, I wanted to make sure I chose the right path toward being a commissioned officer. I was most impressed by the Navy captain's presentation. He said that the NROTC program was selective, that not everyone who applied would qualify, but that those who did would be able to develop morally, mentally, and physically to serve the country with honor, courage, and commitment. He was persuasive, much more so than the other two speakers with programs on campus—not that I needed much persuading. I'd already crossed off the Army based on my brother's input, and never gave any serious consideration to joining the Air Force. In addition, a Chinatown neighbor, who was a Navy officer, told me it was the best of the three programs.

A majority of NROTC midshipmen were on full four-year scholarships, but I was not, having discovered much too late—only after I got into the program—that you had to apply as early as your junior year in high school in a highly competitive process. I did, however, appreciate getting a stipend for books and a subsistence allowance my last two years of college; didn't have to go on cruises and get seasick[3] during the summer, as did scholarship recipients; and, with summers free, was able to do a variety of interesting work and encounter a variety of fascinating people, which I

---

3 Ironically, ocean cruising is now one of my favorite pastimes.

wouldn't have been able to do on a ship. During successive summers, for instance, I became a licensed industrial radiographer, climbing nearly one hundred-foot-high oil refinery towers in Oakland, California; a short order cook and canteen restaurant manager in a Pennsylvania mountain resort; and a door-to-door salesman in New York (more on this later).

Two of my best friends in the NROTC were Ron Wilkins and Terry Thompson. Ron was about six foot four, with the wholesome good looks of an Oklahoma farm boy. He invited me to his home on school breaks to get a glimpse of life in rural Oklahoma. He'd been an electronics technician in the Navy, which sponsored him through the NROTC program. Terry, a former enlisted man in the Navy, and I roomed together at Kingfisher house in our sophomore year and both joined the Marine Option program together. Instead of being commissioned as Navy ensigns, we would become Marine Corps second lieutenants. Fellow Kingfisher House resident John Veccia influenced Terry's decision, as well as mine, to become Marines.

Within minutes of meeting John, he'd let you know he'd been a jarhead and was ultra-proud of it. He hung a framed display in his room of his lance corporal insignia, the Marine Corps emblem (eagle, globe, and anchor), and his service ribbons. His salty stories about life in the Marines made me want to learn more. I watched a rerun of the movie *The D.I.* starring Jack Webb, gaining a new appreciation of what it means to earn the title of "Marine." Webb portrayed a tough Marine drill instructor who set uncompromising standards for those under his command.

I was also influenced by the Marine officers and enlisted men assigned to our NROTC unit. Compared to the Navy guys, they seemed so much more squared away, spit-shined shoes more glossy, uniforms more tailored, posture more military. I also found the Marines more approachable and always available whenever I needed help, while the Navy officers seemed more standoffish. Our NROTC drill instructor was a Marine gunnery sergeant who, when I asked him, taught us hand-to-hand combat and knife fighting, something I really appreciated because it wasn't a formal part of the curriculum then.

There were other reasons why I choose the Marines over the Navy, among them the fact that I got seasick riding on anything rougher than the Staten Island Ferry and didn't want to spend my life at sea. And I thought the Marine *dress blues* was the sharpest-looking uniform of any of the services. But most of all, I wanted a chance to test myself, to see if I was up to the challenge required to earn the coveted title of United States Marine. And I could never resist a challenge.

THE GOOD SAMARITAN

Ron's willingness to go out of his way to do good deeds prompted Terry to do his share as well. Late one night, spotting a car along the shoulder of a country road and stopping to see if he could be of service, he aimed the beam of his flashlight through the mist of a cold drizzling rain at a heavyset woman squatting near the car beside a ditch.

"Ma'am, is there anything I can do to help?" Terry asked with concern.

"Ya ain't got no toilet paper do ya?" she asked with more than a hint of irritation as she shielded her eyes from the light.

"Umm, no ma'am, I don't." Terry replied, embarrassed.

"Then, if ya don't mind, jus' let me do my business!"

That put an end to Terry's Good Samaritan phase. Terry wanted to be an aviator but was so tall that he was afraid he wouldn't get into flight school since he could barely squeeze into a cockpit. Sadly, he would never have the chance to fly, because shortly after getting commissioned and reporting to the US Marine Corps Basic School at Quantico, Virginia, Terry died on one of the most dangerous places on earth: Interstate 95.

THE CHURCH LADY

Ron had seen a classified ad for off-campus housing located within a ten-minute walk from campus. By our junior year, we'd grown tired of dorm living. As we walked over to see the place, Ron mentioned the owner had sounded uptight on the phone and might have reservations about a nonwhite boy from New York.

We walked around to the rear entrance of the house, a two-story white colonial on a quiet street shaded by mature elms. Mrs. Churchwell, a tall, middle-aged woman, came to the doorway and peered at us behind a locked screen door. Ron pulled out the ad from his back pocket, reminded her about their previous conversation, and explained our interest in renting a room. Mrs. Churchwell, inviting us into her living room, described what was available: two small bedrooms with a common entrance.

She emphasized that all tenants must obey house rules, i.e., no smoking, no alcohol, no women, and no cooking. She beamed with pride when she announced she was a good Southern Baptist and a member of the Daughters of the American Revolution. "My ancestors came over on the Mayflower!" she said. Ron said he too was a Southern Baptist and was active in the Campus Crusade for Christ. Her steely gaze turned in my direction. I wondered if she had been expecting me to say something to reassure her that I was no heathen either. I was ready to hum "Onward Christian Soldiers." We were, after all, in the middle of Oral Roberts territory.

Just as I was about to open my mouth, she asked, "You know Tim Lam?" Before I could say "Who?" she explained that he was one of her tenants and, for the next five minutes, described what a wonderful person he was.

"He's a Chinese fella from Hong Kong. I never ever let a foreigner in the house before, but I just had to make an exception in his case when I discovered who his father was," she explained in her nasal twang, pronouncing the name Tim with two syllables, making it sound like Tee-em. She rummaged through a stack of church periodicals until she found an article with an accompanying photo of the senior Dr. Lam. The caption read, "Founding president of Hong Kong Baptist University."

"I'm Chinese too!" I blurted out, trying to link myself in some tenuous way to the tenant who had passed muster.

"Well, I'll take a chance on you, seeing as how I've been nothing but impressed with Tee-em," Mrs. Churchwell declared.

So thanks to Tim, she let Ron and me live at 1020 Monett Avenue. After meeting Tim, I learned why she had been so impressed. He was a genius. He had completed his undergraduate work at Wake Forest University and was on his way to a second master's degree, this one in mechanical engineering. Whenever any of us had problems with math or science, he'd always be able to explain the solutions in understandable terms.

Every Thanksgiving, Mrs. Churchwell would invite all of us to dinner. The dining table would be set with a white tablecloth, fine china, and polished silver. The oven-roasted turkey was served with cranberry sauce, string beans, fresh corn, mashed potatoes, and gravy. Dessert was pecan pie and vanilla ice cream. We were grateful to have a nice home-cooked meal, but it would have been more enjoyable if Mrs. Churchwell and her feisty ninety-year-old mother hadn't traded barbs throughout the meal.

Mrs. Churchwell paid me to vacuum and clean once a week. We got along well until I made the careless mistake of leaving an empty beer bottle in the trash, foolishly thinking it was well hidden by the garbage I'd piled on top. How was I to know that she'd rummage through the trash? She kicked me out shortly after finding the incriminating evidence, sternly warning me that alcohol would lead to my ruin. Unfortunately, Tim had already graduated by then and had returned to Hong Kong, so he wasn't there to intervene on my behalf.

Tim and I stayed in touch over the years, first when I visited him in Hong Kong during an R&R from Vietnam and later during my travels in Asia. Then Tim and I would meet again some thirty years later, when he and his family immigrated to Northern Virginia and bought a beautiful home just fifteen minutes down the road from ours.

It was on that first visit to Hong Kong on a sightseeing tour, during a scenic stop on a hill, that I took a photo of a woman in a flower garden performing slow, dancelike movements that were gentle, elegant, and graceful. I was mesmerized. The tour guide said she was doing the Chinese martial art of taijiquan. At that moment, I knew it was something I just had to learn.

KOSHARE DANCERS

During my last year at OU, I moved into an apartment with Bob Benzin, a fellow Ruf Nek. Bob was in the Naval Enlisted Scientific Education

Program, which sponsored enlisted Marines and sailors through four years of college to study science and engineering. He was able to save on our grocery bills by shopping at a military commissary. Bob was a great cook and didn't mind preparing most of our evening meals in exchange for my cleaning up. I definitely got the better end of the bargain.

Bob majored in physics and entered the submarine service after earning his commission. On school breaks we visited his parents in La Junta, Colorado, where they ran a dry cleaning and laundry business—and they weren't even Chinese! Bob got me hooked on southwestern-style Mexican food. In high school he was a member of the Koshare Indian Dancers, which was part of the Boy Scouts. The dancers maintained Native American culture via ceremonial dance. Bob and I had lost touch over the years until I ran into another former Koshare Dancer who had worked at CIA. He was Bob's high school classmate and helped me reconnect with Bob. We've stayed in touch ever since.

BURGERS, BEER, AND BISCUITS

Food was always on the minds of us hungry students, maybe even more than sex, depending on when we last ate. We frequented several campus eateries, including the Town Tavern, a greasy spoon and sports bar, its walls covered with plywood panels listing Sooner game scores, year by year, since 1947. They served two of my favorite menu items: chicken fried steak and frosty, pint-sized mugs of beer called Sooner Schooners. They didn't check IDs, which made it a popular student hangout since most of OU's undergrads were below the twenty-one-year-old legal drinking age. Coors Beer was on tap and flowed green on St. Patrick's Day.

Most of the local joints served burgers—not the preprocessed tiny patties of the McDonald's variety but real beef that measured five inches in diameter and half an inch thick, that came on buns that you needed both hands to hold, garnished with cheese, lettuce, tomatoes, onions, ketchup, and mustard. For some reason I couldn't understand—maybe as a form of self-punishment or perhaps to find out if any other place besides Oklahoma served such giant-size wonders—Paul, a fellow New Yorker, always ordered a cheeseburger at every lunch or dinner stop we made driving between Oklahoma and NYC, and at every stop always complained about how terribly paper-thin and unadorned the meat paddies were compared with what he'd gotten used to at OU, always sending the waitress back for more meat and more condiments.

"More" was the byword for Stanley, a 1020 Monett housemate, whenever we ate at a diner on Main Street that offered a daily special at a reasonable price, always served with a basket of oven-fresh homemade biscuits. Stanley was a kind-hearted, good ol' country boy, but "couth" was definitely not his middle name. He'd always snap his fingers at the waitress, point to our empty basket, which had already been refilled at least once, and shout "more biscuits!" He wasn't satisfied with just one basket or even two of the fluffy, melt-in-your-mouth biscuits that he'd pour honey on and gobble up for dessert. Finally, the waitress began charging us for the extra baskets, which Stanley attributed to the fact that we were not big tippers.

MOST AND LEAST FAVORITE PROFESSORS

One of my favorite professors was Dr. Huff, who taught advanced calculus, loved his subject, displayed a dry sense of humor, and used expressions like "ad infinitum, ad nauseum" to mock our textbook author's pedantic style and "intuitively obvious to even the most casual observer" to make fun of the author's one-sentence footnote to explain a mathematical axiom requiring twenty pages of proof. My least favorite instructor was Earl Lafon, who taught a required math course all engineering majors had to pass, and who seemed to enjoy belittling students and giving failing grades. I barely passed and was frustrated that I didn't learn much despite my hard work.

Among my electives, my favorite professor was Percy Buchanan, who taught Far Eastern History. He was head of the judo club, which he invited me to join. He'd been an Army officer in World War II, served in the Pacific, spoke fluent Japanese, and was knowledgeable about China. He insinuated that he had close ties to US intelligence and recommended former students to the CIA. It sounded intriguing.

MOST USEFUL CLASSES

My favorite classes were not in my major but in my minor: psychology. The study of human behavior in individuals and in groups was endlessly fascinating because I had a chance to observe it every day: the campus was a living, breathing laboratory. Plus, my psychology and sociology classes had lots of pretty girls whereas my engineering and math classes had very few. As it turned out, my psychology classes (and my organizational behavior classes as an MBA student) would prove to be far more useful when I had to deal with people as a military commander, case officer, martial arts instructor, and acupuncturist.

GRADUATION

In the summer of 1966, I received a bachelor of science degree and, at the same time, a Marine Corps commission. I don't know which made me happier. Our NROTC drill instructor was happy too, ready to salute us brand-new second lieutenants, and we were equally ready—dare I say even eager—to return the salute and hand him a shiny silver dollar. (Tradition requires newly commissioned officers to give a silver dollar to the first enlisted person who salutes them.)

With a major in electrical engineering and minors in math and psychology, it had taken five long years to graduate. College, at least the academics, had, for the most part, been a grind. I was so glad to be done with school that the thought of ever pursuing an advanced degree never even entered my mind. I would have laughed if someone had told me then that my formal academic studies would be ongoing and that I would eventually earn postgraduate degrees in business administration, national security, and Chinese medicine.

CHAPTER 4

THE FEW, THE PROUD,

THE MARINES

Some people spend an entire lifetime wondering if they made a difference in the world. But the Marines don't have that problem.

—RONALD REAGAN

Chief Thompson, our NROTC gunnery instructor, described shelling enemy troops in Korea. "Through my binoculars I saw the Chicoms climbing up the ridge. They were in single file silhouetted against the sky. After firing a spotter round to get the correct range, we let loose salvo after salvo of high-explosive rounds. It was like shooting ducks at the penny arcade!" The chief's story—told in antiseptic fashion—about firing at the enemy from the safety of a ship miles offshore, was one more reason why I wanted to be a Marine instead of a Navy officer. I had a romanticized notion of combat. "If I go into battle, I want to it to be up close and personal," I told myself naively.

ESPRIT DE CORPS

Although the other military services have special units with high esprit, it permeates the entire Marine Corps, from private to general, from office clerk to battlefield commander. In the Corps, there are no special shoulder patches, no special head coverings, and no special boots to differentiate special units from not-so-special units. In the Corps, everyone is just a Marine, and being a Marine is more than enough. Every former or active duty Marine I ever met exuded pride in belonging to an elite brotherhood. This was exemplified on an orientation visit to the Marine Corps Base at Camp Pendleton, California, with my NROTC unit. I would have expected to hear about the glories of the Corps from the base commander or a recruiting officer or drill instructor. But the Corp's most eloquent emissary during our visit was a private, a black Marine bus driver with a mellow baritone voice who drove us around. As he entertained us with a song about his beloved Corps, I couldn't help but be moved by an organization that could instill such deep, genuine, heartfelt pride.

(Sung to the tune of "Ghost Riders in the Sky")

You can have your Army khaki, you can have your Navy blue,
There's just one kind of uniform, I'll introduce to you.
It's not made of gold or silver, but it's the finest ever seen
It's worn with pride and honor, it's called Marine Corps green.
Here's a different sort of fighting man, the best the world has seen.
The Germans called him Devil Dog, but his real name is Marine!
He was born on Parris Island, the land that God forgot.
The bunks are hard, the water's cold, the sun is blazing hot.
He gets up every morning, way before the rising sun,
He runs a hundred miles or more, before the day is done.
He peels a million onions and twice as many spuds,
And when he gets a little time he goes to wash his duds.
He fought on Okinawa, and on Iwo Jima too,
The enemy thought he was a fighting god, when he fought on Peleliu
And when he hit that beachhead, he dug into the sand,

And many a brave Marine, my boy, lies buried in that land.
When the Army or the Navy ever tread from heaven's scene,
They will find their wives are sleeping with United States Marines.
And when he gets to heaven, to St. Peter he will tell,
"Another Marine reporting, sir, I've served my time in hell!"

OFFICER CANDIDATE SCHOOL

During my junior year of college, attending Officer Candidate School (OCS) at Quantico, Virginia, as part of the Marine Option Program, I was assigned to a platoon of forty midshipmen, supervised by two drill instructors under a Marine lieutenant. The training was designed to challenge us mentally, emotionally and physically, to evaluate our leadership potential, and to teach us basic combat skills. Others who had survived the training told me what to expect, including an upperclassman who'd been "recycled" because of problems the previous summer. Although he was smart and physically fit, he said it was all about having the right attitude, and the drill instructors thought he'd been too cocky.

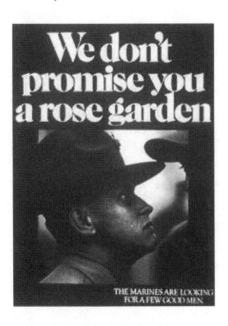

Marine recruiting poster

Before going to OCS, I used the entire school year to prepare for the grueling six weeks, running three miles daily in combat boots to build endurance and increasing the number of pull-ups, push-ups, and sit-ups I needed to do to score well on the physical fitness test. I knew the pace would be unrelenting, the weather hot and humid, and our drill instructors demanding.

George, a fellow Marine Option from Oklahoma, came to New York to visit me before we departed for OCS. Since it was his first trip to New York, I enjoyed showing him my favorite parts of the city. We went to the World's Fair at Flushing Meadows, getting a panoramic view of the world in miniature. As we walked from one nation's exhibition to the next, I hoped that one day I'd be able to visit these interesting places for real.

We drove to Quantico in George's canary yellow Mustang, arriving on one of the hottest days of July. Outside a Quonset hut (a sheet metal structure used in World War II), we waited to process in. With their Smokey Bear hats and crisp military bearing, drill instructors walked by and snarled at us. "They look like they could eat nails for breakfast," George observed. We were exhausted by the time we finished processing, collected our gear, and met our platoon sergeants. After dinner, we marched over to a World War II-style wooden barracks, where we stowed our belongings and cleaned the area, not allowed to bunk down until everything was squared away.

We stumbled out of bed well before dawn to the sound of drill instructors banging garbage cans to wake us, shouting at us to change into physical training gear for a run and calisthenics. *Move your fat ass maggot!* Anyone caught moving too slowly would get severely chewed out, have to do countless push-ups, or be penalized in some imaginatively unpleasant way that only a DI could conjure up. A typical training day included some combination of the following: PT, close-order drill, a three-mile run with full pack and rifle, running the obstacle course, and running the confidence course. We had exercises involving small arms, supporting arms, company-level tactics, first aid, hand-to-hand combat, and pugil stick fighting. Then there were twenty-six-mile forced marches with full pack, plus day and night field exercises.

I found one of the most engaging exercises was actually modeled after some of those used by the Office of Strategic Services, CIA's predecessor organization WWII, to select personnel for espionage assignments. In one of several exercises, we were divided into six-man teams and confronted with a problem that could only be solved if we worked together, such as fording a stream carrying a log or climbing over a wall with a wounded Marine. With no designated group leader, there was ample opportunity to show leadership, not of the John Wayne, I'm-in-charge variety, but rather the kind that called for showing tact when working within a group, volunteering for tasks no one else wanted, and helping guide other team members.

The thing I dreaded most was trekking up the infamous Hill Trail, a steeply sloped trail purposely hosed down to make it slippery and muddy, often the final part of a long run or forced march. Our drill instructors knew how much to push us without going over the edge. Well, most of the time anyway. One midshipman in my platoon suffered heatstroke and was dropped from the program. Nonetheless, we knew our instructors had to endure much tougher training than we did just to become DIs, so we respected them and did our best to earn their approval. DIs have gravelly voices because their vocal cords have been damaged from overuse. As part of their training, they had to scream cadences at the top of their lungs so that they could be heard across a drill field. Their voices are instruments of motivation or intimidation.

My toughest challenge at OCS wasn't physical; it was staying awake, especially after a big meal and during lectures. First aid was the worst. It was hard not falling asleep after a lunch of spaghetti and meatballs when you're sitting in a hot Quonset hut with no air conditioning while an instructor drones on about sucking chest wounds. I tried holding my breath, biting my tongue and clenching my teeth, but that didn't work. Odd, but the one thing that kept me from falling off my chair was watching the guy next to me nodding off, possibly because I had to focus on nudging him before he keeled over.

Horse and Rider

Toward the end of our training, during PT we played horse and rider, one of my favorite games as a kid. Someone got on my shoulders as we paired up and tried to knock down other teams. My team did well staying upright until I tripped. I heard a loud pop, which was my knee giving way. My partner's full weight fell on top of my buckled left leg. Stupidly, I got up and continued to play, not realizing the seriousness of my injury until an x-ray showed a torn knee ligament. Hospitalized that afternoon and for three days with my leg in traction, I was depressed.

When Lieutenant Shadduck, my platoon commander, visited the next day, I braced for bad news, knowing candidates were routinely washed out for physical or psychological reasons. A lucky few were given a second chance to repeat the program the following year if deemed worthy. Fortunately, Lieutenant Shadduck said my performance to date showed I could handle the physical side of training, and since the next phase involved more classroom than fieldwork, he'd let me complete the program without having to recycle. I was grateful. He showed me you don't have to be a rule-bound hard-ass to be a good leader.

I finished the rest of the course hobbling around on crutches with my leg in a cast. During the final field exercise, our company hiked up the Hill Trail to get into a defensive position. I was sitting on a log, with my crutches out of sight, when someone from another platoon staggered past me. With his shirt drenched in sweat from the hike and the ninety-degree heat, he said, "Hey man, you gotta be in fantastic shape. You didn't even break a sweat." I didn't have the heart to tell him I had hitched a ride up the hill on the chow truck.

Lance Lieutenant

"Goddamn it! You laughing at me?" screamed 1st Lieutenant Cobb, the red-faced commander of 4th Platoon. 2nd Lieutenant Nate Wong, the target of Cobb's wrath, clicked his heels, stood at ramrod attention, and shouted back, "Sir, no sir!" Cobb's red hair, freckled complexion, and youthful appearance made him look like Howdy Doody gone wild. He couldn't have been more than a year or two older than the rest of us. Did he overcompensate to make sure we knew he was in charge?

He blew up after catching the tail end of a skit Nate and others in his platoon enacted to lampoon an order for us to carry notebooks in our left hand as we marched to class. We understood the rationale to avoid looking like unruly civilians but felt it was going overboard when a follow-up order specified not only which hand to use but also to hold the notebooks with seams facing downward.

In their skit, Nate and his cohorts conspicuously held their lunch cartons in their left hand, marched to the dumpster in formation, and deposited their empty boxes with military precision. We doubled over laughing, reminded of the silly things we had to do in the name of military uniformity. Cobb wasn't amused, however, not realizing we weren't mocking him but simply releasing the pressure we felt going through the rigors of The Basic School (TBS).

In July 1966, 181 of us were assigned to Company B at TBS in Quantico. We were part of the class of 1-67, newly commissioned officers about to learn how to lead Marines in combat by undergoing six months of intensive war-fighting training at the platoon and company level. Our program had been condensed to twenty-one weeks, making it even more intensive as a result. But Vietnam's demand for fresh blood had exceeded the supply. Every Marine, no matter what his occupational specialty, is expected to be a rifleman first. So the focus at TBS is infantry tactics. The character of every class is unique, shaped by its students, instructors, and the real-world scenarios the students would encounter upon graduation.

Some classes might have a majority of students commissioned via OCS or the Platoon Leaders Class. Ours had mostly gone through NROTC. So aside from having survived OCS, we had also spent four years during college marching around a drill field, spit-shining shoes, and wearing a uniform. This was in addition to getting a stipend or scholarship to study military campaigns, tactics, leadership, and the missions of the Navy and Marine Corps. In other words, as a group, we were well indoctrinated and "gung ho" by the time we arrived at TBS. Knowing that Vietnam loomed on the horizon, we wanted to get the most out of our training. So while flower children were burning bras and draft cards, we were preparing our minds and bodies for the rigors of war.

Most of the staff instructors were topnotch subject experts who willingly shared their combat experience and technical knowledge. In the classroom, they lectured us on leadership, military justice, first aid, and combat intelligence. They gave us tips on how to run the obstacle course and confidence course faster, egged us on during physical training and forced marches, supervised us on the firing range as we tried to qualify with an M-14 rifle and a .45 caliber pistol, taught us hand-to-hand combat, and showed us how to survive in the water by making a float with our pants. From them we learned how to read maps and identify terrain features as we navigated the hills and valleys of Quantico. In the field, we set up radio communications, blew things up with land mines and plastic explosives, fired machine guns and rocket launchers, and called in artillery and air strikes. Throughout our training, we were given different leadership roles during field exercises and simulated combat scenarios so that we could demonstrate and be evaluated on our leadership ability.

On the administrative side, B Company consisted of four platoons, each supervised by a captain or first lieutenant. They were new, and we were the first company they'd supervised. Because they would be judged on how well we did, they kept us on a tight leash. We learned years later that they'd been unnecessarily concerned about controlling a cocky bunch of know-it-alls. And, truth be told, we were cocky. Our ranks were filled with star athletes, class valedictorians, lawyers, and graduates from some of the nation's top schools. Intimidated, they treated us not as the well-motivated junior officers that we were, but as lance lieutenants—more than OCS candidates but less than real lieutenants.

Captain Bartlett, my platoon commander, was arguably the most levelheaded of the bunch. A tall, lanky southerner who described things he liked as "real fine," except it came out sounding like "reeal fan," Bartlett was unlike the other platoon commanders who probably saw the movie *The D.I.* one too many times and tried to act like Jack Webb. Captain Bartlett never raised his voice. So I was taken aback when he called me to his office to chew me out.

"Lieutenant Lee, I'm *reeal* disappointed in your performance lately. You just don't seem motivated," he said as he scanned my midcourse evaluations.

I was dumbfounded. I didn't think I'd been doing badly, but Bartlett, in his low-key way, dressed me down.

"Lieutenant, I expected great things from you, that you'd rank at the top of your peers. What the hell happened on the rifle range?"

I was embarrassed to tell him my rifle had jammed. Not earning at least a marksmanship badge is a cardinal sin in the Marine Corps.

"No excuse, sir! Got shook up when my rifle jammed."

"That's because you didn't have presence of mind. You probably still had time to hit enough bull's-eyes to qualify after you cleared the jam!"

He was right, I'd lost it, wasted precious seconds refocusing. By the time I squeezed off a few well-aimed shots, time had run out. I admitted I wasn't doing as well as I should have, but I wanted to set Bartlett straight.

"Captain, I'm trying my best! I'm as motivated now as I ever was."

"Well, I wanna see the ole Lieutenant Lee. I wanna see you giving it a hundred and ten percent! Understand?"

"Sir, yes, sir!"

I marched out crestfallen.

SELF-EVALUATION

It was time for honest self-evaluation. I should have been doing better. Academically, I had difficulty focusing unless the subject or speaker held my interest. It wasn't as if I hadn't been studying. Just the opposite: I tried too hard. It would only be years later that I would learn how to study effectively. It's a wonder I graduated from college.

At TBS, leadership scenarios saved me from landing at the very bottom of class rankings. Field instructors held my attention with fascinating stories about combat, drawing on their actual experiences to highlight tactical concepts that we'd have to execute, much like a football coach would draw up plays, have us scrimmage, and then critique us afterward. One scenario illustrated envelopment, where you go around the enemy's defenses instead of assaulting from the front, like a quarterback making an end run instead of going up the middle. Yes, this was Sun Tzu's *Art of War* principle of not using force on force, of exploiting your enemy's weaknesses. I loved it.

We were assigned different positions. As a platoon commander you assessed the situation and told subordinates the objective and what to do, all within minutes. To ensure that leaders issue commands to cover key points, the military uses SMEAC, a mnemonic for the "five paragraph order." It means:

> Situation (enemy and friendly units)
> Mission (who, what, where, when, and why)
> Execution (commander's intent, scheme of maneuver, fire support plan, and tasks)
> Administration/Logistics (food, ammunition, supply, etc.)
> Command/Communications (key leader locations, primary and secondary signals)

This mnemonic served me well both in training and during combat but also later as a civilian supervisor coordinating CIA clandestine operations.

One of our instructors, Captain Kelly, was a respected Vietnam vet who taught "fire and maneuver" tactics. One element lays down a base of fire to keep the enemy pinned down while other elements move forward, then roles are switched so that the maneuvering element becomes the base, allowing other elements to advance. During an exercise, where I was assigned as the platoon commander with a mission to assault a fortified enemy position, I huddled with my squad leaders and issued a five-paragraph order as each of them, in turn, repeated the SMEAC sequence with their squads.

I received written feedback the next day via Captain Leopold, one of B Company's administrative platoon commanders. He was not popular due to his gruff manner. While I stood at attention, he read Captain Kelly's glowing evaluation giving me "outstanding" marks for leadership. "You agree with this?" he asked. From his tone of voice, Leopold made it clear he didn't think I deserved such high praise. I simply said "Yes, sir! By your leave, sir," and left his office scratching my head.

LIGHTER MOMENTS

One of my more amusing displays of leadership happened on the way to amphibious warfare training, scheduled for a week at the Naval Amphibious Base located at Little Creek, Virginia, where we would climb down cargo nets from a troop carrier onto small landing craft to practice ship-to-shore assaults. We partied the night before in Quantico, knowing there would be no physical training exercises early the next morning. Unfortunately the five-hour drive to Little Creek seemed excruciatingly long for those of us who had too much beer the night before. When the buses reached a roadside rest stop along I-95, 181 men made a mad dash for the restroom. Long lines snaked around the lone brick building that could accommodate no more than six at a time. Because we were expected to re-board the buses within fifteen minutes, there was no way everyone could get a chance to use the facility. Making a snap command decision, I directed people to fan out into the woods. We were supposed to be officers and gentleman, but decorum gave way to urgency. Little old ladies gasped at the sight of uniformed men hiding behind any available bush or tree, fertilizing the Virginia foliage.

We never had much free time at TBS. When we did, we frequented the Latch String, a Fredericksburg pub run by a former Marine. It was next door to Mary Washington, an all-girls college at the time. With guitars in hand and beer in our bellies, platoon mate Dick Larson and I serenaded college girls and fellow Marines. The song I'd learned at Camp Pendleton from the Marine bus driver was a crowd pleaser. We weren't that good, but we were gratified when people bought us round after round to keep us going.

POSTER MARINE

The high-pressure pace at TBS made us edgy, so much so that I almost came to blows with Van, a "poster" Marine who stood next to me in formation. His spit-shined shoes looked like glass and his utilities (fatigues) were always starched and creased. He'd been in the enlisted reserves and was always "squared away." There was much to admire about Van, except for one annoying trait: he always found fault with others. Late one evening, after an exhausting field exercise, we exchanged heated words as we stood alone, nose-to-nose, in the parking lot behind the Bachelor Officer Quarters.

"Come on, you little scumbag! Go ahead and hit me. I'll let you take the first shot."

Standing with his jaw jutting forward and hands on hips, daring me to throw the first punch, Van presented an inviting target. I assessed the situation. On the one hand, it was so very tempting to rear back and deck him. On the other hand, he was in good shape and might not go down with one shot. What if we both ended up hurt and unable to finish the program?

"Van, I don't want to fight. But if you insist, I'm going all out and won't quit until one of us is dead," I replied in my best Charles Bronson voice.

That got Van to calm down long enough for us to have our first serious conversation. Even though we saw each other every day, because Van was married and lived in Married Officers Quarters, we never had a chance to really get to know each other. I told him that whenever he said anything it was always to complain about something I or someone else did or didn't do.

"Van, why are you constantly on my back?"

"It's because you're unmotivated, Lee! You do well when you're in charge, but you act like you don't care when you're not. It's like you're two different people."

Van's words stung. Being called unmotivated in the Marine Corps is like being called a pervert. All Marines are supposed to be gung-ho.

"Van, I'm quiet by nature and prefer staying in the background. Guess it's partly my personality and partly cultural. But that doesn't mean I don't care!"

Van slowly nodded as if he understood. "OK, sorry if I come across as overly critical. My wife says I'm too much of a perfectionist. She's trying to help me with this."

We began chatting about shared interests instead of our differences. It was midnight by the time we shook hands. Out of that frank encounter came mutual respect. Most importantly, it taught me that my reticence could be misinterpreted as indifference. My inclination to remain in the shadows would serve me well in a future career that called for anonymity, but it would not always be seen as a positive attribute.

Some forty years later, during a reunion with my TBS classmates, we purchased commemorative bricks to line a walkway at the National Marine Corps Museum at Quantico. They were engraved with the names of those classmates who were killed in Vietnam. Van, a fighter pilot, was among them.

THE KING OF BATTLE

Before graduating from TBS, I'd selected infantry as my first of three choices for an MOS (Military Occupational Specialty). Afraid the war would end without me, I wanted to get to Vietnam without delay. Infantry officers went straight over whereas those with other specialties required additional training. I got artillery, my second choice. I was disappointed but not entirely unhappy since it meant a chance to spend time with friends and family before heading overseas and a few more months of advanced training. I would learn that while infantry is the queen of battle, field artillery is king of the battlefield.

In December 1966 I arrived at Fort Sill, Oklahoma, where soldiers and Marines learn fire support at the Army Field Artillery School.[4] I liked directing artillery rounds to hit targets quickly and accurately. An artillery officer has to able to read maps, calculate distances and directions to targets, and determine the types of artillery shells needed to get the job done. It was a set of skills that required mathematical precision that I knew I would soon employ. But I didn't appreciate doing it from a windy mountaintop in the dead of winter. As one student practiced zeroing in on a target, then calling in and adjusting artillery rounds, the rest of us had to sit motionless waiting our turns. Even with three layers of clothing that included thermal underwear, woolens, and outer gear, I was chilled to the bone, the coldest I'd ever been before or since.

My return to Oklahoma brought me back in contact with my college classmate John Veccia, who warmed me up with a gift bottle of Johnny Walker when he came to see me at Ft. Sill. A "cannon cocker" when he was in the Marine Corps, John gave me valuable tips on how to set up an artillery firing position, something I was having difficulty with in class. After college, John joined the Oklahoma City Police Department (he would later be a special agent with the Bureau of Alcohol, Tobacco and Firearms). When I visited him in Oklahoma City, he let me ride around in his patrol car one evening. I found it thrilling driving though the streets of the city with headlights off trying to catch crooks and speeders.

While at Fort Sill, four positions opened for a twelve-week Vietnamese course at the Defense Language Institute in Monterey, California. I thought learning the local language would get me to a frontline unit faster. I was

---

4 "Fire support is long-range firepower provided to a front-line military unit. Typically, fire support is provided by artillery or close air support (usually directed by a forward observer), and is used to shape the battlefield or, more optimistically, define the battle." (From: http://en.wikipedia.org/wiki/Fire_support, accessed January 25, 2014)

determined to avoid a rear-area job away from the action once I got "in-country." Although I didn't score well on the foreign language aptitude test, I talked the head of the Marine unit into letting me go, promising to study hard.

I immediately fell in love with the Monterey Bay area, its scenic ambiance, and fall-like weather all year-round. I graduated first in my class, primarily because I had an easier time learning a tonal language than the other students but also because I finally learned how to study in bite-size chunks of time and material. I set a goal of returning to the Institute to study Mandarin Chinese if I survived my tour in Vietnam.

As I said good-bye to Monterey and my classmates, we kidded each other about how many medals we'd earn, giving play to Napoleon's maxim that "a soldier will fight long and hard for a piece of colored ribbon" but knowing full well that some of us wouldn't make it back, at least not in one piece.

CHAPTER 5

VIETNAM REFLECTIONS

It is well that war is so terrible lest we should grow too fond of it.

—ROBERT E. LEE

I arrived in Vietnam in the summer of 1967 with the Headquarters Battery of the 13th Marine Artillery Regiment, part of the 9th Marine Amphibious Brigade, on a troopship from Okinawa, disembarking at the mouth of the Cua Viet River on the northeast coast of South Vietnam along the demilitarized zone (DMZ) separating the south from North Vietnam— the scene of some of the war's heaviest fighting. I looked around, trying to decide if I should be pleased or not that I had finally gotten my wish to be up close to the action. A bead of sweat dripped off my forehead, vaporizing the instant it fell onto the ship's metallic deck. As we unloaded equipment onto small landing craft, a single shot from an enemy sniper zipped overhead, welcoming us to the war zone.

We motored upriver to Dong Ha, a logistics hub for supplies destined for other parts of I Corps.[5] Although considered a rear area, we were nervous as we waited to join an armed convoy the next day to Khe Sanh, our ultimate destination. Bunking down for the night in a plywood "hooch," a temporary living quarters with a ten-foot-long and two-foot-wide trench dug right outside the entrance, we quickly discovered the trench's utility when the sound of artillery woke us in the middle of the night. "Incoming!" someone yelled, causing us to scramble for the trench. Luckily no one got hurt in the frenzied stampede, but when I got up the next morning, I found a size twelve boot print smack in the middle of my lower back. Had my back not hurt so much I would have laughed at how comical we must have looked, blindly stumbling over each other to squeeze into the narrow trench. Even now I still don't know if it was actually enemy incoming or the sound of our own outgoing rounds. We were newbies and couldn't tell the difference then, but we would soon get plenty of practice.

5 The I Corps Tactical Zone was a corps of the Army of the Republic of Vietnam (ARVN), the army of the nation state of South Vietnam that existed from 1955 to 1975. It was one of four corps the ARVN oversaw. This was the northernmost region of South Vietnam, bordering with North Vietnam. (From Wikipedia http://en.wikipedia.org/wiki/I_Corps_(South_Vietnam), accessed January 25, 2014)

Khe Sanh Combat Base, on the northwestern edge of the DMZ[6], sat in a valley of red clay surrounded by lush green hills and triple-canopied rain forest that hid the infamous Ho Chi Min Trail, a complex network of jungle roads and tunnels the enemy used to infiltrate men and supplies to the south. The scene of heavy fighting in the spring of 1967, it was relatively calm when we arrived that summer.

We set up tents on the western edge of the base and settled into a routine. It was like living in the middle of a giant football field in a huge stadium but surrounded on all sides by hills instead of bleachers. Whoever occupied the hills controlled the ground below. A long airstrip in the middle of the field was one of two ways to move supplies and troops in and out of Khe Sanh. The other was the way we'd come, along Route 9, the east-west highway that stretched just below the DMZ. Both were dangerous. By air, you risked getting shelled on landing or takeoff. By land, you risked getting blown up by a land mine or being ambushed. Dick, a college classmate, was badly wounded while on a mine-clearing operation along Route 9.

I was assigned to the battalion's Fire Direction Center (FDC), responsible for coordinating artillery support for the 26th Marine Regiment. Because the FDC is the brains of an artillery unit, it had to be well shielded from enemy shelling. So the first thing we did when we arrived at Khe Sanh was to bulldoze a giant hole, about forty feet by twenty feet by fifteen feet, and line it with dirt-filled wooden ammunition crates. Because we were too dumb to consider the upcoming monsoon season, it flooded. We spent weeks bailing water and rebuilding. During the wet season, everything turned slimy-green and smelled moldy. In the dry season, a fine dust of red clay covered everything.

---

6 The **Vietnamese Demilitarized Zone** was established as a dividing line between North and South Vietnam as a result of the First Indochina War. During the Second Indochina War (popularly known as the Vietnam War), it became important as the battleground demarcation separating North Vietnamese territory from South Vietnamese territory. http://en.wikipedia.org/wiki/Vietnamese_Demilitarized_Zone, accessed January 25, 2014:

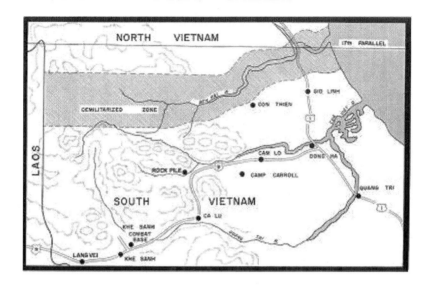

Map of DMZ and Route 9

After a month as a watch officer sitting around a bunker, I badgered my superiors to let me go to the field, either as an forward observer (FO) or to join a combined action platoon[7] where I could use my Vietnamese language skills, although the latter assignment was less likely since it was a job filled by experienced infantry officers. The FDC plots a target on a map, calculates the trajectory needed to hit the target, and issues commands to the guns, but someone has to be close enough to see the target in order to radio the exact location to the FDC and to make corrections after the first round is shot so that subsequent rounds can bracket and destroy the target. That someone is the FO, and I wanted to be that someone, to be the eyes and ears of the artillery unit, to be on the front lines with the infantry.

Sensing I'd keep bugging him, my commanding officer finally sent me to Alpha Battery, which supplied FOs to the rifle companies. I was

---

7 (From Wikipedia: http://en.wikipedia.org/wiki/Combined_Action_Program) The United States Marine Corps operated the Combined Action Program during the Vietnam War, from 1965 to 1971. The concept of combining a squad of Marines with local Popular Forces (PFs) and assigning them a village to protect proved to be a force multiplier.

attached to Delta Company, 1st Battalion, 26th Marine Regiment, under the command of 1st Lieutenant Ernie Spencer, who was also in Monterey with me. My TBS classmates Ross Brown and Walt Chapman were platoon commanders by then and had a good deal of on-the-ground combat experience. It was reassuring, as the new guy on the block, to see familiar faces, knowing I could count on them to teach me what I needed to know.

Life with the infantry was a welcome change, providing a chance to put into practice what I'd learned in training. As a green 2nd lieutenant, I was lucky to have Corporal Mac as assistant leader of our four-man FO team, schooling me on essential survival skills, including how to make a C-ration meal tasty by mixing together various ingredients. Although many guys hated Cs, I was an exception, even learning to like canned ham and lima beans—one of the first rations that others traded.

The makers of Tabasco Sauce published The *Charlie Ration Cookbook* with recipes using only easily found ingredients. The recipes made the meals more palatable if not delicious. For example, mixing turkey loaf with syrup from canned peaches added moisture and sweetness to an otherwise dry and hard-to-swallow meal.

Mac was a crusty field Marine with a talent for scrounging things. Unfortunately, the company gunnery sergeant caught him "finding" something and put him on report. The skipper[8] called me on the carpet. However, instead of giving Mac an Article 15 punishment (for minor offenses that do not warrant a court martial), he realized Mac was a good NCO and left it up to me to discipline him. Because of the incident, I couldn't justify recommending Mac when he came up for promotion. I regretted my decision. I never saw him again after I left Khe Sanh and hope he made sergeant on the next round of promotions.

---

8 In the Marine Corps, "skipper" is a term of respect for a company grade commander, usually a captain.

I listen for incoming

Someone once described combat as 90 percent boredom and 10 percent terror. When not shooting at someone or getting shot at, you're preparing for or recovering from combat. Much time is spent on humdrum but essential chores: maintaining equipment, cleaning weapons, fortifying positions, filling sandbags, digging foxholes, and getting supplies ad infinitum, ad nauseum (as Professor Huff used to say).

During downtimes, I had a chance to wonder why the US high command considered Khe Sanh a base of strategic importance. Whatever the reason, it was apparent that static defense was not a mission the Marines were used to or good at. We had a steep learning curve and, in the interim, would pay dearly while Washington politicians debated courses of action and Saigon generals experimented with a succession of strategies, each apparently no more successful than the last.

Patrolling the area on foot gave me a keen appreciation of the dense terrain around Khe Sanh, which was impossible to fully grasp by simply flying over in a helicopter or by studying aerial and satellite photos. This might explain why some of the ideas crafted by Washington war planners were ridiculously ineffective, most notably the "McNamara Wall" of electronic sensors and the use of Agent Orange to defoliate forested areas. Sadly, these ideas dreamed up by armchair warriors were emblematic of a lack of area knowledge at the highest levels of the US command.

Hiking up and down the hilly terrain on patrol was exhausting because the ground was slippery, especially during the rainy season. On patrols it was a good idea to wear gloves because the so-called "elephant grass," growing ten feet high or more, with its sharp edges, sliced through clothing and flesh when you climbed up and down the surrounding hills. During the dry season, it got unbearably hot, like walking around in a sauna with a full load of combat gear. Because we carried only two canteens per man, we had to ration what we drank so we wouldn't run out before we could find a stream. On long patrols all I could think about was a glass of ice-cold "bug juice," as Marines called Kool-Aid.

Each Marine was loaded down with a weapon, rations, sleeping gear, entrenching tool, canteens, first aid kit, helmet, backpack, etc., weighing anywhere from twenty to forty pounds in all. Our gear was vintage World War II and not well designed. Compared with the Army's well-constructed backpacks with thick shoulder pads, ours had narrow straps that cut off circulation, making our loads seem even heavier. My radio operator Richard Friend carried an additional twenty-five-pound radio. When he sprained his foot and I had to carry his load, I realized how much of a burden he literally shouldered every time we went on patrol. I never took him for granted after that.

My radio operator Richard Friend on patrol

Threats to our existence didn't only appear on two legs. Leeches infested low-lying areas. One Marine was medevacked after a leech crawled up his penis. Ouch! A platoon commander was seriously gored in the leg by an enraged water buffalo. Although I never saw one, a tiger reportedly attacked another Marine. What I personally experienced was running into a bee's nest, another constant worry.

Delta Company set up on Hill 881 South[9], guarding one of the key northern approaches to Khe Sanh. My FO team lived in a nine-by-twelve-by-ten-foot bunker that we dug by hand, lining the inside with dirt-filled ammunition crates, covering the top with metal sheeting and then piling sandbags on top to serve as a roof. Even though it was a combat outpost, it felt safe to return to the hooch at the end of the day, a place that protected us from the rain and enemy fire—a place to sleep, dream, and recuperate.

By candlelight we read dog-eared paperbacks that we passed around like prized possessions: a means of escape, however temporary, from activities that required total vigilance. A great nuisance, not to mention health hazard, were the ever-present rodents the size of cats that shared our living spaces and rations. One got into our bunker and caused us many a sleepless night. Another crawled on top of our chaplain's head.

The explosion of artillery, either our own or the enemy's, often roused us from slumber. Occasionally friendly fire got too close, the result of inattention when plotting friendly positions. Our artillery batteries shot harassing and interdicting (H&I) rounds targeted at routes the enemy was likely to use to attack our own positions. They went off randomly throughout the night. It was hard to tell whether they ever did any damage. A sniper we nicknamed "Luke the Gook" shot at us from an adjacent hill. He never hit any of us, so we decided to leave him alone for fear that someone with better aim would replace him.

---

9 Hill 881 South is replicated in an exhibit at the National Museum of the Marine Corps.

As the winter of 1967 approached, enemy activity increased significantly. Intelligence indicated North Vietnamese Army (NVA) units were preparing to launch large-scale attacks around Tet, the lunar New Year in late January or early February 1968. Khe Sanh was in their cross hairs. At the same time, my tour with Delta Company was drawing to a close, and I had received orders to join an artillery unit in the south.

Before leaving Khe Sanh I zeroed in a ring of preplanned artillery targets that covered primary avenues of approach the enemy would use to attack the Special Forces camp at Lang Vei, down the road from the main compound. Such preplanned targets would enable our forces to call in artillery rounds against the enemy quickly. I vividly recall how isolated the camp appeared, how inadequate their defensive perimeter was, and how precarious their situation seemed. To thank me for bolstering their defensive plan, the Special Forces commander asked if there was anything they could get for me. I requested an Army backpack, but sadly I never got a chance to collect. A month later the NVA surrounded Khe Sanh, attacked the Marine-occupied hills around the base (including 881 South), and overran Lang Vei using tanks. I can only hope that whatever I'd done had at least bought enough time for some of the camp's personnel to get out safely. The Marines at Khe Sanh went on to endure 77 days of daily bombardment by North Vietnamese artillery. I was lucky—very, very lucky—to get out of Khe Sanh unscathed. The man I'd replaced and the man who replaced me were both killed in action.

HEAVY ARTILLERY

I boarded a flight south to join a battery of 155 millimeter and eight-inch self-propelled guns (SPGs), which are long-range cannons mounted on a tank chassis, with a crew of eight manning each gun. We were set up near Chu Lai, a coastal city that was what I'd imagined Vietnam would be like, with rice paddies, villagers, and women walking along the road wearing long, flowing traditional dresses. This pleasant respite in the rear didn't last long, because a few weeks after I arrived we received orders to road march north, back to I Corps in Quang Tri Province.

155 mm self-propelled gun

We set up on the outskirts of Hue, a beautiful city in central Vietnam. During a lull in the fighting, I rode into the city with one of our sergeants whose tour was coming to an end. We stopped at an orphanage run by Catholic nuns because he wanted to adopt a little girl there. He held her gently in his arms and promised to return in a few days to complete the paperwork to take her back to the United States. Then the Tet Offensive started. We shot volley after volley, supporting outnumbered Marines battling the NVA for control of this ancient capital.[10] When the fighting settled down, we went back into town. It was in ruins. The orphanage was destroyed, the little girl was dead, and our sergeant was devastated. Grief over his loss and hatred for the enemy consumed him.

Major Bell, our battery commander was a square-jawed, well over six-feet-tall officer with a ramrod posture, who looked like he'd stepped out of a Marine recruiting poster, having served at the Marine Barracks in Washington, DC, known as "8th & I" because of its location. (The Barracks,

---

10 The Battle of Hué during 1968 was one of the bloodiest and longest battles of the Vietnam War (1959–1975). The Army of the Republic of Vietnam and three under-strengthened US Marine Corps battalions attacked and defeated more than 10,000 entrenched NVA and Viet Cong forces. (From Wikipedia: http://en.wikipedia.org/wiki/Battle accessed January 25, 2014.)

the home of the Marine Corps Commandant, is a showplace for the Marine Corps Band and Silent Drill Team.) A spit-and-polish officer, Bell set rules that made more sense in garrison than in combat. In one of those "am I really in a combat zone?" moments, I encountered Bell one evening on my way to take a shower just as he was emerging from one. As I walked past him, he shouted "Lieutenant Lee, didn't you forget something?" Still clutching the bath towel with my left hand, and dropping the soap in my right hand, I saluted smartly and said, "By your leave, sir!" With only flip-flops on our feet, we were buck naked except for the towels around our waists and the helmets on our heads. But because we were covered (wearing headgear), Bell insisted we follow Marine Corps regulation, which required us to salute if outdoors. Maybe I should have joined the Air Force, with its more relaxed standards? Only kidding, although the flyboys did have the best officers clubs and the most well stocked post exchanges of all the services in Vietnam.

While I was with Bell at our headquarters near Hue, we also had two units dispatched to support the infantry in other locations. One was a 155-mm gun platoon at Camp Evans attached to the Army Air Cavalry and the 101st Airborne Division; the other was an eight-inch SPG platoon supporting Marines along Route 9 near Khe Sanh. After life became more routine, and I got antsy standing watch once again in the FDC, I bugged Major Bell, to let me join one of the dispatched units. "Let me take over a platoon at one of the fire bases, sir!" What finally convinced Major Bell to let me have a command was not my combat experience but my legal know-how.

SIX SIX AND A KICK

When Private Bennots was caught sneaking out of the mess tent with two cans of peaches hidden under his T-shirt, Major Bell wanted to court-martial him, charging him with stealing, being out of uniform (he wasn't wearing a helmet when he exited the mess tent), and failing to obey a lawful order (because he showed up late when told to appear before the first sergeant the following morning). Bell appointed an experienced Mustang (a former enlisted Marine), our unit administrative officer, as prosecuting trial counsel and me as defense counsel.

I tried unsuccessfully to convince Major Bell that he could easily have handled it using Article 15, Nonjudicial Punishment.[11] But he didn't just want any ol' trial. Who knows what would have happened if he let someone get away with stealing peaches, so he went up the chain of command to convene a special court-martial, which carried a maximum penalty of six months forfeiture of pay, six months in the brig, and a bad conduct discharge.[12]

"Look here, Lee, he's guilty. The first sergeant says we shouldn't let him get away with it. I'm not trying to pressure you, just want to see that justice is done."

"Yes, sir, but I have a legal responsibility to defend him to the best of my ability," I replied respectfully.

Bell might have thought that he had stacked the deck against me by assigning the Mustang to be on the opposing side. What he didn't know was that just before deploying to Vietnam I'd spent a month as a trial counsel at Camp Pendleton, getting several cases under my belt, including the special court-martial of a Marine represented by a high-powered civilian lawyer. The lawyer poked holes in my arguments and got the case dismissed. Although I lost, I used my courtroom experience to help my client in Vietnam.

I convinced Bennots that it was in his best interests to plead guilty to stealing peaches since he was caught in the act. But I got him off on all the other charges. Although he had to spend three months in the brig, he was glad he didn't get a longer confinement or bad conduct discharge. Bell was

11   Major Bell had authority to do the following: 1) Admonition or reprimand. 2) Confinement on bread and water/diminished rations. (3) Correctional custody: not more than thirty days. (4) Forfeiture: not more than one half of one month's pay for two months. (5) Reduction: one grade. (6) Extra duties: not more than forty-five days. (7) Restriction: not more than sixty days.

12   A special court-martial sentence can involve forfeiture of two-thirds basic pay per month for one year, and additionally, for enlisted personnel, one-year confinement and/or a bad conduct discharge.

happy that justice was served. And I was happy that two weeks later he let me have a command position.

DO NOT DISTURB

We had two 155-mm SPGs at Camp Evans. Colonel Klink, in charge of the Army unit we were supporting, gave me a hard time whenever our guns were down, and they were down more than they were up. The guns, known as "Long Toms," were 1950s vintage artillery pieces that the Army used during the Korean War and then either converted or displayed as museum artifacts. The Marine Corps, the most underfunded of the services, keep them in its arsenal. With a fifteen-mile range, they were great when they worked. But when they broke down, we couldn't get many replacement parts because they were no longer manufactured, forcing us to cannibalize one gun to service the other until we jerry-rigged a part to fit. This, I found time and again, was symptomatic of the Marine Corps' perverse pride in fighting with outdated equipment. To be fair, the Corps' survival in the face of repeated congressional and Army efforts to dismantle it was in part successful because it was able to demonstrate that it was a lean, mean, fighting machine, with major emphasis on "lean" in times of fiscal constraints.

But when our guns were up and firing, Colonel Klink wasn't happy either. I was on the brink of being insubordinate when he forbade us from shooting H&I rounds after midnight. I would have agreed with him if he had said H&Is were ineffective, but he said the noise kept him from getting a good night's sleep. Being at Camp Evans was too much like being in the rear, so once again I asked to be sent closer to the action.

CA LU FIREBASE

I joined an eight-inch SPG platoon at Ca Lu, a firebase[13] located several miles east of Khe Sanh along Route 9. First serving as executive officer, I

13 A fire support base (FSB, firebase or FB) was a temporary military encampment widely used during the Vietnam War to provide artillery fire support to infantry operating in areas beyond the normal range of fire support from their own base camps. file:// localhost/(http/::en.wikipedia.org:wiki:Fire_support_base, accessed January 30, 2014)

later took over as commander. Being in charge of the lives of forty men and millions of dollars of equipment was an awesome responsibility at any age. I was twenty-five.

The sound of artillery could be frightening and affected people differently. We medevacked one lad who curled up into a fetal position and couldn't stop trembling at the sound of incoming. But the incoming rounds you didn't hear were the deadliest because you didn't have time to dive for cover. One enemy rocket scored a direct hit on our position, wounding four and killing one Marine. He'd been in-country less than a week.

From then on we ordered everyone to wear flak jackets at all times unless they were in a bunker. These padded protective vests weighed about nine pounds. Because crewmen had to haul around two hundred-pound artillery rounds in ninety-degree heat, I made wearing shirts optional.

A general dropped in unannounced as part of his visit to fire bases along the DMZ. From his spit-shined boots and starched utilities, I guessed he was either new to Vietnam or coming up from Saigon. He looked around, asked a few perfunctory questions, and then demanded to know why my men were shirtless.

I took a deep breath before explaining that wearing flak jackets on top of a shirt while hauling around heavy ammo crates might cause heatstroke. His frown indicated he didn't like my answer. But since he wasn't in my direct chain of command, he couldn't tell me what to do. After he hopped back on his helicopter, I imagined him flying back to the rear for a cold beer at the officer's club. I radioed Major Bell to warn him that he might be hearing from the irate general. Given Bell's previous by-the-book attitude, I was relieved when he told me not to worry about it.

HALT! WHO GOES THERE?

My flak jacket hid my rank and USMC insignia, and I carried a submachine gun—standard issue for my unit—instead of the M16 that Marines normally carried so that people who didn't know me couldn't tell that I was an American. When I walked over to Combat Base Vandergrift, just up the road from my encampment, one of my friends there liked to introduce me to his men as "Colonel Lee of the Korean Marines." It wasn't until I started talking that they realized I was an American.

However, sometimes even speaking English didn't guarantee they'd know I was a US Marine. "Hey, you guys got a water tank around here?" I asked two Marines standing outside a bunker taking a smoke break. From their blank expressions, I could tell they hadn't expected English to come out of my mouth. I pulled out my canteen and shook it to show it was empty.

"I think he wants water," one Marine said to the other.

"Oveeeer theeeere, behiiiiind buuuunkeeeer!" they said slowly and loudly.

Thinking I didn't understand them, they spoke even slower and louder while pointing in the direction of the water tank. "Thanks guys!" I said as I walked away, laughing to myself.

CO ROC

In May 1968, about a month after American forces lifted the siege of Khe Sanh and reopened Route 9, our SPGs drove back to the area with the mission of flushing out enemy units around the combat base. Our orders were to conduct an artillery raid, one that would try to knock out the NVA guns that continued to harass the evacuation of the remaining elements of the US Marine compound. The enemy guns were well entrenched at Co Roc, a mountainside position just across the border in Laos and fifteen kilometers west of Khe Sanh. From there, and out of range of Marine artillery at Khe Sanh, the NVA long-range rockets continued to shell the remaining Americans at will.

The NVA gunners were the last remnants of the enemy preventing the final evacuation of our embattled base. Khe Sanh had been the most fiercely contested piece of terrain of the war. Hand-to-hand combat and air strikes forced the NVA to withdraw, but now it seemed as if the enemy was having a last hurrah. Our artillery mission was to do what US planes couldn't. The NVA guns were mounted on tracks. They rolled out to shoot at the Marines, then rolled back deep inside the mountain, where they were impervious to American airstrikes. B-52s couldn't penetrate their fortress; the bombs would just bounce off the mountain. Only our guns, firing straight into the cave, might have a chance of doing any damage.

Self-propelled gun (SPG)

KHE SANH REVISITED

A few days before we deployed, I received orders to scout out a suitable site for our guns. My platoon along with the rest of the battery would follow. We wanted to set up close enough to shoot directly into the mouth of the enemy's stronghold. Artillery pieces are normally indirect fire weapons; for example, they are useful for shooting high-trajectory projectiles that go over mountains to hit targets on the other side. This time we were aiming straight into the mountain.

Johnson, my platoon sergeant, and I set out by jeep for Khe Sanh after sunrise. On a map it didn't look far. From our position at Ca Lu, one of several "forward fire bases" sprinkled along the DMZ, it was a short zigzag line across a few grid squares along Route 9, a road that was supposedly secure, meaning it had been cleared of enemy mines. Intelligence showed no major enemy units blocking our path.

We drove along unpaved roads without stopping, wanting to get there well before sundown so we wouldn't get shot by our own troops as we tried to get inside the base perimeter. As we traveled through the Vietnamese countryside, I marveled at its breathtaking beauty. How nice it would have been to pause, even for just a moment, to soak in the magnificent sights and sounds enveloping us. On our left were steep ravines, dark and deep, lush with green foliage. A bird with a three-foot wingspan, feathers of crimson and gold, beautiful and majestic, swooped across and glided down into the valley below. On our right, jagged rock walls in shades of browns and grays jutted skyward and a waterfall cascaded down the rock face to a rushing stream. This was not the jungles of the south but the highlands of the north, home to indigenous hill tribes.

As our jeep neared Khe Sanh, Sergeant Johnson nudged me and said, "Hey, Lieutenant, look over there!" My gut churned as I stared at the charred remains of an NVA soldier, a twisted body lying grotesquely on the side of the road, a grisly reminder of the horrible carnage each side had inflicted on the other. It was hard not to breathe in the stench, the smell of death, that told of the unimaginable destruction that had taken place here just weeks earlier.

After getting past a security checkpoint, we drove inside the base to link up with the local commander. It was a vastly different place from the one I had left just three months earlier. The runway was still there, pockmarked by enemy rockets, the carcass of a C-130 transport plane lying crumpled in the middle of the tarmac. Gone were the tents that had served as living quarters, and gone were the depots filled with the supplies of war. The few troops that remained lived in bunkers reinforced by dirt-filled sandbags or wooden ammo boxes. Rats were the only creatures unafraid to venture outside in broad daylight, scurrying about scavenging for food.

After establishing liaison with my counterpart, Sergeant Johnson and I found shelter for the night in a bunker that had belonged to Battery A, my former unit. Three months earlier I had slept in the same bunker, on a cot lined with an inflatable mattress, under mosquito netting. Back then, for dinner I'd drive over to the mess hall for a hot meal, then wander over to the "club" for a cold beer. This time Johnson and I heated C- rations for dinner, eating silently, lost in our own thoughts. A rat sauntered across the dirt floor, illuminated by a kerosene lantern, our only light in an otherwise pitch-black bunker. The NVA guns of Co Roc pounded the base throughout the night, rattling our bunker, sending particles of debris down from the ceiling, preventing us from getting much rest.

After a fitful night's sleep, we got up early the next morning to select a site about a kilometer west of the compound. Although it was out in the open, we planned to shoot at the NVA before they could pivot their guns on us, hoping the enemy wouldn't be able to readjust their artillery firing position without becoming vulnerable to US air strikes. By late afternoon, Major Bell and the rest of our battery arrived to take part in the operation, code-named Drum Fire II. One of our guns, however, got stuck on a bridge and had to turn back. Just like tanks, our self-propelled guns had the advantage of mobility, but the sheer bulk of our tracked vehicles made it difficult to negotiate Route 9's rickety bridges.

With everything in place, we set up and prepared to start shooting at first light. Trenches along the side of the road, the handiwork of the enemy, would have made good shelter had they not been cluttered with trash and crawling with venomous creatures. "To hell with it, I'm sleeping outside. I'd rather get hit than stung by a centipede!" someone remarked. Most of us felt the same way, so we slept under a night sky filled with stars—a positive omen, signaling we'd have good visibility to launch our attack the next day.

US artillery firing at the enemy

ARTILLERY DUEL

The first shot we fired was a spotter round, one that an air observer (AO) in a fixed wing aircraft hovering over Co Roc could see and be able to use as a marker to adjust the impact of our subsequent high-explosive rounds. When the AO called in by radio and started berating my FDC chief, I grabbed the handset and asked what was wrong. AOs had a tough job as our eyes and ears, but I had full confidence in my crew and was in no mood to let him browbeat my men. After all, they'd been up all night and would be working nonstop for the next several days while the AO would be back in the rear sipping a cold beer by nightfall.

"We shot that round exactly where you told us. Check your coordinates again!" I barked. The AO thought my crew had made a mistake but realized his own after rechecking his map. After he resent the correct data, we bracketed the target within the next couple of rounds. Once we zeroed in, we "fired for effect," meaning we threw everything we could at the target. Within the next forty-eight hours, we shot well over a thousand high-explosive rounds at Co Roc, cheering when aerial reconnaissance reported that our rounds had set off secondary explosions inside the mountainside cave, meaning we'd caused real damage. Unfortunately, our all-out effort only silenced the enemy guns for a brief two days. Although we had suppressed the NVA gunners long enough to evacuate a few more American units, it wasn't enough. Just as I was about to bid a final good-bye to Khe Sanh, the enemy gave us a farewell surprise.

PARTING SHOTS

As we drove past the front gate of the combat base and onto Route 9, North Vietnamese rockets rained down on us with the roar of what sounded like freight trains smashing into the earth, exploding one after another, and right smack in the middle of our convoy. The earth trembled. I jumped out of my jeep, dived into a roadside trench, and flattened my body against the hard red clay, trying to make myself meld into the ground.

"Oh God, dear God, please get me out of this in one piece! I promise I'll be good forever!" I begged. "Yea, though I walk through the valley of the shadow of death, I will fear no evil," I recited over and over and over.

The explosions were as deafening as they were terrifying. I covered my ears with both hands. Then, just as quickly as the thundering started, it stopped. The sound of jets—our jets—roaring overhead buoyed my spirits. It meant our own fighters might keep the enemy suppressed long enough for us to move out—away from the valley of death. Thank God for aviators. Taking back every bad thing I ever said about jet jockeys, I stood up and surveyed the damage. Miraculously, unbelievably, considering we were in the center of the enemy's bull's-eye, no one in my unit was seriously injured.

When my ears stopped ringing, I realized that I was standing in an NVA-dug trench within a stone's throw of the front gate, one the enemy must have used to get close enough to breech the base's perimeter during the siege of Khe Sanh. How ironic that an enemy-dug trench would save my life. I climbed back into my jeep, its windshield shattered, possibly only seconds after I'd jumped out. I was happy to be alive but couldn't help feeling frustrated. The NVA's parting gesture, an artillery barrage, was like an upraised middle finger, as if to say, "We're down now, but we're not out!"

SHORT TIMER

A month before people leave the field, many get skittish and try to avoid assignments that might get them killed or wounded before they can board a plane home. As I approached my thirty-day mark, I appreciated the lull in enemy activity but knew that idle Marines can get into mischief. Instead of focusing on the enemy they turn on each other. In combat the focus is on survival; everything else is irrelevant. During downtimes, however, minor annoyances can become magnified.

So I kept the men occupied by servicing equipment, retraining, and sharpening their skills. I ordered boxing gloves so they'd have a healthy outlet for pent-up anger. When Major Bell assigned a cook to my unit, we set up a sandbagged mess tent so everyone could eat at least one hot meal a day, a luxury in the field. Private Tyson, my new cook, was high-strung. The first thing he did when he arrived was try to squirm out of guard duty.

"Lieutenant, how am I gonna cook breakfast in the morning when I gotta stand guard at three a.m.?"

"Look, Tyson, we're short-handed. Everyone, including you, has to take his turn!"

To keep him happy, I arranged an earlier shift to give him time to prepare the next day's meals. His ability to transform canned goods into tasty cuisine boosted everyone's morale. When I left Vietnam, he baked a chocolate cake for my wheels-up party.

FIRST MARTIN, NOW BOBBY

A month before I left, Sergeant Johnson came into my bunker with his head down and tears in his eyes. Because of his quiet competence, I had picked him as the senior platoon NCO over another candidate. He was a black Southern gentleman who spoke with a drawl.

"Sir, first it was Martin Luther King; now they got Bobby!"

He had just heard the news of Robert F. Kennedy's assassination over Armed Forces Radio. From Sergeant Johnson's slurred speech, it was obvious he had drunk more than his fair share of beer that night. I tried without success to console him, finally telling him to sleep it off. The next morning neither of us mentioned what had happened. On the surface, things were back to normal. But we both realized the war was being fought not only in Vietnam but also back home. The times they were a-changing, and we'd never be the same.

HOMECOMING

We whooped and hollered as our United Airlines chartered flight touched down at Travis Air Force Base in California. I and every other Marine aboard was glad to be alive, to be in one piece, and to be home after thirteen months in Vietnam. There were no welcome-home ceremonies, no ticker-tape parades, no marching bands, but we hadn't expected any. In July of 1968, public attitudes toward returning veterans ranged from sympathy to indifference to outright disdain, and it was hard to tell which was worse. The story of my friend Hank, whom I had replaced as a forward observer, is illustrative of what some veterans faced when they got back to the States.

Midway through his combat tour, Hank looked forward to a well-earned R&R in Hawaii to meet his wife and newborn son, whom he was seeing for the very first time. As they strolled along Waikiki, a "long-haired hippy" came up to them, spit on his uniform and called Hank a baby killer. Hank, unable to contain his rage, drew back and floored him.

He told me about the incident after his otherwise-joyful fourteen-day visit with his wife and son. It was the last time they saw him alive. I was deeply saddened to learn that Hank was killed in action shortly after returning to combat.

Once home, my friends politely asked me what it was like in Vietnam, but I was hesitant to talk about my combat experiences because, whenever I tried, their eyes would glaze over or they'd change the subject, unable to relate to what I'd been through or understand why I had volunteered to go in the first place. My family had different reactions. My brothers were proud I'd been an officer, but my parents never approved of my becoming a Marine and believed in the Chinese proverb "don't use good iron to make nails; don't use good men to make soldiers." Baba thought the war was stupid and agreed with the growing antiwar sentiment; Mama panicked every time she saw casualty reports on the evening news. Not wanting to add to their mental anguish, none of my letters home ever hinted that I'd ever been in harm's way.

FIGHTING FOR EACH OTHER

Combat is an intense experience, a life-changing experience, an experience that binds men together from all walks of life: ivy leaguers and high school dropouts; frat boys and farm boys; black and white; yellow and brown. Men with nothing in common back home share a common resolve on the battlefield: to survive, to not let the guy next to you down, to never leave a buddy behind. Huddled together in foxholes, we risked life and sanity slugging it out with the NVA in the highlands of Vietnam. As the war continued, and as the expediency of Washington political decisions erased whatever traces remained of our youthful idealism, and as the myopia of the Pentagon's strategy wiped away whatever tactical triumphs we achieved on the ground, we fought on. We fought on not to "push back the red tide of communism," not to "fight for right and freedom," but to fight for each other.

LIFE HAS A FLAVOR THE PROTECTED WILL NEVER KNOW!

These words, indelibly etched in my mind, were scribbled on a handmade cardboard sign dangling from concertina wire on Hill 881 South, the scene of some of the most brutal fighting in the war. We passed the sign each and every time we returned from patrol, a daily reminder of how lucky we were to be alive, how lucky we were to have a chance to fight another day. As strange as it may seem to some, I was grateful to be there. Even with all the physical hardships and emotional traumas we had to endure in combat, I wouldn't have traded any of the experiences I had as a leader of Marines, of having to make decisions that determined whether my men or I would come home alive, of having a level of responsibility that few are given in a lifetime—a level of responsibility that in civilian life would take me another two decades to achieve.

My radio operator, Richard Friend, thought I'd lost my mind when, at the end of an especially draining mission, I'd utter my favorite tongue-in-cheek expression. "Aaah, the good life!" I exclaimed, trying to sound like the Budweiser commercial guy enjoying a cold beer while the song "It's a Good Life" played in my mind. Friend, only half-jokingly, responded, "Dammit, Lieutenant! If you say that just one more time I'm gonna shoot you!" Hungry, thirsty, and sleep-deprived after having been on patrol for the last seventy-two hours, he was in no mood for my offbeat sense of humor.

In Khe Sanh, I vowed that if I every returned to "the world" in one piece, I'd never ever take life for granted again. And not just about the big things but the little ones as well. Things like hot chow, a dry place to sleep, running water, and flush toilets. To remind myself that things can always be worse, I vowed to dig a hole every year, fill it with mud, and lie in it. Although I've never actually carried out that promise physically, I've evoked that image many times mentally, especially when I get too full of myself, complain too much, or take things too seriously.

POISON TOOTH ROULETTE

They say generations of young men in every culture and era throughout history have sought the chance to prove themselves in some form of life-and-death challenge. One might argue that it's the reason why men are so easily recruited for military service or volunteer for dangerous missions or engage in life-threatening hobbies. A character in the John Fowles novel The Magus came up with an efficient way to provide such a challenge without having young men marching off to war.

In the novel, when men reached draft age, they would be presented with a bowl of candy, each piece shaped like a tooth and filled with liquid. One would be filled with poison without an antidote; the rest would be filled with sugar water. It was Russian roulette with poisoned candy instead of bullets.

Just think of all the national treasure we'd save if all the young men could take the poison tooth challenge. But we would need all the politicians who wished to send them off to war to play this game and take the first bite!

2007 KHE SANH VETERANS REUNION

Exactly forty years after setting foot in Vietnam, I attended a Khe Sanh veteran's reunion in Washington, DC, not knowing if I really deserved to be there and feeling quite guilty for having escaped the worst of the war when so many had been killed or seriously injured, physically and emotionally. But I wanted to see my heroes Ernie Spencer, Ross Brown, and others I'd had the honor of serving with, often thinking about them and wondering what their lives were like after Khe Sanh.

It was wonderful to reconnect after so many years with Ross, my Basic School classmate, who had an illustrious career in the Marine Corps as a combat leader and retired as a full colonel. And with Ernie, the commander of our rifle company, who became a shipping executive after leaving the service. He wrote a memoir about his war experience, *Welcome to Vietnam, Macho Man*, as a way to help him deal with PTSD. And just as they had done forty years earlier, they welcomed me back into the fold, making me feel like part of the brotherhood, making me feel like I belonged.

Ross always had a smile on his face, no matter how tough things got in Vietnam, exuding the kind of positive energy that makes you feel good just being around him. Each combat patrol with Ross was lesson in human relations. His men respected him not only because he was a tactically knowledgeable platoon commander, but also because he cared deeply about them as individuals. Ross proved the truth of what Teddy Roosevelt said: "People don't care how much you know until they know how much you care."

I always admired Ernie for being so cool under fire. Even when we were in danger of being hit and I scrambled for cover, he'd walk around in flip-flops puffing on a cigarette, seemingly oblivious to the possibility of getting shot. He demonstrated that when a leader is cool and calm, no matter how bad things get, everyone around you is cool and calm. And when you're cool and calm, you and your subordinate commanders make better decisions, make fewer mistakes—mistakes that can cost lives.

During the reunion, we went to the National Museum of the Marine Corps at Quantico, walking through the Vietnam gallery and visiting an eerily realistic replica of Hill 881 South. It was like going back in time, to the time when I first stepped off the helicopter to join Delta Company as an FO. One of Delta Company's own, now an ordained deacon of the Catholic Church, held a touching memorial service at the museum in remembrance of all those we lost at Khe Sanh.

Ernie mercifully left out of his memoir an incident he kidded me about at the reunion. Recalling my first night on Hill 881 South, he said I rushed into his bunker upon hearing what I thought was incoming, wearing nothing but my underpants and combat boots, unlaced, not having had time to put on anything else. But like any good FO, he noted, I had my binoculars and map with me, ready to call in counter-battery support.

Ernie enjoyed yanking my chain. Ross remembered the time Ernie called all the platoon commanders together on a company operation to discuss the day's patrol route and possible danger points and fire missions. As we huddled around his map spread on the ground, he pointed at various positions and said to me, "Now, Lee, how are we going to kill these f---ing gooks if they hit us here?" Ross laughingly recalled that it was all the other lieutenants could do to keep themselves from totally cracking up.

Ernie Spencer, Ross Brown, and me plotting targets
on an imaginary map at the 2007 Khe Sanh reunion

Ernie hailed from Hawaii and had some Korean blood. We were the only two Asian officers in the regiment. Our gunnery sergeant must have been nearsighted, because he would always mistake me for Ernie.

"Skipper, when do you want me to set up the ambush?" he'd ask me.

"No, Gunny, I'm not the skipper! Remember, he smokes and I don't; and he wears glasses, and I don't," I reminded him.

At the time, Ernie wore eyeglasses and I didn't; now I need glasses and he doesn't.

CHAPTER 6

LOVE AT FIRST BITE

Lovers do not finally meet somewhere. They are in each other
all along.

—RUMI

After Vietnam I returned to the Defense Language Institute in Monterey, California, this time to study Mandarin Chinese. Having grown up speaking pidgin Cantonese, I was ashamed to be illiterate in the language of my ancestors. I relished the chance to learn Mandarin and once again enjoy the good life that Monterey offered.

Monterey is home to Steinbeck's iconic Cannery Row. San Francisco is just two hours north; Carmel, the 17-Mile Drive, Pebble Beach, and the Big Sur are a short drive south. Soon after I got to California, I bought a used Dodge Dart, the first car I'd ever owned, and I loved it. Some say you never forget your first love; I say you never forget your first car.

The Big Sur

I rented a beachside apartment with Burt Vanderclute, an Army artillery officer who was studying Turkish. Burt taught me how to handle a stick shift, letting me drive his red Triumph convertible around town. He was not only generous but also brave to give me the keys to his car whenever I wanted. I was a novice driver and, even with my Dodge Dart's automatic transmission and power steering, it took months before I was able to get in and out of our parking space without denting someone's fender.

BLIND DATE

Burt and his girlfriend, Abby, fixed me up with a blind date, whom they described as "cute with beautiful, waist-length hair." I loved girls with long hair, so I was anxious to meet her.

Abby kneeling on far left, Vicki standing next to her,
with friends practicing Polynesian dances

Things didn't go well on our first date. After dinner we went to a movie, and during the feature film, I closed my eyes briefly. "Hey! Did you just fall asleep on me?" she asked while poking me in the ribs. I explained that I was simply resting my eyes. They were itchy, red, and watery because I had hay fever.

Vicki was attending Monterey Community College, having just moved back to the Monterey peninsula after a year in Oregon. Because she had recently ended a relationship with someone, she told me she wanted to take things slowly. That was fine with me since I hadn't planned on getting into anything serious.

At first it was hard to figure out if she liked me or not. I was clueless when it came to reading women, and she was even shyer than I was. After one or two more dates, I began to wonder if I should continue to ask her out. What made me decide to call on her again was her father, Harry Shishido of the Shishido clan, tied by marriage to Mori Motonari, a famous daimyo (powerful territorial lord) in sixteenth-century Japan.[14]

Her dad and I hit it off right away. He was skilled in judo, had fought as a professional wrestler, and resembled Odd Job, the assassin in the James Bond movie *Goldfinger*. After retiring from the Army, Harry settled in the Monterey area with his wife, Thelma, and daughters Vicki and Sharon. Having spent his entire career in food services, he loved to cook, which was great because I loved to eat. And I could be assured of a good meal because Harry could make Chinese, Japanese, and just about any other type of Asian cuisine.

LOVE AND MARRIAGE

Falling in love was easy in a place as romantic as Monterey. We shopped for trinkets along Cannery Row, attended Bach concerts in Carmel, watched otters playing in the surf, and strolled along the beach at sunset. When we got bored, we'd spend a weekend in San Francisco.

When my parents came to visit me from New York, I introduced them to Vicki and her family, doing so with some trepidation in view of the animosity toward the Japanese that many older Chinese still harbored. Unfortunately, some can be xenophobic. Uncle Henry, for example, said that he once refused to give a bottle of water he was about to discard to a Japanese man sitting next to him who'd asked for a drink.

---

14 From Wikipedia, http://en.wikipedia.org/wiki/Akitakata,_Hiroshima, accessed January 25, 2014.

I knew my parents weren't like that and it would have been out of character for them to veto any plans I might have entertained with Vicki, nor would I have let them. Nonetheless, I was glad they were more open-minded than some of my conservative relatives, and got along well with my future bride and the Shishido clan.

John, my beachside apartment neighbor and a fellow Marine studying Vietnamese, asked me to fix him up with Vicki's sister, Sharon. I hesitated because Sharon had gotten mad at me for setting her up with a blind date once before—to another Marine who was too quiet for her taste. John, however, wouldn't give up. It was love at first sight. They got engaged and married within months of their first date and just before he shipped off to Vietnam.

Vicki and I had a much longer courtship and married three years later. By then she had graduated from the University of California, San Diego, and I had left active duty. We returned to Monterey for our wedding ceremony at the historic Delmonte Hotel on the grounds of the Naval Postgraduate School. John was my best man and Sharon was Vicki's maid of honor.

Naval Postgraduate School

At our reception, I toasted my new father-in-law, thanking him for giving me two out of the three things that are supposed to make a man happy according to Taiwanese custom: to marry a Japanese woman, to live in an American-style house, and to have a Chinese cook at home. There's an old Taiwanese belief that Japanese women are more docile (not true, at least not for Japanese-Americans), that American-style houses are the most comfortable (arguably true), and that Chinese food is the most delicious (absolutely true).

But I'm jumping ahead on the timeline again. I still had two years of active duty to complete. We wouldn't get married until after I moved to Washington, DC, and she graduated from college.

GARRISON DUTY

After language school I attended the Army's Interrogation Course at Fort Holabird, Maryland, in preparation for an assignment to the Marine Corps Interrogation-Translation Teams at Camp Pendleton, California. Working and living in sunny Southern California was a most pleasant experience. We set our own training schedules and were garrisoned at Las Pulgas, away from division headquarters where the G-2, a colonel in charge of intelligence units, oversaw our activities. He left us pretty much alone. I found that working with seasoned officers and senior NCO's who staffed our teams was a headache-free job with none of the morale and disciplinary problems that were surfacing in other outfits.

It was 1970, and news of the My Lai massacre and Kent State shootings dominated the headlines, inflaming the public's outrage over the war and calls for withdrawal. I commiserated with a recent Annapolis graduate who was being harassed by his superiors because he had applied for conscientious objector status.

At least once a week, it wouldn't be at all unusual for me to see a hitch-hiker thumbing a ride along the Interstate who you knew without a doubt was a recruit trying to escape from the Marine Corps Recruit Depot in San Diego. The freshly shaved head and furtive demeanor, not to mention the white t-shirt and utility trousers, gave him away. A Marine colleague in civilian clothes driving into work picked up one of these shaved heads trying to get to Los Angeles. The recruit's smile at catching a ride didn't last long when the officer locked the doors, took the next exit to Camp Pendleton, and deposited the lad with the MP's at the base front gate.

I convinced Vicki to finish her last two years of college at the University of California in La Jolla. We rented an apartment in Pacific Beach near the ocean and within easy commute to Vicki's campus and my office. We loved the carefree California lifestyle that allowed us to enjoy year around outdoor activities, play tennis or swim, and take day trips south to Tijuana or north to Disneyland. Introduced to Mexican food years earlier by my college roommate, I was happy to discover that the San Diego area had some excellent Mexican restaurants. Vicki and I would frequent one or two of them a week so that I could indulge my seemingly insatiable appetite for this tasty cuisine; and when that wasn't enough, we'd pick up some takeout at Taco Bell. Fortunately, I worked out for two hours daily to burn off the extra calories and didn't put on any extra weight.

My Quantico classmates Nate Wong and Andy Vaart were also assigned to the interrogation-translation teams. Nate and I went through artillery and Vietnamese language training together and served in Vietnam around the same time. Andy was studying Chinese in a class ahead of mine at Monterey; he would wind up at the CIA, as did I. It was wonderful spending time with them, and we've remained close ever since. They left active duty a year before me. Nate went to medical school and returned to Hawaii to practice medicine. Andy went to grad school before joining the CIA.

We had six teams, each headed by a captain and staffed by half a dozen officers and senior NCOs conversant in a target foreign language, from Spanish to Serbo-Croatian. We sent individuals overseas for in-country language proficiency training and to Monterey for refresher courses.

I went to Taiwan and lived in the student dorm of a medical college, learning more in two months conversing with native speakers than I did the whole year at language school. While there I met Anita, a lively personality with boundless energy. We practiced taijiquan in a class taught by another dorm resident. It was my first formal introduction to this ancient Chinese martial art, one that incorporates Chinese philosophy and medical theory into its practice to unify body, mind and spirit.

Anita, from a family of talented musicians and a gifted one herself, introduced me to her sister Elizabeth, a classical guitarist. Their charming mother, wanting Elizabeth to attend grad school in America, saw me as a vehicle to a visa. Fortunately, Elizabeth gave me a heads up that her mother would approach me, allowing me enough time to come up with an excuse. "Madam, I'm honored you think I'm worthy of your daughter's hand, but my job doesn't permit me to marry." It was partially true. My drill instructor once said to me, "Maggot, if the Marine Corps wanted you to have a wife, they'd have issued you one!"

Elizabeth, however, had no problems getting to the United States on her own. She eventually received her advanced degree in microbiology and later became a medical doctor. Anita also immigrated to America and got her PhD in pharmacology. Years later both sisters returned to their roots and now practice Chinese medicine. We had no idea when we first met in Taiwan that our career paths would coincide a lifetime later.

In my last six months at Camp Pendleton, I was put in charge of all six teams. Our mission in garrison was to improve our area knowledge and interrogation skills as well as our language proficiency. We devised training scenarios and took turns role-playing prisoners of war and interrogators. Those who had served in Vietnam as interrogators confirmed what had been drummed into us in school: torturing prisoners doesn't work because they'll tell you anything, including lies and half-truths, just to get you to stop. Extracting reliable information using noncoercive techniques, in their experience, proved to be far more effective.

One of those experts was Tony, a staff sergeant and Vietnam vet. One day when he was coming to work, a sentry at the main gate stopped him even though Tony was in uniform and normally would have been waved through. The sentry thought Tony was an imposter because his appearance didn't match up with the campaign ribbons he was wearing, including a Bronze Star on Tony's chest. Tony had let his afro grow a bit too long since he was being discharged in a few days. The sentry gave him a hard time until Tony pulled out his military ID to prove he was a real Marine.

Tony spoke fluent Mandarin, had an infectious laugh and a sarcastic sense of humor. More often than not he'd find some way to make you the butt of a joke but all in good fun. He helped me find a one-bedroom studio in his apartment complex when I wanted to move off base. The more I got to know him, the more I appreciated his cool competence and professional work ethic. During his off duty hours, he moonlighted as a waiter to save enough money to go back to college. After leaving the Marine Corps, Tony earned a degree in international relations. We didn't know it at the time, but we would see each other again and get a chance to rekindle our friendship two years later in Langley, Virginia.

DESERT MIRAGE

While I was at Camp Pendleton, my brother-in-law John returned from Vietnam and was assigned to the Marine base at 29 Palms, in the California desert about a three-hour drive inland from San Diego. The first time Vicki and I visited John and Sharon at 29 Palms we arrived late at night and checked into a motel. When I looked out the motel window and saw thousands of bright lights illuminating the skyline, it appeared to be a well-populated oasis. "This is like Las Vegas, not the desolated dump I'd imagined it would be," I said to Vicki. However, the next morning when I opened the curtains I was astonished to see nothing but sand, cactus, and tumbleweed. The lights I saw the night before looked much closer than they actually were and gave the optical illusion of a bustling metropolis.

Compared to the other military services, the Marine Corps has far fewer assignment locations one would consider garden spots. This was an important factor, although not the only one, in deciding what I wanted to do next. As the end of my active duty commitment drew near, I wondered if I should stay in the Corps or get out. If I stayed, there was a good chance I'd wind up at 29 Palms or Camp Lejeune in North Carolina, another isolated place, at least in my New York bred eyes.

Nonetheless, I would have seriously considered staying in if the Corps had had something like the Army's foreign area officers program. The program was designed to develop officers with expertise in a specific region or country by having them get advanced language training, a postgraduate degree, and a follow-on overseas assignment in their selected area of study. I'm happy that Marine officers now have a chance to be sponsored for a similar program, but when I was on active duty the Marines didn't place much emphasis on intelligence-related activities. Indeed, regular line officers could not select intelligence as a primary occupational specialty. If rank is any indication of where the Corps placed its resources at the time, the Commandant's assistant chief of staff for intelligence, unlike his others chiefs, was a colonel and not a general.

I was glad when Washington promised to end the war and bring our troops home, but I didn't relish becoming a peacetime Marine. I have great respect for my TBS classmates who stayed in during the height of anti-military hysteria. The Marine Corps had prepared them to go to war, but nothing could have prepared them for the onslaught of public condemnation for having served in Vietnam. And nothing could have prepared them to become babysitters for those disenchanted Marines in their ranks who had been drafted into service by court order. I salute those TBS classmates who kept the faith. It was their leadership that helped produce future Marine warriors, warriors who have acquitted themselves so magnificently on the battlefields of Iraq and Afghanistan.

But I didn't have the fortitude to endure what my classmates faced during that troubling period, and began interviewing with prospective civilian employers. Before long I had several job offers, including an unexpected one that would turn my then even-keeled existence into a far less tranquil one.

SECOND PATH

SPY

CHAPTER 7

BREAKING COVER

And ye shall know the truth, and the truth shall make you free.[15]

—JOHN 8:32

I was grateful when informed I'd be getting a medal, especially since it was only a few months earlier that I had imagined myself being marched out of the headquarters building in handcuffs. Instead, I'd be receiving the CIA's Career Intelligence Medal, a US flag that had been flown over the headquarters building, and other mementos celebrating my thirty years of service at a private awards ceremony in my honor.

I looked forward to inviting my family and Agency colleagues to the ceremony. Whatever I'd accomplished during my career wouldn't have been possible without the hard work of some of the brightest, most dedicated people I'd ever known. And it wouldn't have been possible without the love and support of my family. So I wanted to use this special occasion to tell my

---

15   This is inscribed on the wall of the CIA's main lobby, characterizing the Agency's intelligence mission.

colleagues what a privilege it was just to be on the same team. And, most of all, to thank Vicki, Jenjen, and Marisa for never complaining about our peripatetic lifestyle, about having to move every three or four years, and about my frequent absences. But first I had to tell my daughters where I really worked.

Jenjen and Marisa had gotten permission to miss classes at McLean High School so that they could attend what they thought would be my retirement ceremony. A week before the event, Vicki and I discussed how to tell our teenage daughters that I worked for the Agency. Would they be mad we hadn't told them sooner? A CIA colleague said he'd waited till his son turned twenty-one before telling him where he really worked. When his son didn't believe him, he took him to CIA Headquarters to prove it.

We called a family meeting and told Jenjen and Marisa they were the first among our family and friends to know my true employer. I had never told my parents, brothers, or other relatives. I said I had to maintain cover all these years to protect those whose lives or careers might have been jeopardized because of their association with a known CIA officer.

Jenjen said matter-of-factly, "Dad, I suspected all along you worked for the CIA." Marisa claimed she already knew; her friend said her father, an overt CIA employee, had worked for me overseas. I felt relieved they reacted positively but was a bit disappointed they were so cavalier about what I thought would be a surprise revelation.

"Maybe we shouldn't have told them till we actually drove onto the compound," I said to Vicki.

"They might have jumped out of the car at the sight of the heavily armed security guards!" Vicki laughed.

LANGLEY, VIRGINIA

It was a month after 9/11, so security at Langley was extra tight, with guards in full body armor carrying automatic rifles. On the day of the ceremony, we drove past the brick guardhouse at the main entrance on Route 123. I pointed to the roadside memorial decorated with fresh flowers. Eight years earlier a Pakistani terrorist had parked his pickup here during the morning rush hour and methodically gunned down two agency officers and wounded three others.

Past the visitor's center, beyond the barricades, a winding road led to the original headquarters building. The vibrant autumn colors lent the wooded area a secluded beauty. It looked more like an idyllic college campus than a typical government compound. The serenity outside was belied by the hectic pace of life within—emblematic of the double life I had once led.

Vicki and the girls accompanied me up the steps of the main entrance, passing a bronze statue of Nathan Hale,[16] the first American executed for spying for his country. An imposing and instantly recognizable seal of eagle, shield and compass sixteen feet in diameter was inlaid on the gray

---

16 From the CIA website: This statue captures the spirit of the moment before his execution—a twenty-one-year-old man prepared to meet his death for honor and country, hands and feet bound, face resolute, and eyes on the horizon. His last words, "I regret that I have but one life to lose for my country," circle the base around his feet.

granite floor of the lobby. On the left side of the lobby, we admired the CIA Memorial Wall with black stars etched on white marble, each star representing an Agency officer who died in service. As we posed for photos and waited for the ceremony to begin, I mentally retraced the first time I'd ever walked into the building three decades earlier.

Jenjen, Vicki, me, and Marisa in the CIA lobby

It was the fall of 1971. I had goose bumps as I stared at the giant CIA emblem and walked across the marbled lobby. At that moment I had the feeling that my life would be forever changed.

MR. SMITH COMES FROM WASHINGTON

Funny, but I never even applied for a job at the CIA. Before leaving the Marines I'd already accepted an offer from Electronic Data Systems (EDS), a computer software company founded by Ross Perot. A phone call from a Mr. Smith, however, made me reconsider.

"Hello, this is Bob Smith," said the caller. "I'm with the CIA."

"Who? Can you speak a little louder?"

"I sent you employment application forms and wondered why you hadn't completed them yet. Did you get them?"

"I did, but I've already accepted a job offer and will be starting work soon." I didn't mention I was about to trash all twenty-odd pages of the paperwork that had arrived a week earlier in an unmarked manila envelope.

"Look, I'll be in San Diego next week. Let's get together."

"Well, OK."

I couldn't pass up a chance to meet the mysterious caller. And I was a big James Bond fan.

In a cryptic follow-up phone call, Mr. Smith provided instructions for our meeting. We each described ourselves physically and an article of clothing we'd be wearing. "Oh, by the way," he said, "don't tell anyone about the meeting."

On the appointed day, I waited in a hotel lobby, expecting him to pop up from behind one of the potted palms. Finally, a large man with gray hair extended his hand to shake mine. We went to his room, where he reviewed the forms it had taken a week for me to fill out listing dates, times, places, addresses of every place I'd ever been, and every school I had ever attended since sixth grade.

"Captain Lee, you have qualifications that would be useful to several Agency components. What kind of career do you want?" During my job search, I'd interviewed with several companies and had practiced answering the same question, so now I gave my all-purpose reply.

"Mr. Smith, my dream job would make use of my engineering degree, military experience, language skills, and desire to work overseas. Not a nine-to-five kind of job. Big salary and perks aren't major considerations."

My concern wasn't about finding a job but finding the right one. I didn't have anything specific in mind, but I did have clear ideas about what would make me happy. The Marine Corps had whetted my appetite for overseas travel, and I was looking for a company with operations abroad. After the exhilaration of combat, I doubted I'd be able to sit still at a routine job. With EDS I would make a handsome salary while getting top-notch training as a software systems engineer, a field with growth potential. But EDS had a reputation for being starchy and didn't offer overseas positions at the time.

At the end of my meeting with Mr. Smith, intrigued by the Agency mystique, I agreed to go for interviews at CIA headquarters. Besides, it was an expenses-paid trip to the East Coast, giving me a chance to attend my cousin's wedding in New York after I finished in Washington.

BE CAREFUL WHAT YOU WISH FOR!

I arrived a day before my first interview. It had been five years since I'd visited the nation's capital. It was summer, and the city was as hot and muggy as I remembered it being during weekend escapes from Quantico. I took a bus tour of the local sights, reminding me of why I always enjoyed the city's stately architecture, friendly inhabitants, and Southern charm.

Mr. Smith had arranged an interview with the Technical Services Division (TSD), which was responsible for clandestine technical operations. Its offices at the time weren't at Langley but in the old Navy Annex across from the State Department—the same spaces occupied by Allen Dulles, the Agency's first director. TSD was composed of specialists who used various technologies to support espionage operations around the world. If you think of clandestine ops as being carried out by a *Mission: Impossible* team, then the TSD "tech" would be the Greg Morris character—the one installing spy gear.

TSD hired all kinds of talents: artists who made disguises, cabinetmakers who fabricated concealments, paramilitary types who devised explosives, and electronics specialists who installed surveillance devices.

TAKING UP THE CHALLENGE

My initial interview was not the one-on-one kind I'd been used to. A secretary led me to a large conference room. Seated on high-backed leather chairs around a rectangular table were more than a dozen representatives from various TSD branches. They peppered me with questions about my academic and professional interests, travels, etc. A Chinese speaker popped in to talk to me in Mandarin, trying to gauge my fluency. Someone asked me a question in Spanish, making me regret I had listed having had Spanish training in the Marines. Someone asked for examples of how well I worked under pressure.

After an hour, the secretary took me to a wood-paneled office and introduced me to TSD's chief of operations, a bald, stocky man with a bushy mustache chomping on an unlit cigar and sounding like a New York taxi driver. Dispensing with small talk, he said, "I think you'd do well here. If you pass the security screening, psychological testing, and polygraph, I'd like you to join us."

When I asked what I'd be doing, he said he couldn't tell me. "It's about espionage" was all he would say. Afterward, I met Earl, TSD's chief of personnel, who offered me a starting salary $10,000 below what I'd be making with EDS.

Weighing the pros and cons I said, "Earl, I've already got a job lined up with a company offering an attractive salary, excellent advancement opportunities, performance bonuses, and the location of my choice. You, on the other hand, can't guarantee where I'll be working, can't tell me what I'll be doing, and are offering substantially less pay. So why should I take this job?"

Earl responded in a low-key, no-pressure way, neither trying to sell me on how important or exciting the work would be nor trying to appeal to my patriotism. Instead he simply said, "We can't promise you many things, but the one thing I can guarantee if you join the Agency is this: it'll be a challenge."

I was amazed that Earl uttered the one thing I could never resist: a challenge! It was like he had read my mind. I hadn't survived the war to settle down to a nine-to-five job. And I definitely was more interested in a challenging career than in making money. Earl's straightforward answer sealed my fate.

SUPER TECH

Pete looked at the map as I maneuvered the rental car through morning traffic, not used to driving a stick shift, especially around a strange city. *CRUNCH!* I slammed on the brake, but it was too late as my bumper smashed into the rear end of a taxi in the middle of rush hour on my first TDY (temporary duty) assignment overseas. A police cruiser pulled up behind, red lights flashing. Just what I didn't need. Spies are supposed to be inconspicuous. I imagined being James Bond but felt like Maxwell Smart.

As the taxi driver got out of his shiny car to survey his dented rear fender, I braced for a tongue-lashing. To my surprise, he simply shrugged his shoulders and acted as if getting rear-ended was an everyday event. The policeman motioned us to follow him to the police station. I apologized to the taxi driver using hand and arm gestures since I didn't speak the local language. We were supposed to see the CIA station chief that morning but got to our meeting two hours late.

Pete, a TSD engineer, and I were there to test an electronic tracking system at the request of Bob, the deputy chief of station. People called him "Super Tech" because he loved gadgets and technical operations and could conceal a microdot[17] with a razorblade better than a TSD tech could with more sophisticated tools.

Although the tracking system didn't work as well as we had hoped, the trip gave me a feel for overseas life and reinforced my desire for a permanent assignment overseas, a major reason I'd joined the Agency. Although TSD had positions overseas, the slots and locations were much more limited than those for case officers. So after returning home I explored ways to switch career paths.

---

17 In 1870 during the Franco-Prussian War, messages were sent by carrier pigeon. A French photographer used a photo shrinking technique to permit each pigeon to a carry high volume of messages. The microdot technique was used by many countries to pass messages through insecure postal channels. Source: en.wikipedia.org/wiki/Microdot; accessed June 2014.

WHEN ONE DOOR CLOSES

Deciding I'd rather be Peter Graves than Greg Morris on the *Impossible Missions Force*, I asked colleagues and TSD management how to go about it, but fellow techs tried to talk me out of it. "Nah, don't become a case officer; they're a bunch of prima donnas," a coworker warned. My ops chief said, "They probably shopped your file already and weren't interested. So forget about it and get back to work." I understood management's reluctance to let me go since they'd invested time and money training me.

Because of my military experience and engineering degree, I was assigned to TSD's Special Devices Branch, responsible for supporting paramilitary operations and deploying electronic tracking devices. I respected my branch chief —Wally, a former paramilitary officer—and I didn't want to seem like a disgruntled employee after just a short time on the job.

Just as I was about to give up, Bob sent a message to Wally asking if I could replace Ted, his station technical operations officer (TOPS). I was excited but apprehensive about replacing Ted, an experienced tech who spoke the local language. Could I fill his shoes? And why would Bob, whom I'd just met, want me? "He probably just likes the cut of your jib," Wally surmised. When Wally said he'd support my decision if I wanted the job, I was extremely grateful he'd sponsor me for an intensive yearlong training program while I occupied a branch slot, one he couldn't refill until I deployed overseas.

TOPS officers are jacks-of-all-trades assigned to an overseas station as singletons to support clandestine operations. Although they're from one of TSD's operational branches (such as audio surveillance, disguise, documents, etc.), they're cross-trained in other TSD disciplines and need to be familiar with all the technical capabilities available from TSD (and now the Office of Technical Services, its successor).

Let's say a station identifies a terrorist cell operating from a safe house and recruits a cell member as an access agent to help mount a technical operation. If it's simple, such as supplying the agent with a concealed recorder or camera to record a meeting or to take photos, the station's TOPS officer may already have the equipment on hand. However, if it's more complex (e.g., breaking into the safe house to download information from a target computer or implanting audio and video surveillance devices), the station might need more resources. Then the TOPS officer would request additional technical expertise, and the station might request more case officers from a neighboring station or from headquarters.

Just Call me Hammerhead

"You've got one hour to defeat at least fifteen of the twenty locks," said Ken. "Go!"

I took a sip of cream soda. Ken, our instructor, kept cases of his favorite soft drink in a refrigerator next to our workbench in a windowless room of a one-story warehouse cum safe house. I stared at the assortment of locks mounted on a three-by-six-foot oak board. I'd practiced on similar models before. Most were "pin tumblers," the kinds of locks used on front doors of houses, or garage padlocks. Others with foreign markings were unfamiliar to me. Two of us were taking the final "advanced locks and picks" exam.

"Only ten minutes left!" Ken announced. I watched Rick, an experienced tech, out of the corner of my eye as he opened all fifteen of the locks without breaking a sweat, while I still had another four to go. If I had a hammer then, I would've been tempted to smash open the remaining ones. But that wouldn't have been very surreptitious, which was the point of the exercise.

My mind wandered off to a story about a tech who, after several unsuccessful tries to pick a lock during a real operation, hammered it open, attempting to cover up the mess by making it to look like a burglary. From then on everyone called him Hammerhead.

"Time's up!" Ken said, "Don't worry, Hon. Not many get through all the locks. I made it tough to let you know what it's like to try to manipulate a lock under pressure." To brighten our spirits, Ken pulled out a couple of bottles of cream soda. Every time I have one, I think of Ken and the locks I couldn't open.

PHOTOS, MICRODOTS, EXPLOSIVES

In photo class, before digital cameras were invented, I learned how to develop and enlarge black-and-white film. And how to make concealed cameras by detaching the lens from the camera body and triggering the shutter with a remote release. One resourceful female officer, by hiding the lens in her bra, got clear, identifying face shots of targets staring directly at the camera.

In one of our practice exercises, we had to use a concealed camera to take photos of a meeting between a case officer and a target at a local airport. One tech was literally an out-of-the-box thinker, installing a lens in a red-and-white popcorn box, filling the box with the real thing, and snapping photos while strolling around the airport munching popcorn. Unfortunately, people kept disrupting his photo taking by asking him where he had purchased the snack. The airport didn't have any popcorn vendors, so he had to come up with an answer, "Oh, I bought it before I got to the airport."

I learned the art of secret writing, a technique as old as spying, which required preparing and sending secret messages hidden in plain sight. Early-era spies used lemon juice or urine to write a message on a sheet of paper that when dry would be invisible to the naked eye. The intended recipient could make the text reappear by applying heat or a special chemical to the paper. We learned covert ways to open letters and practiced "trapping" letters or envelopes to see if they'd been tampered with. We buried microdots that, to a casual observer, would appear to be a period at the end of a sentence in a letter, magazine, book, or anything with text, but which are, in fact, microfilm with photographs of documents that have been reduced down to the size of a period.

My own branch was in charge of explosives and demolition training. We practiced blowing things up with shaped charges made with coffee cans packed with C4, a plastic explosive, and capped with a metal cone. Once the C4 detonates, the cone would be propelled forward like a bullet. One of our instructors, a former US Navy underwater demolitions expert, had a favorite saying: "A neat charge is a happy charge!" He said it to emphasize the importance of careful preparation to achieve maximum effect without blowing ourselves up.

YOUR MUSTACHE IS CROOKED

Our disguise specialists used Hollywood consultants for technical advice. They could change someone's appearance dramatically by creating custom-made disguises—a complicated, multi-step process. A plaster cast is first made of the person's face to create a form-fitting mold. Different materials are then used to craft a lifelike mask.

Fitted with one that turned me into a white, middle-aged male with brown hair and neatly trimmed beard, I wanted to see if it could fool Mike, one of my officemates. Letting our secretary in on the prank, I asked her to tell Mike a Mr. Brown from the audit staff wanted to talk with him. Mike started to sweat.

"I can't understand why they'd want to talk with me!" he said with furrowed brow.

The next day our secretary brought Mike into a conference room where I was waiting in disguise.

"Hello, I'm Steve Brown. Please have a seat," I said without trying to alter my speech in any way. Mike sat down in a chair about five feet away from mine, looking straight at me, obviously nervous, unsmiling, but with no hint that he recognized me.

"Mike, you haven't been padding your expense account, have you?" I asked with a straight face.

As we reviewed Mike's understanding of travel accounting, his jaw tightened and his fists clenched. I was amazed my disguise had fooled him and had a hard time suppressing an urge to burst out laughing. Mike's jaw dropped when I pulled off the mask, but it's he who would have had the last laugh if he had known that years later a budget officer from the office of security would be scrutinizing my own personal finances.

As a TOPS officer, I only had to learn the basics of disguise, including the use of wigs, hair coloring, and makeup. Our instructor warned us not to drink hot beverages when wearing a mustache because heat can cause the glue holding the disguise in place to melt. He made his point by relating an amusing story of a case officer who used a mustache disguise to meet an agent. At the end of the meeting, the officer drank some coffee before remembering that heat could wilt the disguise. So he went to the men's room to make sure the mustache was still secure and decided to freshen it up with a squirt of hairspray.

Upon returning to the table, he knew something was amiss when the agent stared at him bug-eyed. The officer, to his chagrin, understood the reason for the agent's startled reaction after seeing his own reflection in the mirror. The hairs of his fake mustache were jutting straight out at a ninety-degree angle, looking like it had an erection.

CHAPTER 8

THE CLANDESTINE SERVICE

Secret operations are essential in war; upon them the army relies to make its every move.

—Sun Tzu

When my good friend Andy Vaart visited me overseas on business, I was anxious to show him around, having been in Asia for six months studying Mandarin. We'd shared parallel careers starting as Marine 2nd lieutenants at The Basic School; we studied Mandarin at the Defense Language Institute in Monterey; and we were assigned to the same outfit at Camp Pendleton. Both of us later wound up at the Agency, he as an intelligence analyst and I as an ops officer. At Langley we often met for lunch with other Chinese speakers to maintain our conversational skills.

After greeting Andy at his hotel, we took a taxi to the National Museum. I gave the driver directions in what I thought was passable, if not flawless, Mandarin. Confident my language proficiency had improved since I last saw Andy, I wanted to show off my new fluency as we made our way around town chatting with the locals. The Chinese are relatively tolerant of foreigners trying to speak their native tongue and fulsomely praise you even if you butcher their language.

"My God! Where did you learn your Mandarin?" asked the driver incredulously as he turned around to stare in my direction. My chest puffed up as I waited for him to say something like "Oh my, you speak Chinese so well!" Instead he looked down his nose at me and remarked, "Your Mandarin stinks! You should be ashamed!" I thought New York cabbies were rude, but they were Miss Manners compared to this guy. He turned his attention back to the road but continued to hurl insults my way. It wasn't until I explained that I wasn't a native and was born in the United States that he finally shut up.

I've never been under the illusion that I speak fluent Chinese even when others think I should. Of course, with a name like Hon and not John, I'm never offended when people assume I was born in Beijing and not Brooklyn. Having grown up on the streets of New York's Chinatown, I spoke pidgin Cantonese, could get by with simple phrases, but was functionally illiterate. Regretting I hadn't paid more attention when I attended Chinese language school as a kid, I was thankful that the Agency gave me a chance to polish my Mandarin.

RIGHT HAND MEETS LEFT

The opportunity, however, appeared only after navigating a bureaucratic maze, one that required a change in career paths. I began talking with operations officers who might help me make the switch, including a senior officer who taught a class on clandestine operations for non-case officers. He described life in the field and introduced our class to the rudiments of tradecraft, including how to elicit information from a prospective target at a cocktail party. I felt an adrenaline rush when I tried my hand at recruiting and debriefing during a training exercise and knew this was what I wanted to do.

When I asked the instructor if he knew of any openings in the Directorate of Operations (DO), he said, "There's a shortage of people like you, so I'll call my contacts in the East Asia Division to arrange an interview." I was encouraged by his offer to help but disappointed to learn that what he had in mind was a position for native Chinese speakers who transcribed audio surveillance intercepts. I thanked him but explained I wasn't interested in being a transcriber even if my Chinese had been fluent enough, which it wasn't.

Although I interviewed for several DO positions, no one could add me to their rolls because of a government-wide hiring freeze. I was about to give up when I met Don, head of DO career management. When he encouraged me to apply for the Career Training Program (CTP), I said I'd asked about the program when I first interviewed with technical services but was informed that the CTP office had reviewed my file and wasn't interested. Don shook his head as he thumbed through my file, saying there was no indication that was so. He explained that the CTP was a pipeline for young officers with potential to be the Agency's future leaders. Career trainees went through a year or more of training and rotational assignments before being assigned to one of the Agency's four directorates (operations, analysis, science and technology, or administration). In practice, most career trainees wound up in operations or analysis.

CAREER TRAINING PROGRAM

Since I'd already completed the security and psychological screening, my main hurdle was getting past interviews with two senior officers who served as guidance counselors for the program. The Directorate of Intelligence (DI) rep didn't endorse my application because he said my academic credentials couldn't compete with applicants he had interviewed for the upcoming class, and there were only a few slots left. Many had advanced degrees in international relations, including at least one with a Harvard PhD. There were just too many candidates vying for too few positions. As he reviewed my file, he casually mentioned that someone who was a DO officer and CTP graduate had recommended me for Agency employment. I was pleased to learn that he was a former Marine Corps buddy. Until that moment neither of us knew the other was working here, a common occurrence in the compartmented world of the CIA.

My interview with Tom, the DO rep, went better but not by much. Tom was underwhelmed by my cursory knowledge of international affairs, mediocre college transcripts, and rudimentary foreign language skills. He gave me a provisional pass but said I'd need the head of CTP, Mr. Hopkins, to break the tie. I had a restless night's sleep as I mulled over what I'd say to convince him I was suitable.

As hopeful as I was apprehensive, and as thankful for the opportunity as I was aware that I might not make it, I went for my final interview with Mr. Hopkins. He looked like a thinner Anthony Hopkins but was more Dutch uncle than Hannibal Lecter. When asked why I'd make a good case officer, I was prepared to tell him about my combat experience as a Marine officer and ability to work under pressure. I was going to say my engineering degree would be an asset in an increasingly sophisticated technical world. And I was going to tell him my ethnicity would allow me to fit in where others couldn't.

But I'd already said all those things before to all the people I had hoped could help me, like the DI rep and the DO rep. It didn't work. Tired of hearing myself touting a laundry list of my own virtues, and knowing that the art of persuasion was one of the keys to being a good recruiter—the mark of a successful case officer—I decided to take a completely different tack: I talked about my summer job. I told Mr. Hopkins that during college I'd sold an educational program door-to-door in New York City, and at one point scored the highest sales in the company nationally. I used the story to illustrate that I could persuade people to let me into their living rooms and to buy a product they'd never heard of from someone they'd never met before.

After listening to my monologue, Mr. Hopkins didn't say a word for what seemed like the longest, longest time as I sat across from him. We were separated by one of those big executive desks piled high with stacks of personnel files, across what seemed like an unbridgeable chasm that separated me from my dream job. Then, getting up from his chair, closing the gap between us, and smiling, he extended his hand and said, "Mr. Lee, I'm going to give you a chance to prove yourself!" My spirits soaring, I shook his hand, thanking him profusely, promising I'd try my best not to let him down. Who would have thought that a summer job as a salesman would help me get my foot in the door to becoming a clandestine operations officer?

FLASHBACK

Want Ad: *No Experience Needed, High Income, Good People Skills Required*

Home from college for the summer, I answered a New York Times help wanted ad, hoping it wouldn't be in a sleazy backroom office making telephone sales calls, hoping it wouldn't be like the job I had for a week of people slamming the phone on me. On that job it didn't take long for people to realize I was trying to sell magazines and for them to hang up or to curse at me. The only conversation lasting longer than a minute was with a youngish-sounding girl who said she wanted to buy a subscription but didn't have money. When I asked to speak with her mother, she said she couldn't come to the phone, explaining that her mother had just died. After that I didn't want to have anything to do with sales.

I went for the job interview at a midtown Manhattan office near Park Avenue. Judging from its location and expensive office décor, this was no shoestring operation but, as I had feared, it was all about sales. As I was about to walk out, a stunningly attractive receptionist grabbed my arm and persuaded me to fill out an application. Then I, along with a dozen other applicants, met Mr. Charles, the head of *Parents* magazine's education division. Charles said he wanted self-starters to market a "crib to college" program. *Parents* magazine, he explained, was a respected organization that provided expert advice to parents on education, psychology, and health. They were offering a new set of educational tools to help kids achieve academic success.

The program included a set of encyclopedias written in a lively style that would appeal to students of all ages. Also included was a series of books covering science, math, English, and history. In addition, kids had access to the "Answer Man," allowing them to get written responses to academic questions. It cost almost $300 and could be paid in monthly installments. Even in 1964 dollars, it was not cheap; today it would cost about $2,000.

Charles introduced his team leaders, who talked with infectious enthusiasm about why they had joined. They liked a nonroutine job and meeting interesting people. Teams of sales reps assembled in the morning, drove to different parts of the city, and fanned out to cover a several-block area to sell the program door-to-door.

LIFE OF A SALESMAN

Knocking on doors wasn't appealing. I pictured Willy Loman returning home every night, head down, shoulders slumped, arms dragging. Yet I was attracted by the chance to observe human behavior close up. "It's a great way to learn how to deal with all kinds of people from all walks of life," Charles said. It fascinated me how people interacted. Psychology was my minor in college, with social psychology and organizational behavior being my favorite electives—bits of lightness to balance the heavy rigors of math and engineering courses. Moreover, since I was an introvert, I thought the job would help my people skills. And it looked like a good product developed by a reputable company with a worthwhile goal: helping kids to get a head start in school and in life.

I put aside my reservations when I learned that new sales reps would be mentored on how to handle prospective buyers and be given a how-to manual with suggested answers to counter possible buyer objections. All we had to do was follow the script, they said. I signed up and returned for classes about the product, contracts, and how to close a sale. The manual was brimming with useful sales tips. *Look for homes with venetian blinds, not pull-down shades. Pull-downs mean they can't afford it. Don't try to sell to your relatives when you're learning the ropes. Applying the "no man is a prophet in his own country" rule, your relatives will dismiss what you have to say. Their doubts will lower your self-confidence.*

The following Monday I was supposed to observe a sales call with a seasoned rep. But no one was available, so on my very first day out, I went alone, feeling the adrenaline rush of hopeful anticipation as I walked up to the first house.

KNOCK, KNOCK, WHO'S THERE?

Standing on the steps of a two-story row house in a middle-class neighborhood, taking an extra deep breath, and summoning my courage, I knocked on the front door.

"Who is it?" asked a woman from behind the door.

"It's about the school," said I, trying to keep my voice steady. *Don't say you want to sell something or you won't get in.*

"What school?" the woman wanted to know.

"I'd like to talk to you about your children's education."

"OK, wait a minute" she responded.

It was an interminably long minute as I stood waiting, imagining her calling the cops: "Hello officer, there's a guy outside my house claiming to be from the school..." Who could blame her for being suspicious?

Just when I thought it best to move down the block before the paddy wagon came, I heard the click of the door bolt slide open. A man in his late twenties and still in his PJ's appeared; his wife must have gotten him out of bed. I apologized for any inconvenience and said I wanted to discuss a program that could benefit his children.

James, the husband, invited me to sit down. He said he had a four-year-old son and his wife was expecting another child soon. The plastic tablecloth and spare furnishings indicated that the family was not well off. *No way these folks can afford this,* I thought, but I went through the "crib through college" pitch anyway, just for practice. To my surprise, James seemed enthusiastic about the program and asked his wife to join us—always a good sign. *Whenever possible, make the presentation when both husband and wife are available.*

I went over the pitch again with Clare, but before I could finish, James said he wanted to buy the program. His only dilemma was the expense. I told him that he could pay over a three-year period, amounting to only twenty-five cents a day. When the couple signed the contract, I wanted to jump up and down with joy. Instead, I thanked them sincerely, waved good-bye, and went to the next house buoyed with confidence.

By the time I met up with my team that afternoon, I'd had several doors slammed in my face but had completed four other presentations and sold one additional program that day. My team leader couldn't believe my success the first day out. "Chalk it up to beginner's luck!" I told her with a big grin.

DON'T BUY, DAMMIT!

One of my most memorable calls was on the Abrams family in Brooklyn. Mr. Abrams, a retired postal worker, welcomed me into his detached two-story house. He and his wife offered me lemonade as they listened to my pitch, asking how the program might help their grandchildren, who ran around us in circles making as much noise as they could, rambunctious eight-year-old twins who lived next door to the Abrams. I tried to filter out the ruckus as they played cowboys and Indians, shooting me with cap pistols and toy bows and arrows.

About halfway through my presentation, their mother appeared and demanded to know what was going on. Mr. Abrams introduced Stella, his daughter-in-law. When she learned I was trying to sell something, she hollered, "Don't buy! Don't buy!" Mr. Abrams tried to calm her down. "Just let the poor guy finish, please." Stella stormed out but ten minutes later reappeared with another woman she brought along for support. They both yelled louder and louder, "Don't buy, dammit! Don't buy!"

Never pitch a group; if one person reacts negatively they'll reinforce everyone else's concerns. An experienced salesman would have put his brochures away and left, but I didn't know any better. Although I should have made a graceful exit, Stella's tirade just made me more determined as I tried to counter every argument she voiced.

By then several neighbors had joined the fray. Finally, after fifteen minutes of heated back-and-forth, Mr. Abrams raised his hand and shouted, "Stop, enough already! Where do I sign?" I had Stella to thank for the sale. From their body language, she and her in-laws didn't get along. Mr. Abrams, I surmised, made the purchase out of spite.

A MASTER SALESMAN

By the end of my second week, I finally had a chance to follow a real pro on a sales call. Arnie told me to let him take the lead as we approached the house. When he rang the doorbell, a woman stuck her head out of the second-floor window.

"Whaddya want?" she asked.

"It's about school!" he mumbled softly so the woman had to come downstairs to hear.

"Who? What'd you say?" the woman shouted.

"The school. It's about the school," Arnie responded.

After Mrs. Jones came down and invited us in, Arnie laid out our program and explained its benefits. Mrs. Jones listened as Arnie finished describing how it would help her children. She finally said, "I like the program but just can't afford it."

With that, Arnie abruptly pushed his chair back and stood up. Grabbing his trouser leg, he pointed at a patched-up hole. "Mrs. Jones, I haven't bought a new suit in ten years! Know why?" She shook her head. "It's because I sacrifice for my kids, for their education. All you have to do is put away twenty-five cents a day, Mrs. Jones. Is that asking too much?"

Mrs. Jones seemed taken aback as she stared at the man in her living room holding his crotch. I thought she'd kick us out once she had regained her composure. Instead, she wiped a tear from her eyes and slowly nodded as Arnie pulled out a contract from his briefcase and asked if she wanted to pay with cash or check. When she signed on the dotted line, I knew I'd witnessed a master salesman at work.

As we left Mrs. Jones's house, Arnie told me, "Potential customers decide to buy something because they want to and not because you trick or coerce them into it. You merely present them the opportunity and help them reaffirm they're making the right decision." Years later, Arnie's advice would help me persuade people to become spies.

Clandestine Training

In 1972 I joined a class of officers selected for the Career Training Program. We started with three-month interim assignments to help us make a career choice among the Agency's four directorates: operations (DO), intelligence (DI), science and technology (DDS&T), or administration (DA). In practice, everyone in my class had been screened and would become either case officers in the DO's Clandestine Service or intelligence analysts in the DI.

I had two interim assignments, one as an operations "country desk" officer, and the other as an intelligence analyst for strategic military issues. In both the DO and DI, the world is carved into geographical or functional areas, e.g., Africa, Latin America, Counterterrorism, Counternarcotics, etc.

Because offices at CIA headquarters were always shorthanded, career trainees were welcomed as extra help that wouldn't use up their own hard-to-get personnel slots. But we were often given menial jobs since we were there for only three months. During my DI interim, I catalogued the movement of military units in a country of intelligence interest. My CT advisor Tom got angry when he found out I was doing clerical work instead of analysis and chastised me for not making better use of my time.

In truth, I wasn't confident in my ability to take on a writing assignment, so I was satisfied doing research. Nonetheless, I knew Tom was right and asked the office director to give me more substantive work. By the end of the assignment I'd published a paper on an armed insurgency. Years later, when I became a supervisor, I tried to give CTs as much responsibility as they could handle. They never failed to meet and often exceeded my expectations.

Camp Swampy

The most stimulating part of the program for me was tradecraft training at "the Farm," a clandestine site that's been widely reported in the press as being in Virginia. We affectionately called it Camp Swampy because it was located in a marshy area that smelled like swamp gas when the wind blew the wrong way. With barbed wire fences surrounding the compound, sealed-off areas for firing ranges, parachute towers, a small runway, a mess hall, and barracks-style officer's quarters, I felt like I was back in the Marine Corps.

However, this was the Agency's boot camp for spies. This was where we learned how to recruit and handle agents, mount surveillance, avoid being surveilled, communicate covertly, and other esoteric skills needed to operate securely and effectively in the field. Following well-scripted training scenarios, we pretended to be members of a CIA station team assigned to the Republic of Virginia. According to the script, it was a country friendly to the United States but it shared a border with the People's Republic of West Virginia, which posed a threat to US interests.

Our instructors were veteran ops officers with years of field experience. They served as our advisors, instructors, and role players. In scenarios designed to teach us how to be case officers, they acted the part of foreign agents, double agents, and provocateurs. They evaluated our skills and provided feedback after each exercise. Although the pace of training was stressful, I had fun and couldn't believe I was getting paid to do things I saw in the movies. One of my favorite courses was "crash and bang," where we learned how to crash through roadblocks while firing a weapon. The course was euphemistically called "Defensive Driving."

My military and tech ops experience came in handy. For example, having attended the US Army's Interrogation Course, I knew how to debrief someone and elicit information efficiently. At the Defense Language Institute, I had learned how to memorize and recall information without taking notes. And my TOPS training allowed me to skip tech ops classes and exercises, giving me extra time to focus on other parts of the course.

YOUR WRITING SUCKS!

I was embarrassed when my instructors returned my intelligence reports with big, red correction marks. I felt like a kid in grade school. You don't have to be Hemingway to be a good ops officer, but lives depend on being able to convey information clearly, succinctly, and accurately.

As an engineering major in college, and later as a Marine officer, I didn't have much need to refine my writing skills. To make matters worse,

I was a hunt-and-peck typist despite having taken typing in high school. At the Farm, a decade before personal computers, I used up many a bottle of whiteout correction fluid. If I had to name an invention that made life easier for me, word processing would definitely be on the shortlist!

ROLE PLAYING

I snuck into the back of the two-story brick building without attracting attention and slid into a seat in the back row of the auditorium. Participants on stage sat around a horseshoe-shaped conference table while political rivals presented their agendas. My target was a tall, slim man who talked about why people should vote for him.

I tied a red bandana around my forehead, unsheathed a three-foot long sword, and rushed down the aisle. With sword raised and handle gripped tightly, I let out a blood curdling "A-I-Y-A-A-H!" and lunged forward. A shot rang out a split second before I reached my target. Clutching my chest, I slumped to the floor. As they dragged my limp body away, the guy who shot me shouted, "You know who this is? It's crazy Sockamoto of the Red Army!"

That ended my thespian appearance during a covert action exercise. With the exception of the guy who shot me using a pistol loaded with blanks, none of my classmates knew I'd appear in the guise of "Sockamoto." It was my attempt to add levity to the serious business of covert action. We were learning about political influence operations, one of the Agency's most controversial areas.

CHAPTER 9

ANATOMY OF RECRUITMENT

The habits and language of clandestinity can intoxicate even its own practitioners.

—WILLIAM COLBY

In the late 1990s, the CIA's Directorate of Intelligence surveyed analysts across the intelligence community and asked which collectors added the most value to their work. Among those rated were open source information, State Department reporting, satellite imagery, signals and communications intelligence, and human intelligence. Clandestine reporting from human sources ranked at the very top.

When it comes to divining the plans and intentions of adversaries, there's no substitute for having someone with access to the inner circle of an Osama bin Laden or a Kim Jong Il. But recruiting someone like that can take years. Vetting and training them takes even longer. The following illustrates the recruitment of a human asset or agent.[18]

PATIENCE PAYS OFF

The air was crisp and smelled of fall as I walked through the plaza, using a circuitous route to ensure I wasn't followed, on my way to meet Mitch. If I saw someone anywhere along the way twice, it could be a coincidence. But if I spotted the same person three times, I knew I was being tailed and would abort the meeting. I arrived at the safe house with some takeout. Eating lunch while I debriefed Mitch saved time since he couldn't be absent from his embassy for too long without arousing suspicion. Mitch was a midlevel foreign ministry official and pro-American. He enjoyed the modest salary I gave him so that he could save for his kids' education, but he was a reluctant spy. As the Agency's budget began to shrink, I had to decide whether or not to keep him on our payroll.

Mitch refused to report on his own government but was willing to provide information on other diplomats. I hoped he'd start to provide intelligence as I gained his trust, reasoning that Mitch could prove his worth as he ascended the promotion ladder. In the meantime, I made the most of Mitch's contacts. He was friendly with Adam, a diplomat from a country of priority interest to US policymakers.

COURTSHIP

Recruiting is like dating: it takes time to build a relationship before popping the question. Some men think they can increase their odds by propositioning every girl they meet, hoping at least one will say yes. Some intelligence officers try a variation of this cold pitch by asking a recruitment

---

18 Spy jargon: Intelligence terms can be confusing. In the FBI, staff officers carry badges and are called special agents. In the CIA, an agent or asset is someone, usually a foreign national, who provides information or assistance to the Agency. CIA officers who run agents are called case officers. One of a case officer's primary jobs is to recruit assets, also called sources, who report information of intelligence value. Not all agents are sources. Some provide support, for example, safe house keepers. Other assets could be access agents or "cutouts" that can help us make contact with a potential source.

target to spy without any attempt at foreplay. I know of an intelligence service that does it over the phone. What's next, robocalls? To me, cold calls are a bad gambit because it could make a prospective target skittish, trigger a security clampdown by the target's own intelligence service, and close the door to a more methodical approach. In my experience the best recruitments occur when the case officer and target develop mutual trust, and building trust takes time.

THE SCRIPT

Mitch told me Adam was not as straight-laced as others from his embassy. He was approachable, liked to have fun, dated a local woman, enjoyed good food, and liked the theater.

"Mitch, can you help me meet Adam?"

"No way! I don't want to do anything that could blow back on me. I'm already taking enough risk just meeting with you."

"I understand your concern. Your safety is primary, and I wouldn't do anything to jeopardize it."

"Well, if that's true, you wouldn't ask me to introduce you to him! If he found out you're CIA, my career and possibly life would be in danger!"

"Just listen to what I have in mind. First, you won't have to introduce me directly. I want you to invite Adam and his girlfriend to a show. During intermission I'll just happen to run into you accidentally. That's all you have to do. I'll take care of the rest. Second, I'll be going as 'Joe Chin' and will introduce myself as an Asian consultant for multinationals."

It took several more meetings to convince Mitch that I would distance him from any repercussions in a future relationship I might establish with the target. Mitch reluctantly consented to set up a chance encounter.

ACT ONE, SCENE ONE

The theater lobby was packed during intermission. I watched them approach the refreshment stand, where I stood with drink in hand. I waved and said, "Hi! You look familiar. I'm Joe Chin. Sorry, but I forgot your name." I pretended I didn't remember Mitch's name, purposely botching it and calling him Mike. "I think we met at a National Day reception some time ago," I said.

Adam, not a hail-fellow-well-met kind of guy, didn't say much as I tried to make small talk. Of medium height and build, he sported a neatly trimmed mustache. His buxom girlfriend flashed a toothy smile. We exchanged cards. Just before returning to our seats, I said, "Hey, I know a great restaurant around the corner. Let's go for drinks and something to eat after the show. My treat!" All agreed.

When I saw Mitch the next day, he was all smiles. "I can't believe how well everything turned out! You really put Adam at ease," he said. "He didn't seem the least suspicious." I complimented Mitch for keeping his nerves under control and thanked him for giving me the chance to meet an important target.

My initial meetings with Adam were social, getting together over a meal while assessing his personality and motivations. Was he a risk taker, someone who would agree to become a spy? Did he have access to information worth stealing? I wanted a second opinion. Case officers can become overly enamored with a target and lose objectivity.

I brought in a husband-and-wife ops team with expertise on Adam's country. They lived in an upscale safe house and had well-backstopped alias personas. Playing the role of wealthy clients, they strengthened my bona fides as a financial risk advisor. After meeting Adam and forming their own opinion about his potential, they gave me two thumbs-up. Next, an Agency behavioral psychologist did a psychological assessment on him, confirming my belief that Adam had the makings of a good spy.

I knew via independent sources that Adam harbored no ill will toward Americans even though he despised US government policy. Although he never directly criticized his own government, it was run by a tyrannical regime, so I had no doubt he was not enthralled with what was going on back home; it was a nation in turmoil, where he personally faced a bleak future. With approval from Langley, I turned my relationship with Adam from a social into a commercial one.

"I need a knowledgeable consultant about your area of the world— someone like you." He sat still for several minutes, as if deep in thought.

Then he said, "What is it you are asking of me?"

I took a deep breath and remembered my door-to-door salesman training. *Don't go for the sale immediately, but get the prospective buyer used to saying yes. Don't ask Mrs. Jones if she would like to buy a set of encyclopedias for five hundred dollars. Instead, start with "Do you value your children's education?"*

So I asked, "Can you advise me on the types of industries your country will need in the next couple of years?" I explained that I wanted an in-depth risk/benefit analysis for clients who wanted to invest there.

"I can do that," he said without further hesitation.

Over the next month, I asked him for more detailed information in exchange for a monthly "retainer." Getting him to accept payment showed a willingness to break embassy rules by moonlighting. Although a far cry from getting him to spy, it was a start.

HIGHER STAKES

I slowly upped the ante, telling Adam that one of my clients was a US government think tank.

"Do you mind if I pass along your information?" I asked. "Your identity would be kept strictly confidential."

The color drained from his face. He quizzed me on how I could protect his identity. I said we'd give him a code name and the client wouldn't know his true name. I held my breath. We were at a swanky restaurant, so I knew he wouldn't make a scene. He'd either walk out or continue our relationship.

He sat quietly for a couple of minutes, then said, "Sure, no problem." From then on I debriefed him in detail about economic, political, and social issues.

DAISY CHAIN

In the next phase of this "daisy chain," I'd planned to introduce Adam to the US "think tank" representative who would task Adam to collect sensitive information. In the final phase, the representative would introduce him to a CIA officer who would run Adam clandestinely after ensuring Adam wasn't a double agent reporting to his own security service. The ultimate goal was to train him in covert communications in order to transmit intelligence to us when he returned home.

Just as I was about to bring in the think tank rep, Adam announced he'd received orders to pack up and leave for a new assignment. He was being transferred to a third world country and would be leaving town within a week. "I don't like it but have no choice," he said with a frown. He didn't want to give up the good life or his girlfriend.

I notified the station in the country where he would be going and asked if they had an officer who could take over the case. Greg, the officer selected to handle Adam, flew in to discuss the case with me. Greg's station chief, whom I knew and trusted from a previous assignment, assured me that Greg was a top-notch officer. I wasn't disappointed. Greg had a competent, easygoing manner I thought would be a perfect fit for Adam.

ALL IN

During my next meeting with Adam, I said "I've enjoyed our time together and thank you for providing me with information to help understand your country. Because it's been going so well, I want to continue this consultancy relationship by introducing you to a trusted friend assigned to the country where you'll be posted."

Adam was no fool. If he hadn't already suspected that I had an affiliation with US intelligence, this confirmed it. When he didn't balk, I assured him that my friend would take extraordinary measures to protect his security. I promised he would continue receiving payments via Greg as a way to build a personal nest egg for his future. Adam met Greg shortly after arriving at his new posting, and the Station reported that the relationship was going well.

POSTSCRIPT

For security reasons intelligence officers adhere to the "need to know" principle. This means not discussing classified information about an operation that you're not directly involved with. So when I didn't hear anything more about Adam, I didn't ask.

However, a few years later an officer who was supporting the case told me that Adam had returned to his home country after his last overseas assignment and was providing highly valuable intelligence. In the ensuing years, his country went through enormous change. I'd like to think that Adam's reporting helped US policymakers reach more informed decisions about an area of the world that continues to affect vital national security interests. Most of all, I sincerely hope that he's alive and happy and enjoying the good life. He earned it.

And what about Mitch? Twenty years later he'd risen to the highest levels of his ministry. We still gave him a monthly payment but more as a token of appreciation since he no longer needed to augment his salary. He was now providing his case officer with information about his country's economic, trade, and political policies. But in his mind, he didn't do this as a spy. He did it to influence US decisions affecting his country, believing his information would get more attention in Washington via the CIA than through regular US embassy reporting channels.

CHAPTER 10

HEARTACHE AND HEART SHOCK

Life's but a walking shadow, a poor player that struts and frets his hour upon the stage, and then is heard no more....

—SHAKESPEARE

Vicki and I were visiting my parents in New York City in the winter of 1978. It was almost Christmas, but it was not a time for celebration. My brother Yun had died of a heart attack weeks earlier. He would have been forty-five. I apologized to my parents for not returning from overseas in time for Yun's memorial service. I couldn't imagine how painful it must have been to bury a son. Baba said they used up quite a few boxes of Kleenex, but he and Mama seemed able to move beyond their grief, believing that the physical body is just a temporary container for the immortal soul.

We reserved a table in a Chinatown restaurant for a family gathering and set two extra places for Tony and his girlfriend. I thought my family would enjoy meeting Tony, who spoke Chinese and could make anyone laugh. And what we needed then was a good laugh to brighten up our spirits.

Tony, Andy Vaart, and I had served together at Camp Pendleton. After Tony left the Marines and earned his degree in Asian Studies, I believed he'd make an excellent case officer. Because I was undercover and Andy wasn't, I suggested he send Tony a CIA job application to ensure it reached the Career Training office. (I was afraid it would get lost, as mine had been, in the bureaucracy.) As I had hoped, Tony was selected for the Career Training Program.

The first day Tony reported for duty, Andy arranged to have lunch with him in the Agency cafeteria. Tony didn't know I was also working there, so he was pleasantly surprised when I showed up. It was great to build on the friendship that we had started in the Marine Corps. We also shared an interest in Chinese martial arts.

I was delighted to learn that Tony, while going to college in Los Angeles, had studied Shaolin kung fu. It turned out his teacher was none other than Kam Yuen, my boyhood friend from New York's Chinatown. Talk about a small world! Tony brought me up-to-date on Kam's activities as a stunt coordinator and advisor to the popular *Kung Fu* television series.

I introduced Tony to my kung fu teacher in Washington. During weekends we'd work out together in Washington's Chinatown, a small area compared to New York's or San Francisco's. When Vicki and I went overseas, Tony visited us on vacation. Whenever I introduced him to Chinese-speaking acquaintances, they would invariably tell me afterward how impressed they were with not only his language fluency but also his gregarious personality. I was so proud of him.

I was happy to hear that Tony had gotten a field assignment and was in New York visiting his girlfriend the same time we were there visiting my parents. I looked forward to seeing him during our brief stay—not sharing details about Tony with my family other than to say that we were in the Marines together. We waited for him at the restaurant, agreeing to meet there at six, but it was already seven-thirty, and it wasn't like him to be late. No one answered the telephone when I called him, and the waiter said no one had left a message for me.

I'd been with Tony earlier in the day to go shopping. He loved good clothes and bought almost two thousand dollars' worth. But he seemed moody, not his usual upbeat self. When I asked if there was anything bothering him, he said he'd had a fight with his girlfriend. She wanted to break up, and he didn't. I remembered Tony telling me that she was blond and attractive. Tony seemed hopeful that he could win her back and was going to see her that afternoon.

"Well, Tony, you always were a sucker for blondes. Why not invite her to dinner with my family tonight?" I suggested.

"OK," he said.

Tony never showed up. I never met his girlfriend. They were dead. It was on the front page of the morning paper. "Man shoots girlfriend, kills self." I read and reread the headline in shock. *Why, why, oh why, dear God?* I couldn't believe it, didn't want to believe it, refused to believe it. A bone-deep sense of guilt engulfed me. Why didn't I see it coming? The signs of depression. The sudden mood change. The extravagant clothing purchase.

Over the next twenty-four hours, I contacted people who worked with him to help me piece things together, to understand Tony's mindset, to understand why he would do such a thing. I learned that he had a good relationship with his chief but worked in a competitive and not particularly supportive office environment, an environment with colleagues who didn't see Tony the way I did. I felt responsible. I'd brought Tony into the Agency. *How could I have let this happen?!*

I called Andy to break the tragic news and cry on his shoulder. I'd lost more than just a friend; I'd lost another brother. And Andy felt entirely the same way. I know he's also often thought of Tony and what happened. Was there something left over from his Vietnam experience? He'd been in the worst of it during Tet in Hue. Had it to do with being the rare African American case officer in an unusual operational environment? Or none of the above? Now, these many years later, we'll never know.

YOUR MONEY OR YOUR LIFE!

On one of our early field assignments, Vicki and I learned that life abroad is no cocktail party. We were assigned to a capital city that was hot and humid even in the hours before dawn. Sound asleep, with the air conditioner on full blast, we had no clue anyone had crept into our bedroom, the constant drone of the air conditioner muffling the sound of footsteps—no clue until we heard whispering inches above us.

I woke up groggily, thinking our housekeeper had arrived early. When I opened my eyes I saw three people around us. One stood near the foot of the bed, another on my side, the third on Vicki's. Was this a nightmare or were these real-life intruders? Their flashlight beams shining in my eyes kept me from seeing clearly, but they appeared to have stockings over the faces.

"Don't move or we'll stab you to death!" one hissed.

Inspired by the memory of Uncle Henry's cook fending off burglars with his bare hands, and in my best imitation of Bruce Lee, I flung off the bed covers and attempted to strike out at the intruders. My flailing arms met cold steel. The burglars were armed with foot-long razor-sharp knives, the kind that they probably had taped to their bodies as they, I would later surmise, climbed into our apartment through an open kitchen window.

"Stop or we'll kill her!" said the man hovering over Vicki, speaking the local language I understood but Vicki didn't. This was good, because not understanding what they said, she reacted with more anger than fright; bad because her anger wasn't directed at them but at me.

She elbowed me in the ribs and asked, in a tone she usually used when I did something dumb, "Hon, did you leave the front door unlocked again?!" My attention, however, was focused on the burglar pressing the tip of his knife blade against my Adam's apple.

"Where's the money?" he demanded.

"We don't have any other than what's in my wallet," I insisted.

Minutes passed. Feeling the bed sheet moist from my own sweat, blood trickling down from cuts on my face into my eyes, I wondered what would happen next. It didn't take long to find out as they gagged and blindfolded us, making us lie facedown, tying our hands behind our backs and taping our legs together. Immobilized, all I could do was listen closely as they rummaged through dresser drawers, going room to room in search of valuables. Then I heard the sound of running water in the bathroom and felt a wet cloth on my face. One of them was wiping the blood off my forehead.

Could this be an act of kindness or did they want to make sure I didn't bleed to death? Maybe they weren't trying to hurt us after all, I thought. But would they suddenly turn violent again if they found the safe?

I prayed they wouldn't discover the steel, three-cubic-foot safe in the kitchen area left by the previous tenants, chastising myself for not getting rid of the thing when we moved in. Although empty, it was locked. I didn't have the combination but was certain the burglars wouldn't believe me. Would they torture us to get it open? Because the safe was an ugly, gray monstrosity, we had turned it around to face a corner wall in the kitchen area so that the combination dial and handle weren't visible if you just walked by it, especially in the dark.

A thousand thoughts raced through my mind, thoughts on how to get them to leave before they stumbled on the safe, thoughts on what I'd say and do if they found the safe. Then the buzzer sounded.

"What was that?" they wanted to know. "Is it to summon the police? Tell us the truth or we'll cut you again!"

"You're right, the buzzer is an alarm to alert the police," I replied. "You'd better scram because they'll be here any minute."

What I knew and they didn't was that one of them must have accidentally pressed a buzzer that sounded in the unoccupied maid's quarters in the back. Whether they believed me or not, within a few minutes I could no longer hear anything except the hum from the air conditioner. When I figured they were gone, we struggled free, getting one hand loose and then the other. Finally getting untangled, Vicki and I held each other in silent embrace, knowing we were lucky to be alive and, aside from a few minor cuts, had escaped unharmed—physically if not emotionally.

I called our security officer to report what had happened and asked him to contact the police. I wasn't hopeful the culprits would be caught. Burglaries were common in this neighborhood, and the police had little success or inclination trying to catch petty criminals.

They'd stolen my watch and camera, but not much else. Vicki had kept her jewelry in a safe deposit box. Police confirmed my belief that the thieves had shimmied up a drainpipe that led from ground level up three stories and past the open kitchen window of our apartment—not an easy climb. We suspected the building security guard was in on it. Unfortunately for us, they'd picked the wrong apartment and were probably after the rich couple living next door, a shipping tycoon who rode around town with his beautiful wife in a chauffeured Rolls Royce.

CHAPTER 11

SUPERTEAMS AND HIT MEN

Talent wins games, but teamwork and intelligence win championships.

—MICHAEL JORDAN

One of my most enjoyable assignments personally and professionally was as branch chief at a large station in a cosmopolitan city, one with access to domestic help, healthcare for Mama, who by this time was living with us, a top-notch international school for the kids, and available work at the embassy for Vicki.

Larry, the chief of station, reminded me of Clint Eastwood: a seasoned pro and man of few words who gave subordinates plenty of rope but sent you home if you screwed up. Over 10 percent of his hundred-plus staff left short-of-tour. I appreciated his management style. Many found him detached because he seldom walked around to chat with the troops, even though he invited each person in the station to his home for dinner at least once during that person's tour. Active on the international school board, he believed it was our civic duty to contribute to the community.

Rick, our chief of operations, was a chain-smoking workaholic who couldn't understand why younger officers focused more on home life than work. On a previous tour at the station, after he got caught sneaking into the country on a false passport, the station had to cash in favors with high-ranking liaison officials to bail him out of jail. When our liaison asked what he was up to, Rick quipped, "Oh, I was just trying to test your border security!"

Rick, married to a local woman, knew the culture and spoke the language well. His twin boys, tiny Pee-wee Hermans, were mischievous. When no one was watching, they dumped a bag of frozen shrimp into the clothes dryer as their maid was doing the wash. Unable to get rid of the strong, fishy odor, Rick had to trash the dryer and the clothes.

HAPPY DAYS

Until I'd convinced her to give up her apartment in New York and join us overseas, Mama had been living by herself. Baba had passed away six years earlier. It wasn't an easy decision for her or for us. What would happen if she got sick? She was close to eighty years old. Could she cope with a major change at this late stage in her life? Hesitant at first, she finally agreed to move with us overseas, surprising herself and us by adjusting quickly to her new surroundings, made easier when a station officer's wife graciously included Mama in activities with embassy spouses. When Mama wasn't out shopping or playing cards with her new friends, she'd go for a walk in a nearby park.

Our family took advantage of the city's many cultural attractions, fine restaurants, and sporting venues. Vicki and I took golf lessons, the kids learned to play tennis, we went swimming at a sports club and vacationed at a local beach resort, and Mama joined a morning exercise class.

With such a pleasant living environment, you'd think people would be happy, but station morale was low, and there was more competition than cooperation. Because case officers are rewarded for recruiting agents, they jealously guard their contacts, even if another officer might be a better match. Agent spotting, assessing, and handling, while essential to intelligence collection, are, as a rule, given less weight in performance evaluations than recruitment. The reality is that not everyone is a good recruiter.

Tired of spending more time resolving interpersonal squabbles than managing operations, I discovered a book entitled *The Superteam Solution*, which described how teamwork creates synergy, underscoring what I'd learned in school and in combat. In the Marines, "gung-ho" describes someone with great esprit de corps, a phrase actually Chinese in origin and meaning "working together in harmony." And that harmony was what I was after, so I put the book's concepts into practice when Rick became deputy chief of station and I replaced him as chief of operations. We formed superteams, with team leaders responsible for getting officers throughout the station to work on our highest priorities. Branch managers agreed to give officers good grades on annual performance evaluations not just for recruitments but also for sharing leads and contributing to team success. Operations' tempo increased and morale improved when officers pooled their talents instead of competing against one another.

NEW ASSIGNMENT, OLD CHALLENGES

A month before the end of my tour, I found Mama lying on the floor unable to move and mumbling incoherently. She'd stumbled on her way to the bathroom. At first her doctor misdiagnosed her as suffering from dementia, but a CAT scan showed a blood clot on her brain. After surgery she slowly regained her speech and most motor functions, but she had great difficulty walking unassisted.

I took her to New York before heading off to a new job as deputy chief of station in Mazetland.[19] There was no way that I could have taken her with us to third world Mazetland, where US embassy staff flew to a neighboring country even for routine dental work. My brother Bork and his wife Lang reluctantly agreed to look after her. I felt guilty. Their small duplex

---

19 Throughout this memoir, the real names of CIA assets, officers and locations have been changed for security reasons.

was cramped, and they weren't in the best of health themselves. I left with a heavy heart, swearing I'd take over Mama's care when I returned from my assignment in three years.

After arriving in Mazetland, we moved into what looked like a nice house. Loud scratching noises woke us our first night. Rats. Big ones. The next morning I discovered they'd gnawed through my computer printer cables. We used cages to trap the cat-sized rodents, but they remained a nuisance our entire tour.

We realized too late we should have brought our maid Bonnie from our last post. She did everything: cooked, cleaned, and even washed the car. In Mazetland the clear division of labor for domestic help required us not only to hire a cook, but also a maid, a gardener, a driver, and a guard. We didn't complain to the folks back home, knowing they'd just roll their eyes.

HERE'S THE BEEF!

We hired Sam, a cook, based on recommendations from an American couple. They said Sam had worked for many American families and knew what they liked. Indeed, when we interviewed him, he pulled out a well-worn copy of Favorite Recipes, published by the American Embassy Wives Club.

Having spent a month in temporary quarters looking for housing, and tired of eating out, Vicki and I looked forward to what Sam would cook his first day on the job. I arrived home from work to the tantalizing aroma of freshly prepared food, the table set with fine china, crystal glassware, and polished silver.

After a nice chicken broth and a cucumber-and-tomato salad whetting our appetite for the main course, Sam marched out from the kitchen with a large covered serving platter. My mouth watered. He lifted the lid with a flourish to reveal his culinary creation: hamburgers and french fries!

"Oh, wonderful," I said, trying not to offend Sam, having heard he was temperamental. Sam probably wanted to get us acclimated, I thought. But the second night, Sam served Salisbury steak, boiled potatoes, and lemon meringue pie for dessert. It was good, the kids liked it, but I'd expected some local food. "It's great you know so many American recipes," I said, "but we'd really like to try some dishes with a local flavor." He grinned and gave me a thumbs-up.

The next evening Sam did prepare something indigenous: a tangy sauce made from locally grown spices but served over meatloaf and mashed potatoes. We had chocolate cream pie for dessert, and I had to admit his pies were fantastic. Once we convinced him we didn't want meat and potatoes at every meal, he started cooking native dishes that were delicious.

LATE AND EARLY BLOOMERS

Moving from one foreign environment to a completely different one every two or three years can be stressful, especially on children. Some become more psychologically resilient as a result of the experience while others have just the opposite reaction. So we were glad Jenjen and Marisa had each other to play with, making it easier for them to adjust to a new country. They seemed to be doing well at the international school, joined the Brownie troop, and learned to play local musical instruments.

The only problem was Marisa's English: it sounded broken and she wasn't speaking in complete sentences. Because her second-grade teacher was not a native English speaker, and worrying that our daughter was picking up bad habits, Vicki and I went to a parent-teacher conference prepared to request that she be transferred to another class or put in a remedial speech class. We changed our minds and put our worries to rest after meeting her teacher, whose English was flawless. Without our asking she showed us a sample of Marisa's written work. We were relieved to see that it was not only grammatically correct but also much more expressive than we had ever observed at home.

We realized that Marisa didn't have a speech problem at all; she was just quiet and had always let Jenjen do most of the talking for her. Jenjen, two plus years older than Marisa, was an early bloomer who had started talking in complete sentences at least six months before anyone else in her age group. One of her grade school teachers thought Jenjen would make a good lawyer because she was so articulate. She certainly didn't inherit her oratory skills from us, Vicki and I observed, since we were both on the quiet side. Must have been a latent gene.

HELP US, COVEY

Station officers were intelligent, enthusiastic, and hardworking but engaged in endless griping about colleagues and branch managers. So with a nod from the chief of station, I had them form cross-branch teams, just as I'd done on my previous assignment, but this time I had teams present a group solution to resolve interpersonal conflicts based on principles from Stephen Covey's *The 7 Habits of Highly Effective People*. At first there was considerable grumbling, but everyone eventually humored me and went along, no doubt to get me off their backs. In the end they came up with some innovative ideas to address problems in more constructive ways than I could have imagined.

I couldn't stop laughing when, at the end of their presentations, they all broke out into a musical parody of the Beach Boys' hit "Help Me Rhonda." The station reports officer penned the below lyrics. I really appreciated their sense of humor and the good-natured way my boss and the other station officers went along with my unorthodox problem-solving method.

Well since we read your book we've an idea in our heads
Better get our act together or Hon is gonna make us see red
The Seven Habits sound so fine
But they've been driving us out of our minds
You gotta help us, Covey, help us synergize our lives
(bah bah bah bah bah bah bah bah)
Help us, Covey, help, help us, Covey
Help us, Covey, (yeah) synergize our lives
We've been thinkin' win win and seeking first to understand
Been to the emotional bank, got deposit slips in our hands
Well, Covey, you caught our eye
And we can tell you seven reasons why
You gotta help us, Covey; help us synergize our lives

Help us, Covey, help, help us, Covey (bah)
Help us, Covey, help, help us, Covey
Help us, Covey, (yeah) synergize our lives
Gonna be proactive and seek that politically correct balance
Been sharpening our saws and pooling our collective talents
Still we're finding it hard to believe
That Hon has nothing left up his sleeve
You gotta help us, Covey, help us synergize our lives
Help us, Covey, help, help us, Covey (bah)
Help us, Covey, help, help us, Covey
Help us, Covey, (yeah) synergize our lives

Sure, I had them go through a time-consuming exercise to improve teamwork so that we'd be more productive operationally, but there was another unstated reason, perhaps even more important, for getting them to support each other. Without that support, I worried that the emotional stresses and strains I'd already detected could lead to physical and psychological meltdown, especially among young, first-tour officers. They were the most vulnerable among us, without a shoulder to lean on that they would've gotten back home. Over the years I'd seen too many small emotional tears lead to big cracks, resulting in too many broken marriages, too many officers sent home short-of-tour for drinking problems, and too many illnesses due to psychosomatic causes. And then there was always the thought of Tony wedged deeply in the recesses of my mind, the thought that his life might have ended less tragically had his fellow officers, myself included, been more supportive.

HIT MEN

Of course there's nothing like an external threat to take your mind off internal problems, and that's exactly what happened on January 17, 1991. The date also marked the start of US air strikes to push Iraqi troops out of Kuwait, a conflict Saddam Hussein proclaimed would be the "mother of all battles."

At the same time this was happening, we received reports that CIA explosives experts had just finished investigating an attempted bombing in another country in which the bomber blew himself up. They found his severed arm on a tree and other body parts scattered nearby. They said that he belonged to one of dozens of Iraqi hit squads Saddam had dispatched around the world to kill Americans at the same time the US forces were being deployed in the desert against him. All of us felt threatened.

RIDING HIGH

During my three-year assignment in Mazetland, an Inspector General's team from Langley visited us for two weeks to review our activities and interview everyone, concluding that station morale was high, our people well led, and programs well managed. This, along with being awarded a meritorious unit citation for our efforts against a priority "hard target" made me proud of what we had done as a team. When the IG team attributed the station's cohesiveness in large measure to my people-oriented leadership, my head swelled, only to pop like a toy balloon on my next assignment, an assignment that would make me question my people skills, deflate my self-image, and derail my next promotion.

CHAPTER 12

LANGLEY LABYRINTH

Rumor travels faster, but it don't stay put as long as truth.

—WILL ROGERS

COUNTING BEANS AND DODGING DAGGERS

After three back-to-back assignments abroad, we were ready to head home. Nine-year-old Jenjen and seven-year-old Marisa had spent most of their lives overseas and needed to experience life in America. We drove across the country, stopping in Monterey, California, to visit Vicki's folks, with stops at Disneyland and the Grand Canyon. The kids liked Disneyland but loved Las Vegas, where we stayed at Circus Circus and took in acrobatic shows and kids' games.

We picked up Mama in New York, still not fully recovered, thanking Bork and his wife Lang for nursing her back to better health. She still needed a walker and help negotiating stairs. We sent for our former maid, Bonnie—the one who did everything—to help with homecare. We fixed up a lower-level bedroom for Mama in our Virginia house. Located only four miles from the CIA compound, it took more time for me to walk from the Langley parking lot to the main headquarters building than to drive to work.

My home division chief had offered me a job to head a worldwide program focused against a priority target, but it was work I'd done before, first as deputy, then as acting chief. I had travelled to places I'd never been to before, including sub-Saharan Africa, South America, and the Middle East, to drum up activity against what most other nations considered a pariah state. Although the position would come with a larger mandate and staff, I turned it down, which didn't endear me to my division chief, because I wanted to try something entirely different: to learn how budgetary decisions were made. As a field manager, I'd been frustrated by severe funding cuts dictated by what I called mindless bureaucrats with green eyeshades.

I soon became one of them in my new position as chief of the plans and programs group, which was part of the Operations and Resources Management Staff (ORMS). My group helped evaluate clandestine operations and allocate funding for the Directorate of Operations, not the kind of work case officers normally seek since case officers are promoted on how well they recruit and run operations, not for their skills in bean counting. But for me, it was eye-opening sitting in on program reviews, listening to component chiefs horse-trade for resources, and getting a panoramic view of clandestine operations around the world.

Tough choices had to be made in an era of diminished resources. This was in the early '90s: the Berlin Wall was down, the White House and Congress demanded a "post-Cold War peace dividend," and the Agency had to decide what to keep and what to discard among competing priorities. CIA facilities around the world had to be cut or closed, and it would take years to rebuild our clandestine capabilities. As George Tenet observed in the aftermath of 9/11, the FBI at the time had more special agents in New York City alone than the CIA had case officers worldwide.

CORRIDOR GOSSIP

I respected the officers in my group who were all midlevel ranking staff officers with over ten years in the Agency. I appreciated their willingness to help me learn the intricacies of the budgeting process and thought I was developing a good working relationship with them. That is until I overheard one of them making gagging noises unmercifully ridiculing a paper I'd prepared for the Agency front office. Too dumbfounded to say anything, and not wanting to embarrass them by bringing it up, I kept quiet and let the incident pass, knowing they often made snide comments about others as just a harmless way to let off steam. I found it disconcerting that in our face-to-face daily interactions, they were all sweetness and light, giving me no hint they'd been unhappy with me as their boss. I would soon learn, thirdhand, that they'd complained about me not only among themselves but also to others as well.

I learned the extent of their dissatisfaction only after I asked a member of my promotion panel[20] for feedback on why I hadn't been promoted from GS-15 to SIS-1. He told me candidly that it was because Jill, my division representative on the panel, had told members that "I didn't get along with people." I was stunned, never having had any formal or informal feedback

---

20   It was a directorate-wide selection of GS15s to SIS-1. The panel had representatives from each DO line component. How each component ranked its officers had a significant impact on the panel's overall judgment on who should get promoted. A GS-15 is roughly equivalent to a full colonel and a Senior Intelligence Service (SIS) -1 would be a brigadier general.

from anyone about my not getting along with others; indeed, it was quite the opposite. I was puzzled that Jill, whom I'd never met, spoken to, or worked with, could make such a damning accusation. All I knew about her, aside from being a senior officer in my home division's front office, was that she'd worked in ORMS before and often lunched with two of my female officers.

I didn't think these officers had intentionally set out to scuttle my promotion. And even though promotion panels are prohibited by regulation from considering hearsay information, I'm sure Jill was just trying to do her job. Having served on a directorate-wide promotion panel, I knew it was hard to decide who would make the cut, with limited headroom allowing for less than 3 percent of operations officers promoted to the executive ranks in any given year. And I wasn't nearly as upset about not making the cut—knowing there were others more qualified than me—as much as I was upset about hearing what was being said about me: a distorted version of the truth, much like what happens when a story is passed along from one person to the next, ad nauseum, until the original of what was initially said is unrecognizable.

Trying to decipher the cause of their animus, I wondered if maybe my officers viewed me as an interloper intruding on their domain. Or maybe they resented my coming in as chief while they were stuck in a case officer-centric hierarchy without the same career and promotion opportunities as their ops officer peers. And yet, as painful as it was to face my own shortcomings, I knew I had to make allowance for the possibility that they had a legitimate reason for their complaints. To find out, I introduced myself to Jill, trying not to put her on the defensive, and asking her directly for candid feedback, sincerely hoping that I could undo whatever it was I'd done to tick my people off. She simply said that my officers had complained that I didn't value their opinions. Although I left Jill's office with many questions left unanswered, based on her feedback, I knew I had to do a better job of managing my disgruntled officers. I decided to solicit their advice much more often, and make sure they knew I valued their expertise.

With a tarnished hallway reputation, I began kissing my future as a senior Agency manager good-bye. Then a ray of sunshine broke through my dark mood by way of a memo, one totally unsolicited and unexpected, written by Jerry, a Professional Trainee[21] assigned to my group. Addressed to his career counselor, with a courtesy copy sent to me, Jerry described in rather glowing terms my daily interaction with my staff, noting how I welcomed everyone's input, how I gave him as much responsibility as he could handle, trusted him to do the job, and how I was always available whenever he or anyone needed help. I felt like framing it: a positive portrait to balance out the negative caricature others had bought at face value. But there was no one else to vouch for me because everyone who knew me as a manager was still in the field. Wishing to avoid even mentioning that my people skills were suspect since I feared doing so would do nothing but spread the rumor further, I consulted Fred.

"Fred, I'm really discouraged, not because I didn't get promoted, but because of the reason I didn't get it. It seems people are ready to believe the worst about you even if they've never met you. And there's no way for me to get promoted without my division's endorsement."

"Hon, corridor gossip trumps whatever's in your official file. And no one in the division front office knows you because you've been away from the flagpole too long. You gotta learn how to manage up!"

Fred was a friend from my home division who was adept at bureaucratic infighting, so I knew he was right. But I found office politics taxing and so much more stressful than fieldwork. Plus I wasn't even getting hazardous duty pay. So after less than a year at ORMS, I decided to step out of the headquarters cauldron, recharge my mental batteries, and attend the National War College. Before leaving, however, I took care of some unfinished business by giving my officers, the same ones who'd complained about me, exactly what they deserved: cash awards for exceptional job performance.

---

21 Professional Trainees are selected from internal hires based on career potential. They undergo a program of training and rotational assignments that parallel the one Career Trainees undergo.

NATIONAL WAR COLLEGE

Roosevelt Hall

The National War College at Fort McNair in Washington, DC, looked more like an Ivy League campus than a military post. Our classes were in Roosevelt Hall, a Beaux Arts-style building that had been designated a National Historical Landmark. Officers destined for flag rank were selected to attend. Each year the Agency sends one officer from each directorate to the college. I knew being away from a CIA operational component for yet another year would not position me for promotion, but I had always dreamed of going to the War College. It enjoyed a reputation for academic rigor, a top-notch faculty, and outstanding guest speakers.

The yearlong program provided a chance to discuss, debate, and research topics dealing with the elements of national power, ranging from politics and diplomacy to economics and military strategy. Interacting with leading experts and exchanging views with the best and brightest was intellectually stimulating and emotionally rejuvenating. In hindsight, what started out as a stumbling block at ORMS led to one of my life's most broadening professional experiences.

At graduation, I received my diploma as a "distinguished graduate" from our commencement speaker, John Deutch, an MIT-trained scientist who had just taken over as CIA Director. His strong technical focus would provide the impetus for an operation of enormous consequence, one that would impact a future assignment. Funny how things are connected.

When Colonel Jack Glasgow, my classmate at Marine Corp Basic School and the Dean of Students at the War College, sent me a congratulatory e-mail, I replied, "This one's for TBS B Company 1-67!" I'd graduated in the top 10 percent of the class—happy to make up for my poor performance at Quantico decades earlier—an achievement that wouldn't have been possible had it not been for the training I'd received in the Marine Reserves, training that would ultimately lead to separate but related experiences.

MOBILIZATION TRAINING UNIT

Right after joining CIA, I also joined a Marine Corps Reserve Mobilization Training Unit (MTU) within the Agency, consisting of volunteers who didn't get paid like their regular reserve counterparts but who could receive credits toward military retirement by participating in meetings, training, drills, and two-week annual active duty assignments. Less concerned at the time with retirement perks, I joined to maintain my connection to the Corps after leaving full-time active duty. However, I had great difficulty earning the minimum fifty credits required to remain current in the reserves, especially overseas. Unable to attend regular meetings, as I did back home, I earned credits by completing projects via mail for the unit, doing correspondence courses, and finding a military attaché willing to let me do two weeks of active duty, often in a neighboring country, always paying out-of-pocket for travel—doing so because the Marine Corps didn't pay for active duty assignments abroad.

When a DI analyst took over the Agency's MTU, he was completely unsympathetic to my plight as an operations officer overseas, perhaps feeling, with some justification, that my contributions to his unit were insufficient to keep me on the rolls. He kicked me out. I was miffed at the time, but it was the best thing that could have happened and led me, upon my next return to the States, to find another unit, this time a public affairs MTU.

I hoped a tour in public affairs would help hone my written and oral communications skills, something I desperately needed, as I attended workshops on public speaking, got my hands on just about every how-to book on writing on the market, and went to a two-week public affairs course for officers. While I still have a long way to go in becoming a skillful writer, had it not been for this training, I wouldn't have had the confidence to put pen to paper, to touch fingers to keyboard, to start on this memoir or to author a paper while at NWC that won the Chairman of the Joint Chiefs of Staff distinguished essay award.

At the tail end of the public affairs course, the Marine Corps published its annual selection list for promotion. Being eligible for promotion to lieutenant colonel, with fingers crossed, I nervously scanned the list. I didn't make it. Of course I was disappointed but didn't really let it bother me until an officer from Headquarters Marine Corps called a week later to tell me that since I had been passed over twice, according to regulations, I'd no longer be able to stay in the reserves. With all the time, money, and effort I'd invested trying to maintain my status, and still five years short of being eligible for military retirement, my link to my beloved Corps was abruptly severed. I felt unmoored, like a boat without an anchor, drifting out to sea. *What could I do but accept my fate?*

Fortunately for me, Major Ed Horne, a liaison officer for the reserves whom I'd met at the public affairs course, thought otherwise. After reviewing and seeing gaps in my record, he recommended I obtain missing fitness reports from my Agency unit and send copies, along with any recommendations, to Marine Corps Headquarters to at least keep me on the rolls even if I didn't get promoted. The officer who gave me the bad news the first time again said no. The law says up or out, he confirmed in written correspondence. It looked official. It looked final. I was ready to give up. But Ed wouldn't let me, instructing me to resubmit my appeal to the Board for Correction of Naval Records. Six months later, the unthinkable happened: I got promoted. Not only that, but the board backdated the promotion two and a half years to when the first promotion panel met. So thanks to Ed Horne, I fought city hall and won, enabling me to stay in the reserves and retire five years later with full military benefits. But these benefits are still secondary to the reward of maintaining formal ties and the chance to give back to an organization that's given so much to me.

My last active duty assignment in the reserves was with the division of public affairs at Marine Corps Headquarters, giving me a chance to see firsthand why the Corps has been able to maintain such a positive public image and why Harry S Truman was quoted as saying, "They have a propaganda machine that is almost equal to Stalin's." Marine Corps public affairs has worked closely for years with the J. Walter Thompson ad agency to craft ads that are, according to an unofficial USMC advertising gallery website, "unique in that they appeal not to monetary or educational incentives but to the intangible benefits of simply being a Marine."

As a public affairs officer, I learned how to handle press and public inquiries, a skill that unfortunately I had to use when the barracks for the 1st Battalion 8th Marine Regiment in Beirut was struck by two truck bombs in 1983, killing 299 American and French servicemen[22]. It was heartrending trying to remain calm, trying to console wives worried about their husbands and parents worried about their sons. They feared the worst, shocked by what they were seeing on CNN, asking questions for which we, in the hours immediately after the blast, had no answers. I discovered later that Larry Gerlach, a TBS classmate, had been the battalion commander. Blown out of the building and sustaining life-threatening injuries, he had to undergo months of hospitalization and rehabilitation. At a TBS reunion years later, I was more than happy to see that Larry, although having to use a wheelchair and crutches to get around, was doing well and had been able to put his life back together.

ANOTHER CHANCE FOR REDEMPTION

After graduating from the National War College, I was resigned to making up for lost time with my home component, but didn't look forward to

---

22 http://en.wikipedia.org/wiki/1983_Beirut_barracks_bombing

spending another tour at headquarters, so I was thrilled when Mel, my former ORMS boss, called to suggest another overseas assignment.

"Hon, how'd you like to be chief of station in Ozlandia?" Mel asked. He'd just taken over as head of a geographic division, and Ozlandia was in his domain. Mel was a well-respected leader with a good sense of humor. "What starts out goofy just gets goofier!" he'd say about idiotic proposals that came across his desk.

I appreciated Mel's offer, flattered by it, and was grateful that he still had confidence in me as a manager despite the dustup at ORMS. And it's not every day you get to be chief, even in a small pond like Ozlandia, since there were many applicants competing for a limited number of chief-of-station assignments. "Mel, let me talk it over with Vicki and I'll get back to you within a week," I said.

Vicki, unselfish as usual, said I should take the job even though it meant sacrificing hers and not knowing if she'd find work in Ozlandia. We had to consider the kids. They liked being back in Virginia, had made new friends, and would have to move again after only two years. But they said yes after learning Ozlandia was clean, we'd live in a nice, rat-free house, and they'd go a private school, expenses paid. We worried about Mama, who still had difficulty walking. Could she handle yet another relocation so soon after moving from New York? Fortunately, Ozlandia had good healthcare available should she need it, and we'd be able to bring our maid, Bonnie, to look after her.

CHAPTER 13

OPERATION NINJA

It is only the enlightened ruler and the wise general who will use the highest intelligence of the army for purposes of spying and thereby they achieve great results.

—SUN TZU

On the surface, being chief of station in Ozlandia was a hassle-free job. Ozlandian and American political interests coincided, and our intelligence and security services shared information against compatible targets. Some even thought of it as a pre-retirement sinecure, a way to cap off a career in a cosmopolitan city.

Below the surface, however, things were far from languid. Aside from dealing with a variety of priority issues, including counterterrorism, there was the matter of our host government counterparts to contend with. They were usually helpful but sometimes irritatingly obstructive. Why? Because, among other reasons, Ozlandia's internal security service (ISS) never got over an incident when they caught one of our station officers trying to recruit a Soviet official without coordinating with them. But rather than apologize, our then station chief wrote a scathing letter to the head of ISS and, in essence, questioned their manhood. The contents of the letter never made it into the archives at Langley, but I have no doubt that it's part of the ISS institutional memory. Is it any wonder they thought Americans were arrogant? My predecessor put our liaison[23] relationship on firmer footing by immersing himself in the culture and hosting an extravagant annual holiday party for officers from each of the host government organizations that worked with us.

While Ozlandian liaison's upper management had some of the best people I've ever known, dealing at the working level was often frustrating. When CIA intelligence analysts visited ISS headquarters to provide information of interest to the host service, our station escort officer was denied entrance to their compound. Barry, the ISS liaison handler, said our officer hadn't registered with their service. Although he could have issued a temporary visitor's pass, he wanted to make the point that we had to follow his rules. *Beware of people with small powers*, as one of my friends liked to say.

Another problem was convincing ISS to send information to our station electronically for relay to Langley. They insisted that Ozlandia's ISS representative in Washington, DC, must hand-carry everything in hard copy to CIA headquarters because they thought it would give him greater access. This created a huge backlog of unprocessed counterterrorist information. It took months of negotiation to resolve the problem.

THE STATION TEAM

I convinced my career trainee classmate Frank to be my deputy, knowing he'd be able to develop good relationships with our ISS counterparts. A street-smart case officer fluent in five foreign languages, he was great with people. When you talked with him, he'd give you his undivided attention and act like whatever you said was interesting where others would have tuned out long before. Besides Frank, I was lucky to have other competent officers who got along well (for the most part), since teamwork is essential

---

23 "Liaison" in CIA terminology refers to a relationship with an intelligence or security service to share information and possibly work together on issues of common interest.

in a small community. And it helped that everyone had a good sense of humor, including Homer, a senior intelligence analyst.

Homer joked about the old stereotype of analysts being introverts. "You know how you can tell an intelligence analyst when you meet one?" he'd ask. "He's the guy who is looking down at his shoes when he shakes your hand." "Do you know how you can tell an extroverted analyst? He's looking down at your shoes!" Homer didn't fit that stereotype: he was gregarious and developed an excellent network of contacts within the Ozlandian intelligence community.

THREE HATS

I had three primary roles as chief of station. First, I managed the station. Second, I was the ambassador's primary intelligence advisor. And third, I was the senior US intelligence representative in the country. The importance of the last role was not well understood even within the US intelligence community. On any given day, there might be one or more intelligence operations going on in Ozlandia, carried out by different US military, security, and intelligence organizations. Ozlandian liaison loves to play one US entity off against another. The station chief is responsible for ensuring that one activity doesn't bump up against another and for keeping the ambassador apprised.

Unlike the backbiting atmosphere that exists among turf-conscious government agencies in Washington, I found the field more collegial and enjoyed productive personal and professional relationships with members of the US country team. Interpersonal conflicts can crop up anywhere, of course, but people in the field, who have to band together in a foreign and sometimes hostile environment, have a greater incentive to work things out. Either that or go home. In Washington, where there are countless ways to circumvent a colleague or boss or agency or policy, there's less inclination to work together harmoniously. I truly feel people in Washington often have it harder than those in the field, having to deal with longer commutes in horrendous traffic and having to rush to get home after an exhausting day at the office, with little time to bond with colleagues socially.

MISSION POSSIBLE

"Hon, give me your candid assessment," Mel, my division chief, said after I'd been briefed on a complex operation involving my station.

"If all the pieces fit together, it could work, but right now it's just wishful thinking," I replied. My predecessor, Cal, had informed me that the Director was putting pressure on everyone involved to make it happen. "This is the hottest thing the Agency has going right now," Cal said. I thought it was hyperbole but didn't say anything, thinking everyone always feels his op is the most important. And besides, Cal would have to know about every other operation in order to make such a bold claim.

But I started to change my opinion as I listened to Lex (chief of technical operations for another geographic division) describe the operation. It was designed to collect intelligence on Brockville, a country hostile to the United States, by tapping Brockville's communications system. Lex was optimistic; I wasn't. As he explained the operational, technical, and logistical problems that needed to be resolved, I knew it was a long shot. A mission ops team equipped with spy gear had to access the target without arousing suspicion, identify the right communications link, tap it, and send the data home. Although the CIA had a station in Brockville, Americans couldn't move around the city without being closely surveilled.

Lex had identified a target communications node that sat beside the Ozlandian Embassy in Brockville, and that's where I came in. My predecessor had done the spadework by obtaining approval from the highest levels of the Ozlandian government to partner with us. This wasn't an easy decision for their government because public disclosure of Ozlandia's connection with a CIA operation in Brockville would be politically disastrous.

RICKETY RELATIONS

My role as COS was to facilitate the partnership at the operational level, working with my liaison counterpart Ricky, chief of Ozlandia's Foreign Intelligence Service. He was meticulous, whether it was about operations or food; if we ate Italian, he'd insist the pasta be prepared al dente and would send it back if not perfect.

Ricky restricted knowledge of the operation to a handful of his staff and requested we do likewise. We assured him our "bigot[24]" list would be short, knowing he'd be appalled by the actual number on it. The US side would include officers from two US agencies, senior officers from two CIA geographic divisions, personnel from two field stations, and engineers and technical ops officers from two CIA science and technology offices. However, true to our word, only a handful knew about the Ozlandian liaison's role.

Ricky, his deputy, and his technical advisor said they'd work with us if we agreed to certain ground rules: (1) the operation would be jointly managed; (2) the mission team would consist of an equal number of Ozlandian and American officers; and (3) both sides would share all intelligence collected. Because trying to solve complex problems under tight deadlines was stressful, it didn't take long before tempers flared. More than once, Ricky's side felt they were being treated as junior partners and threatened to walk out. I tried to be an honest broker, soothing egos when necessary and making frequent trips with Ricky and his staff to meet with their CIA counterparts to iron out disagreements.

TEAM NINJA

Equipment was built using CIA headquarters officers and security-cleared contractors, none of whom knew the final destination of their handiwork. Craftsmen modified objects to make them appear different from what they truly were. The most important gear was state-of-the-art technology that would allow our team to tap the communications link without interrupting the existing system. The technical pieces had to be assembled, implanted, and resealed to make them appear like integral parts of the original. Plus,

---

24 Bigot List: a list of the names of those privy to a sensitive intelligence operation. It dates back to World War II, when Allied orders for officers were stamped TO GIB for those being sent to Gibraltar for the invasion of North Africa; later their orders were stamped BIG OT (TO GIB backward) when they were sent back to begin planning Operation Overlord, the invasion of Normandy. (From Wikipedia: http://en.wikipedia.org/wiki/BIGOT_list)

it had to be weatherproof. It was like performing open-heart surgery under battlefield conditions, with the risk of getting shot.

The joint mission team included an experienced CIA officer who had spent his career getting into and out of tight places surreptitiously. The others were telecom specialists. They spent months practicing on a mock-up.

At a planning session, someone floated the idea of outfitting the team in black ninja-style outfits so that they could blend into the darkened environment they'd be working in. I argued against it, recommending they wear work clothes consistent with their cover. Although the team was in danger of being spotted by a police or military patrol, they also had to worry about attracting the attention of a casual or not-so-casual observer. Better to look like workmen than spies.

After months of planning and training, the team arrived on location and began frustrating, dirty, and backbreaking work. Tools broke, equipment malfunctioned, parts didn't fit, and colors wouldn't match, requiring shipping things home to be fixed and then shipped back again.

Spy movies don't show Tom Cruise restoring things to their original condition after a break-in, but in real life this is essential to a clandestine mission. Fortunately, the CIA's "second-story" officers are well versed in restoration and repair: it's part of their training as tech ops officers. By day the team renovated the embassy; by night they tapped into the communications link adjacent to the building. On their initial forays, they couldn't get a good signal from the tap. Each time the team ventured out, our station officers in Brockville monitored them, tuning to the radio frequencies of the police and security services, listening for unusual transmissions, ready to alert our team to abort the mission at the first sign of danger.

Finally, we were all elated when Brockville station, which served as a relay, finally reported getting a clear signal from the tap. With the data retransmitted home for decryption and analysis, we anxiously waited to find out if it had all been worth it.

VICTORY HAS A THOUSAND FATHERS

I didn't recognize most of the faces in the CIA's Awards Suite as the Director addressed the standing-room-only crowd, calling the operation a huge success, one that yielded critical intelligence for the White House. He praised everyone who contributed but didn't get into specifics, not saying where the operation took place or what was collected. But everyone could tell it was significant just from the medals he handed out. Each member of the CIA mission ops team received the Intelligence Star, awarded "for outstanding service rendered with distinction under conditions of grave risk."

Cal, my predecessor, was awarded the Intelligence Medal of Merit for "the performance of especially meritorious service that contributed significantly to the mission of the Agency." Brockville and Ozlandia stations each received Meritorious Unit Citations.

When I returned to Ozlandia, Ricky handed out a souvenir: a plain white coffee mug with a hand-painted picture of a rat. He said one of the team members was almost bitten by a rat during the operation and thought the creature bore a striking resemblance to Lex, whom Ricky jokingly thought had disguised himself as a rodent to check on the team's progress. I sent Lex a mug as a reminder that great things can happen when talented people work as a team without worrying about who gets credit.

MAMA FALLS AGAIN

I was in Langley accompanying Ozlandian visitors when I got a message to call home. I held my breath, knowing Vicki seldom called unless it was an emergency. "Your mother fell, but she's OK," Vicki said, trying to sound reassuring. I booked the next flight home and took Mama to see a doctor. She had fractured her hip, unable to move without pain. The doctor recommended surgery, a simple procedure, he said, consisting of inserting screws into her hip joint to hold it together. Already weak and not very mobile to begin with, Mama didn't mend well. The painkillers on top of her medications for hypertension and depression hastened her mental and physical decline. She became more despondent, more demanding, and more difficult for the whole family.

Taking her to medical appointments and looking into healthcare options, locally and for the longer term, drained my energy. I was grateful that Frank and others in the station took up the slack at work. Although I still had a year remaining on my assignment, given Mama's continued deterioration, I knew we had to get back to the United States full-time earlier than intended.

CHAPTER 14

THE GOOD, BAD, AND UGLY

*If you can meet with triumph and disaster, and treat those two
impostors just the same....*

—RUDYARD KIPLING

Before returning to headquarters, I was ecstatic, almost giddy, when I
received news of my promotion to SIS. Unlike the last go-round, when I
felt like an orphan, this time I received endorsements from both the chief
of my current division as well as my home component. I was lucky to have
made it since I knew many officers, some far more competent than me, had
retired after a productive Agency career without ever having reached the
senior ranks. The real work of the Agency, just as it is in the military, is
done not by flag-ranked officers, but by company and field grade leaders.

That said, I hoped that as an SIS officer I'd be able to broaden my
knowledge beyond the directorate of operations, giving me a chance to
be of greater service to the Agency and even to the U.S intelligence community. At the time, while case officers were encouraged to seek a rotational assignment outside the DO, few did so, thinking that being "out of
sight, out of mind" wouldn't be career-advancing. My promotion, however,

provided me with the wiggle room I needed since SISers aren't bound to a home component. So I politely declined an offer to head a "denied area[25]" program in the DO and instead applied for a position in the DI as deputy chief of the Collection Requirements and Evaluation Staff (CRES).

With officers assigned to each DI analytical office and the Agency's twenty-four-hour operations center, CRES relays intelligence requirements from all-source analysts to collectors across the intelligence community—including the Directorate of Operations, the National Security Agency, the State Department, the Treasury Department, and the National Reconnaissance Office—and prioritizes the tasking of surveillance satellites at the national level.

My boss, Jim Simon, one of the most brilliant people I've ever worked for, was a seasoned analyst and manager who gave me a chance to see how the DI worked up close. He believed I could help bridge the cultural gap between DO case officers and DI analysts. When I first joined the Agency, there used to be physical barriers separating the two directorates. The physical barriers are long gone, but cultural barriers remain. No matter how much intelligence is collected by spies, it's worthless without good analysis.

I learned how national intelligence priorities were set during meetings chaired by Charlie Allen.[26] Charlie would present a collection priority (for example, Osama bin Laden), and then get updates from each community representative on what his or her organization was doing against the target, badgering, cajoling, or haranguing people if he didn't think they were doing enough. He had no statutory authority over any of them, but they cooperated with him out of respect.

---

25   In a country considered a so-called "denied area," officers are subject to intense surveillance by local security and intelligence services. So before being deployed overseas, case officers are required to undergo additional tradecraft training so that they can operate securely and handle or communicate with assets without being detected.

26   Allen would later become head of intelligence for the Department of Homeland Security after retiring from the CIA.

FROM BAD TO WORSE

While things were going well at work, things at home were not. Mama became less responsive to medications, wasn't eating, and finally required hospitalization. When she was discharged, I found a good nursing home nearby to provide round-the-clock care. But she never fully recovered and died shortly before her ninetieth birthday. As much as I appreciated the treatment she had received, I saw the limitations of our healthcare system and of Western medicine. What's to prevent any of us from spending the remaining moments of our lives on breathing tubes? What can be done to keep people stronger and able to transition through the twilight of life with dignity?

I toyed with the idea of studying Chinese medicine, something I'd always wanted to do. Although I was eligible for early retirement, I wondered if I should give up a profession I still loved. Afraid to make a hasty decision, I decided to punt by returning to more familiar terrain.

CLANDESTINE INFORMATION TECHNOLOGY OFFICE

I served on a senior panel that addressed technical portions of the Agency's Strategic Plan, one recognizing cyberspace as a new frontier that required not only greater funding, personnel and training, but also long-range goals on what and how we would steal secrets in the digital age.

While on the panel, I got to know Jim Gosler, director of the Clandestine Information Technology Office (CITO), and subsequently became his chief of operations. CITO was jointly managed by the directorate of science and technology and the directorate of operations and staffed with some of the most talented case officers, engineers, technicians, analysts, and support personnel that I'd ever met in the Agency. Our mission was to "exploit information technology for intelligence purposes."

Jim, brought in from Sandia National Laboratories for his technical brilliance, liked to take apart slot machines and figure out how they worked in his spare time. Well over six feet tall, he wore coke-bottle-thick glasses, and stuffed his shirt pocket with pens. Despite his somewhat geeky appearance, he had no problems thinking clandestinely. He used to tell case officers, "I can't imagine ever doing the types of things you guys do." I think Jim would have done well in the field but might have had problems blending into a crowd.

During a familiarization trip to Asia, Jim and two Agency companions were returning from a very long evening walk. After several hours, all three really needed to find a men's room. Unfortunately, their search only yielded a primitive cement block building with slit trenches. As Jim entered the dimly lit building, it became disgustingly evident that this indeed was a toilet. It took a long time for his vision to adapt to the darkness. As he navigated across the slimy floor and held his breath to escape the stench, he positioned himself and unzipped his pants. Seconds before he was to relieve himself, he looked down and as his eyes finally adjusted, he saw the whites of a local's eyes squatting over the hole in the ground doing his business. The sight of a foreigner's hulking figure standing over him and getting ready to find relief must have been terrifying. The guy screamed. Jim screamed even louder and made a quick exit. His two buddies made sure this story was immediately and widely disseminated.

HOMECOMING

Working in CITO was like returning home, since I had started as a technical operations officer almost three decades earlier and now was coming back full circle. I enjoyed learning about emerging cyberspace technologies and seeing the cutting-edge work that our officers were doing against everything from nuclear proliferation to counterterrorist targets. The work was engrossing but the bureaucracy frustrating. I had to attend countless meetings within the CIA and with other US spy agencies to define evolving roles and missions in this as-yet-uncharted territory. Each organization was competing for a piece of the action.

Fed up with the never-ending turf battles endemic to headquarters, I wondered whether I should continue at the Agency or seek early retirement to do something different. On the one hand, having already been promoted to SIS-3, could I climb up the next rung with a little more luck and hard work? On the other hand, at age fifty-seven, could I delay much longer if I wanted to launch a new career? But my decision would have to wait. What was supposed to be a routine security reinvestigation would turn into a nightmare that would put my life on hold.

POLYGRAPH NIGHTMARE

About every five years, the CIA's office of security updates employee security clearances, which includes a reinvestigation and a polygraph exam. Although passing a so-call "lie detector" test is just one of many factors considered in the reinvestigation process, it's heavily weighted. Since I had no problems passing before, I wasn't worried about it.

But after the polygrapher unhooked me from the machine, he told me he had trouble getting a clear reading on my charts and asked me to return the following day. Although annoyed at having to retest, I'd heard that polygraphers were being very cautious ever since the CIA double agent Aldrich Ames[27] had passed two polygraphs while spying for the Soviets. Polygraphers were under the gun not to screw up again. So it wasn't at all unusual when people were asked to retest a second or even a third time.

The next day another polygrapher administered the test, but unlike the first one who interviewed me, this guy was gruff and conducted the exam like an interrogation. After the test, he said I had reacted to questions about divulging classified information and working for a foreign government. When he asked if I felt guilty about anything, I said I had plenty

---

27 In 2003 the National Academy of Sciences issued a report entitled "The Polygraph and Lie Detection." The NAS found that the majority of polygraph research was "unreliable, unscientific, and biased," concluding that fifty-seven of the approximately eighty research studies that the American Polygraph Association relies on were significantly flawed. (From The National Academies Press, http://www.nap.edu/openbook.php?record_id=10420&page=1, accessed January 25, 2014)

to feel guilty about but nothing related to the two "relevant"[28] questions. After running the test again, he said my charts showed "inconclusive" and terminated the exam.

"What's going to happen now?" I asked, flabbergasted at the results.

"My supervisor will double-check your charts and someone will get back to you," he replied.

That someone was Joe from the Agency's counterespionage unit, which conducts investigations of staff employees to uncover moles. Joe told me that after reviewing my charts again, they concluded that there was "deception indicated" to the relevant questions.

"Don't discuss this with anyone. We're required to inform your supervisor, but no one else needs to know," Joe warned.

I told Brian, CITO's deputy chief, that I'd flunked the polygraph and asked for his advice. He'd been my boss in a previous assignment, and I was sure he knew I wasn't a double agent. He sympathized with my predicament, telling me about another senior officer who had experienced the same difficulty recently. He said the officer chose to retire rather than endure a lengthy investigation and advised me to do the same.

"Why put yourself through the hassle? Hon, It's just not worth it."

Two other Agency colleagues, whom I was absolutely positive had answered the relevant questions truthfully, had also failed their polygraph exams recently. One chose retirement. The other, not eligible for retirement and not wanting to resign, suffered through endless grilling and line-by-line scrutiny of all his financial records, of which he had many. I personally knew others who had failed their pre-employment exams, people who never

---

28 Some of the questions asked are "irrelevant" ("Is your name Chris?"); others are "probable-lie" control questions that most people will lie about ("Have you ever stolen money?"); and the remainder are "relevant questions" of interest to the tester. The different types of questions alternate. You pass the test if your physiological responses during the probable-lie control questions are more intense than those during the relevant questions. If this is not the case, the tester attempts to elicit admissions during a post-test interview. For example, the tester might say, "Your situation will only get worse if we don't clear this up." (From Wikipedia: http://en.wikipedia.org/wiki/Polygraph, accessed January 25, 2014.)

had access to classified information, yet their responses to the same "relevant" questions were judged as showing "deception indicated."

I believe all were the result of false positives.[29] Polygraphs measure reactions and not lies. If a test subject reacts more strongly to a relevant question than a control question designed to provoke a stronger reaction, then the subject is thought to be lying. Having helped set up the polygraph for dozens of my own agents, I was aware that false positives were a big problem. When one of my high-level agents took the exam, the polygrapher said he was being deceptive because his charts showed a strong reaction to "Are you working for another intelligence service?" but not to any of the control questions, including "Have you ever stolen anything?" Knowing the agent prided himself on being a devoted family man, I suggested substituting "Are you a good father?" for a control question. I knew he'd feel guilty about this topic no matter how he answered it. Sure enough, he reacted much more strongly to the new question and passed the exam.

Some critics of the polygraph believe the rate of false positives is as high as 60 percent, although advocates say it's less than 10 percent. Despite this, I did, and still do, believe that it's a useful interrogation tool. In the hands of a skilled polygrapher, its value primarily lies in getting people to make admissions. Since I hadn't done anything wrong, I had nothing to admit that pertained to the relevant questions.

Although eligible for early retirement, I refused to leave under a cloud of suspicion and was determined to clear my name no matter how long it took. I knew it would be a lengthy process, but I wasn't mentally prepared for just how long it would take. Joe had to dig through my personnel records and operational files. With thirty years of data, it was laborious detective work.

---

29 "A 1997 survey of 421 psychologists estimated the test's average validity at about 61 percent, a little better than chance." Dan Vergano (September 9, 2002). "Telling the truth about lie detectors," *USA Today*. Retrieved from usatoday.com January 25, 2014.

When he apparently didn't find anything significant, Joe transferred my case to the FBI. After the Aldrich Ames[30] disaster and other botched counterespionage cases, the CIA was required to let the Bureau investigate any Agency employee who had failed a polygraph. Coming under suspicion for wrongdoing couldn't possibly have come at a worse time for me. It was during a decade or more of double agent cases involving CIA or FBI officers. High-profile cases, aside from Ames, included Robert Hanssen, Harold Nicholson, Edward Lee Howard, Douglas Groat, and Larry Wu-Tai Chin. Add another dozen major cases involving personnel from NSA, the military, and other US government agencies convicted of espionage and you can understand why there was heightened vigilance, if not paranoia, during this period.

Joe introduced me to two FBI special agents, Jackie and Kate, who questioned me and covered much of the same ground Joe did. I would have been more annoyed with their inane questions had they not been as young and attractive as they were. Maybe this won't be so bad after all, I thought optimistically.

Joe had said it would have been counterproductive for me to take another polygraph exam because I was already hypersensitive to the relevant questions. Although I wanted to retest, I knew he was right because my blood pressure shot up just thinking about the questions—not because I wasn't truthful but because I knew those were the questions that would determine my fate. However, Jackie and Kate thought it would be a good idea to have it done by an examiner from the Bureau. I agreed.

---

30 Ames was a CIA ops officer who passed several polygraph exams; He was arrested in 1993 for selling secrets to the KGB. Hanssen was an FBI agent convicted in 2001 for passing secrets to Moscow. Nicholson was a CIA ops officer who pleaded guilty in 1997 for passing classified information to Russia. Howard was a CIA ops officer who fled to Soviet Union in 1985 to avoid arrest for allegedly selling secrets to Soviets. Groat was a CIA technican indicted April 1998 on espionage and extortion charges. Chin was a CIA Chinese translator accused in 1985 of spying for China; he killed himself in his jail cell. (From Wikipedia, http://en.wikipedia.org/wiki/Aldrich_Ames and related links, accessed January 25, 2014.)

The Bureau polygrapher's manner was different from my last encounter with the Agency examiner. I liked how he tried to put me at ease during the pretest, carefully previewing each question he'd ask. After the exam, while waiting for him to review my charts, I felt I'd passed this time, having had a good night's sleep, being as relaxed as I could be under the circumstances, and having answered each question truthfully. But when he returned to the room, he had a frown on his face. I'd flunked again! I asked him to rerun the test, but he just shook his head and packed up his machine.

I went home dejected. Even though I hadn't done anything wrong I was embarrassed, even ashamed, that people might find out I'd flunked multiple times. I imagined my security badge yanked from my neck and being escorted unceremoniously out of the building, with a big "F" tattooed across my forehead.

The FBI continued its investigation. I waited for them to bring me in for more questions, but all I got was silence. Then, after months of agonized waiting, I received a call from Jackie and Kate summoning me to their downtown office. They had concluded their investigation, they said, and the ball was back in Joe's court. I knew they hadn't uncovered any wrongdoing.

Just when I thought the end of my ordeal was near, Joe introduced me to a CIA finance officer who asked to see all my tax, banking, and financial records. *BANG!* No longer able to contain my bottled-up anger, I erupted and slammed my fist on the table, hard. Papers flew in the air. I shouted at them, mad that they had waited almost a year to get to my finances. Why couldn't they have done this at the start, I demanded to know. After I calmed down, Joe explained that the Agency couldn't move forward until the Bureau had completed its work.

At one point I told Joe I was going to write something up for the official record. "Hallelujah!" Joe exclaimed with a big smile on his face. I was surprised and demoralized by his comment. Was he really expecting me to write a confession? What I submitted for the record was not a confession but a statement that I didn't do anything wrong, expressing outrage over the snail's pace of the reinvestigation, and criticizing the

Agency's overreliance on the polygraph, a flawed and unscientific process at best.

During the various stages of the reinvestigation, I experienced all five stages of grief. First came denial and isolation. I couldn't believe this was happening to me, feeling alone, unable to confide in anyone, not even Vicki, and I wouldn't have told anyone even if allowed to, afraid that people would gossip about my flunking. Secondly, I was angry, incensed that anyone would question my integrity and mad at the system for allowing this to happen after giving my soul to the Agency. Thirdly, I bargained, threatening to complain to the Director about bureaucratic incompetence resulting in needless delay. Were they purposely stalling and hoping that I'd quit? Well, I wasn't going to give them the satisfaction, I said. Fourthly, I became more depressed, suffering emotional trauma that was tougher than any I'd faced in combat. Finally, I accepted the process instead of fighting it, reigning in my emotions, realizing that my investigators were simply doing their jobs and were required to follow step-by-step procedures. Had I been smart enough to skip the first four stages, I could have avoided a great deal of self-inflicted torture.

In retrospect, my interlocutors had treated me with respect. During the reinvestigation, I reported to work every day, just as I had before, and no one in my office treated me any differently, at least as far as I could tell. The worst part of the whole fiasco was not knowing when it would be over as I waited week after endless week for a final verdict.

When my office was being reorganized, I found myself in limbo. I didn't want to look for a new job because it would mean informing any new boss that I was going through a counterespionage investigation. Why would anyone want to hire me? And after getting burned at ORMS by corridor gossip, I didn't want to tell any more people than absolutely necessary. I feared that word would ricochet through the hallways that I was a serial polygraph flunker. For people who are supposed to keep secrets, too many of them can't seem to resist spreading rumors.

Finally, a year and a half after my ordeal began, Joe gave me the all-clear. I felt like a hangman's noose had been lifted from my neck. I pondered my future. With CITO being restructured as the Information Operations Center, I had to decide whether to look for another assignment or begin full-time studies in Chinese medicine. Should I forgo a steady paycheck for an uncertain future outside the nest?

The reinvestigation, although emotionally draining, provided at least two valuable lessons. First, it reminded me that there are no guarantees in life, so it was foolish to base my happiness on circumstances that could and literally did change in a heartbeat. Second, I'd been too focused on protecting my reputation and status and not enough on things that were more enduring, that couldn't be taken away so easily.

But what were those things that I should have been pursuing? Certainly it wasn't a fancier job title, a closer parking space or a bigger corner office. Realizing I'd have to look beyond the corridors of Langley for the answers, I submitted the paperwork to retire.

THIRD PATH

TEACHER

CHAPTER 15

LEARN KUNG FU - KARATE!

*"The best thing for being sad," replied Merlin...is to learn
something.*

That's the only thing that never fails."

—T.H. WHITE, THE ONCE AND FUTURE KING

If it hadn't been for martial arts to channel my pent-up frustrations during
the reinvestigation, I would have gone bonkers. Working out with Ray
Menan, my martial arts brother, provided a timely safety valve. We had the
same teacher, the late Dean Chin, a leading figure in the kung fu community
and in Washington, DC's Chinatown. Ray and I formed a partnership to
preserve our teacher's legacy by promoting traditional Chinese martial arts.
We began teaching kung fu and taijiquan classes a couple of times a week
at a local recreation center.

During this same period, Stephan Berwick, a Chen-style taijiquan
instructor, provided another outlet to channel my energies. Upon learning that he was a protégé of Ren Guangyi, a well-known taijiquan master whose DVD series on the Chen style I had purchased years earlier,

I immediately enrolled in Stephan's class. Learning a new martial arts style was just what I needed to stay mentally and physically balanced. Stephan had trained in China with top masters, starred in Hong Kong action films, coauthored books on taijiquan, published countless articles on martial arts, and had recently written, directed and coproduced a film starring his teacher.

MARTIAL ARTS FLASHBACKS

Many of the teachers who inspired my martial arts zeal were not as well known. Among those I'll never forget is Rico Mercado, one of my first karate instructors.

Sensei Rico Mercado (far right)

Blood trickled down Sensei's[31] forehead as he knelt before a stack of inch-thick concrete slabs stacked on top of each other and propped up by cinderblocks. He'd split the top slab on his first try but couldn't smash

---

31 Sensei is a Japanese term of respect for teacher.

through the bottom two. With teeth clenched, he aimed his forehead at the remaining slabs. THUMP, THUMP…THUMP! I cringed at the sound of skull hitting concrete. "Sensei, it's OK. Why not try again tomorrow?" I tried to pull him away, knowing he wouldn't give up until his head or the slabs gave way—and the slabs were winning.

Lance Corporal Mercado, my instructor at Camp Pendleton, was a street-smart Puerto Rican from New York City whose single-minded focus inspired me. Everyday at noon, four or five of us worked out for two hours. I was the novice in the group. My sparring partner, Lt. Steve Scarano, chose to wear a white belt, probably to make me feel better, even though he was a black belt in terms of skill. His lack of ego set the tone for the group. Steve and I were the most fanatical, never missing a day of practice, often training together on weekends.

Although Sensei taught Japanese-style karate, his admiration for kung fu nudged me toward my Chinese martial arts roots. He often visited Chinatown in Los Angeles hoping to meet Bruce Lee, someone whom I didn't know anything about and before anyone knew the difference between kung fu and chop suey. Sensei loved watching Bruce on TV playing Kato, the Green Hornet's sidekick. He had a huge collection of Karate Illustrated and Black Belt magazines and read everything he could about his hero.

His idolization of Bruce Lee had a halo effect upon all things Chinese. "I like going to Chinatown just to watch how people walk. They're so graceful!" he exclaimed as he strutted around the dojo trying to mimic how he thought Chinese men walked. He walked around like a penguin, but I didn't say anything to shatter his positive stereotype.

In 1971, right after I completed active duty with the Marines and moved to Washington, DC, to start working at the Agency, I searched for a martial arts school. A TV commercial grabbed my attention, showing a pint-size kid dressed in a white uniform kicking over his head and shouting, "Nobody bothers me!" He was the son of Jhoon Rhee, the father of American tae kwon do. I decided to enroll at his school, until I took a stroll through Chinatown.

HOY LEE

I passed a storefront with a hand-painted sign in the window: "LEARN KUNG FU – KARATE!" Standing outside was a guy in his early twenties, wearing black horn-rimmed glasses with his hair plastered back in a style popular in the sixties. He looked like a wiry Chinese John Travolta, making me leery because he reminded me of a wiry kid in third grade nicknamed Chicken had knocked me out with a sucker punch during recess.

"Who's the teacher here?" I asked.

"Me! What ya wanna know?" he said. I recognized a Hong Kong brusqueness to this man.

"You teach both kung fu and karate?"

"Naah. I put karate 'cause nobody knows what kung fu is."

"I'm interested in learning more."

"Come back tomorrow and try it! I'm Hoy Lee."

I returned the next evening, walking onto a creaky wood floor and into a room no bigger than fifteen by twenty feet and reeking of stale sweat, with an altar painted red against the far wall, and a statue of Guan Gong, patron saint of Chinese martial arts, mounted on the right side of the altar. Students limbered up before class, a sprinkling of white and Asian among mostly black faces.

KUNG FU JOE

A trim black guy in his early twenties called the class to attention and led us through warm-ups. People called him "Kung Fu Joe." Hoy emerged in a black satin uniform, changing from street tough to martial artist, demonstrating how to do a flying triple jump kick: leaping off the ground, kicking his right foot above his head, then snapping his left foot even higher, and finally whipping his right instep around before landing on the ground like a cat. We all tried it, but no one got off more than two kicks.

Hoy and Joe, before taking up kung fu, had studied Burmese kickboxing. At first Hoy didn't tell anyone he was learning the Chinese martial arts. When Joe saw Hoy's supercharged moves, he asked for his secret. After persistent questioning, Hoy told him it was kung fu. "What's that?" Joe asked. Hoy showed him a tiger claw technique, one of many kung fu movements imitating how animals react offensively or defensively. A kung fu practitioner is not only supposed to move like a tiger, for example, but also summon that animal's ferocious spirit. When Joe begged for more, Hoy introduced him to Dean Chin. After that Joe breathed kung fu, ate kung fu, and dreamed kung fu. I marveled at his uncanny ability to watch someone do a complex series of movements then perform the sequence, often better than the person who showed it to him.

I break a concrete slab on Hoy's stomach

KUNG FU FORMS

Just as there are many styles of dance (e.g., ballroom, ballet, hip-hop, jazz), there are many styles of martial arts. Jow Ga Kung Fu is a hybrid of three styles, two from southern China and one from northern China. Dozens of routines called "forms," performed with or without weapons and with or without a partner, are used to teach, practice, and preserve a style's signature combat techniques.

Imagine selecting Muhammad Ali's best moves, arranging them in a sequence, and using them to teach people the art of Ali boxing. It wouldn't be just about how to throw or dodge a punch but also gaining a sense of Ali's unique style, timing, and tempo. That's what martial arts forms are all about. I was impressed by one of the students, a teenager sporting a huge afro and executing a form with obvious skill. Compared with more linear movements of the Japanese and Korean styles I'd practiced in the Marines, the kung fu techniques he demonstrated were more circular and fluid. A youngish-looking black woman watching him looked like his sister, but she turned out to be his mother. This was Barbara Mims and her son, Deric. Barbara, ten years later, would become my daughter's godmother.

Watching students sparring, I saw that their techniques were practical and could be used on the street. At the time, I was more interested in kung fu's martial applications than its artistic expression. Jow Ga seemed to offer both. Kung Fu Joe, for example, took home as many first-place trophies in sparring as he did in forms competition.

YOUNG MASTER

The person who really sparked my desire to learn Jow Ga kung fu was Sifu[32] Dean Chin, who introduced the style to America when he emigrated from Hong Kong in the late 1960s. Partnering with Hoy to open a school on H Street in Washington, DC, the school was officially known as the Jow Ga Kung Fu Association. The first Chinese martial arts school established in the nation's capital, as well as the first in the area to open its doors to non-Chinese—something unheard of at the time, causing much finger wagging

---

32 Sifu is an honorific Cantonese term of address for someone who has achieved a high level of mastery or skill in an art or trade. It's synonomous with "Master" when used in Chinese martial arts; Sifu (shifu in Mandarin) and the title "Master" are used interchangeably in this memoir. Adam Hsu, in his book, *The Sword Polisher's Record: The Way of Kung-Fu,* provides a good explanation of correct and incorrect ways to address Chinese martial arts teachers.

among the old-timers in the Chinese martial arts community—the school received threatening challenges. "Close down or we'll close it for you." In feudal China, a martial arts master never taught outsiders because they didn't want rivals learning their secrets.

Hoy, who had first learned Jow Ga from a co-worker and liked the style more than others he'd studied, invited Dean to share his Jow Ga expertise with the general public. Hoy affectionately referred to Dean as "Sifu Jai," which means "young master." Master Chin was in his mid-twenties, of medium height and build, with a slightly crooked smile, and a haircut like Alfred E. Newman's of Mad magazine—not the image of a kung fu master. But, when he put on a kung fu uniform he magically transformed into a powerful warrior. I watched enthralled when he demonstrated a technique while holding the shaft of a spear, cracking the solid wooden pole in half with mere flick of his wrist.[33] His ordinary looks when dressed in street attire hid the extraordinary abilities he began to develop at age six as a child prodigy, eventually becoming expert in several martial arts styles.

I've always been leery of individuals and organizations that claim a monopoly on skills or knowledge. So one of the things I respected about Dean was his openness toward other martial arts teachers and styles. Because he was confident enough in his own abilities, he never felt the need to disparage others. Indeed, he believed you could always learn from others, and often invited masters from different schools (even if they were business competitors) to practice in our spaces or as guest instructors to teach us forms, some that he'd integrate into our core curriculum. Rooted in tradition, but not anchored to the past, he streamlined old routines and created new ones. We were not only able to learn Jow Ga, but also techniques from other styles he'd studied, including Eagle Claw, White Eyebrow, and Wing Chun. A man well ahead of his time, he orga-

---

33 The force Dean used to crack the shaft was generated internally from his core, not externally by muscle power. Bruce Lee called it "inch power," others call it "jing" or internal force.

nized a martial arts tournament open to all styles in 1974 that included full-contact sparring—a first for the Nation's Capital.

CHIEF OF STAFF

Living within a fifteen-minute walk to the school—and, being single then and thus having lots of free time—I attended classes four to five days a week and took private lessons with Master Chin whenever possible. Because the student population was small, with no more than ten per class, he gave us individual attention. That would change after Dean got married, started working full-time, and pursued an engineering degree.

I became even more deeply involved in the school when Dean appointed me his chief of staff two years after I joined the school. I felt a personal stake in the school's success not only out of respect for my teacher but also because he had given me stock shares in the business. Those shares were not worth much in dollars but were worth the world in friendship. When my senior kung fu brothers Hoy and Deric left town (Hoy to start his own business and Deric to attend college), Paul Adkins and I were put in charge. By the time I left for an overseas assignment a few years later, I was happy that the school was doing well. As I look back fondly on those early days in Chinatown and all the hard work we put into making the school successful, I'm especially pleased to see that many of the youngsters and teenagers we helped train would eventually become sifus with their own schools and leaders in their communities.

Me and Paul Adkins at far right leading a performance in Chinatown, 1973

TRAGEDY

Dean and I became closer as the years passed, with Vicki and I staying at his house on home leave and he staying at ours on his visits overseas. He was gregarious, liked to entertain, and had a wide circle of contacts, including well-known kung fu movie stars. I loved going out with him and was always guaranteed a good meal since he knew the owners of some of the city's top restaurants. Dean was a good conversationalist, with an opinion on any subject—even if he knew nothing about it.

Dean Chin and me

In 1984, while visiting Washington, DC, for a few days on leave, I called Dean up to see if he was going to a Jow Ga school picnic that weekend. He said he hadn't planned to, but since I was in town, he agreed to go with me. On the phone he sounded detached, distant, not his normal outgoing self. It had been two years since my last visit and neither of us was good at keeping in touch via letter, so I was anxious to see him. I learned from one of his assistant instructors that Dean had recently gotten divorced, had to move back in with his father, and was having some financial problems.

When I arrived at his doorstep, I saw a dramatically changed man. Whenever we had gotten together before, he'd do most of the talking while I did most of the listening. Now it was the other way around; now I had to pry things from him. He told me that he'd gone through a painful divorce and had to pay exorbitant bills from a lawyer that he'd counted on as a friend. He was angry that he'd been fired from his engineering job at the Navy Department and that he'd lost his security clearances after a supervisor launched an investigation into why he entertained so many foreign contacts. They claimed that his expenses didn't match his income, ignoring the fact that his ex-wife was from a wealthy family and had bankrolled him until their divorce. The investigators didn't understand that as a prominent leader in the Chinese community, Dean was obligated to play host to a broad range of contacts.

I learned later that he'd been seeing a psychiatrist and was on antidepressants. Adding to his woes, his senior students and instructors had splintered into rival factions. The fate of his beloved school, the one thing—perhaps the only thing—he had left, was no longer in his hands.

A year later, while still abroad, I read in agony a news clipping enclosed in a letter from home. I was devastated. Dean's body was discovered in the woods along the George Washington Parkway. Gossip columnists in the Hong Kong press speculated it was a Chinese mob hit, that Dean was deep in debt because of a bad business deal, and that loan sharks had been out to get him. Given his state of mind when I saw him last, I suspected otherwise. According to a reliable source of mine, police reports didn't indicate foul play.

I felt powerless and guilty, wishing that I'd been there for him, wishing that I could've done more for him. Dean was an esteemed teacher and close friend. His sudden, and still-unexplained, death was one of the saddest days of my life.

SHARING DREAMS

Ray and I had hoped that by teaming up we'd avoid the negative karma that had split the Jow Ga Kung Fu family in America. But after a brief honeymoon, I knew we'd have to resolve differences that hindered our budding relationship, a relationship that would become not only one of the most rewarding but also one of the most challenging in my life. Ray and I had shared a passion for kung fu and began training together on weekends in the mid-1990s. After practice, while stuffing ourselves on Burrito

Supremes from Taco Bell, with the hot sauce probably helping ignite our imaginations, we dreamed about starting our own school.

Our vision took shape in 1999 after attending the first international Jow Ga Kung Fu tournament in Singapore. Going as observers, feeling awkward that we didn't bring any students (kung fu instructors are judged by the caliber of their students), envying those able to field a team willing to travel such a long distance to compete, we vowed that one day we'd bring our own students to Asia.

During the tournament we obtained the approval of Chan Man Cheung, the grand master of our Jow Ga system, to start our own school. A year later, we cofounded the Jow Ga Shaolin Institute. While continuing to hold classes at other people's martial arts studios and at county recreation centers, we began searching for a more permanent place, a place where we could hang our martial arts banners and pictures, a place where we could establish a real martial arts center, a place of our own.

CHAPTER 16

IN SEARCH OF A TRUE MASTER

The true teacher knocks down the idol that the student makes of him.

—RUMI

Before he passed away, I sought Dean Chin's guidance on how I might improve my martial arts skills. He said that because of my previous training in karate and other so-called hard styles, my movements were too stiff. Having studied Northern Shaolin himself, Dean recommended that I look for a teacher in a style who could help me balance the hard with the soft. Soon after that, I began my search for a master in northern style Chinese martial arts.

During my travels in China, as I strolled through a Shanghai park (parks and open spaces in China were where most people practiced martial arts), I came upon one group of practitioners that immediately caught my attention. They were unlike any others I'd seen before, and I'd been look-ing across almost every park in the city for weeks. I watched in awe as they kicked and punched their way across the length of a practice area that was twice as large as any used by other groups. Judging from their crisp tech-niques and fluid movements, I knew they were special.

They told me they were practicing Mizong Quan, a combination of Shaolin, Taijiquan, Xingyi and Bagua,[34] and that their teacher was a Master Lu Junhai. Although he was away on business, I didn't wait for his return to sign up for classes, believing that whoever had produced such good students had to be good himself. I would meet Master Lu the following week, after he finished working as a technical advisor for a Chinese television series called Heroes of the Marsh, based on a novel that just happened to be my favorite Chinese classic. Coincidence?

After training with him for several years, almost two decades would pass before we'd meet again, only this time in the suburbs of London. I'd lost touch with him until one of his students in England, Mr. Tay, sent me an e-mail. He'd been searching on the Internet for other Mizong Quan practitioners when he found the website for the school that Ray and I had established. So when Ray told me he was going to a business conference in England, I piggybacked on his trip to see my old teacher.

In June 2001, Ray and I traveled to London on a red-eye from Dulles, arriving at Heathrow the next morning not having slept all night due to a screaming baby in the next row. I traveled light since I'd be there for only three days to see my martial arts teacher. Ray had a large carry-on plus two twenty-eight-inch suitcases—his own plus his wife's. She'd join him the next day for a weeklong conference in Brighton. We realized too late that taking the Tube from the airport to town was a lousy idea because London train stations didn't have escalators or elevators, so toting heavy luggage up and down stairs was tiring.

After emerging sweaty from the station, we got lost walking in circles until we found the hotel I'd booked online. The price was right, and it was centrally located, but it didn't deserve the two-and-a-half-star rating. No elevators, lumpy mattresses, and a room so tiny the two of us couldn't walk across it at the same time. We were exhausted by the time Mr. Tay picked us up and escorted us to Essex for afternoon training with Master Lu.

---

34 Shaolin is classified as an external style, while taijiquan, xingyi and bagua are classified as internal styles of kung fu.

Tay was Master Lu's sponsor as well as student. He had travelled all over China for a year on behalf of a Chinese herb company interested in hiring an "authentic martial arts master" to teach kung fu and taijiquan in England. He learned that Master Lu was a sixth-generation heir to the Shaolin Mizong kung fu system and the world's foremost expert on Qingping Jian, the crown jewel of Chinese swordsmanship. You'd think that in a country where there were over a billion people, finding a true martial arts master wouldn't be hard. But many masters and their traditional Chinese martial arts styles disappeared during the Cultural Revolution.

We took the hour's train ride to Essex, the home of Master Lu and his wife. He was waiting for us at the station. His hair was grayer and there was less of it, but his smile was still warm, his eyes still sparkled, and his face still unblemished despite the passage of time.

"Lao le!" he said as we embraced, meaning "old now." I didn't know if he meant he was old or I was; he'd just celebrated his sixtieth birthday.

"Master Lu, this is my kung fu brother Ray, a research scientist here for a conference," I said. Ray pumped Lu's outstretched hand with both of his.

"Master, I'm so glad to finally meet you. Hon's told me so much about you."

LET'S SEE WHACHA YOU GOT

To make the most of our limited time, Master Lu offered to teach us a weapon routine that afternoon before we joined his regular evening class. We walked from the train station to a Boy Scout meeting hall he rented for classes. But first he wanted to see what I remembered. He could recall each of the routines he'd taught me and asked me to perform Luohan Quan (known as "Buddha warrior fists"), one of the longest in the system; it starts slowly and speeds up to a finish. Fortunately, I'd practiced it before the trip. Forgetting a routine would have been disrespectful; it would have meant that I didn't value his teaching and the time he'd spent teaching me.

Master Lu then invited Ray to show what he could do. It takes just a few seconds to judge someone's skill. I was hoping Ray would do a Jow Ga routine to demonstrate his many years of dedicated training, but he performed the sixth routine of Qingping Jian,[35] the last and most difficult in this system. Ray darted across the room, thrusting, slashing, and dodging imaginary opponents. Master Lu frowned, but not because Ray's performance was bad. On the contrary, it was good—and that was the problem. The system was a closely guarded family heirloom, handed down only from master to trusted disciple and not to be taught openly to outsiders. And Ray, a man he didn't know anything about, was, in Master Lu's mind, an outsider.

"Where did he learn that?" Master Lu asked, a bit sternly.

"I taught him, Master," I replied nervously.

Master Lu relaxed when I vouched for Ray as a trusted kung fu brother, a serious martial artist and a person of good moral character, emphasizing that Ray had promised he wouldn't teach anyone without permission. But Master Lu still wasn't smiling, and he explained his reluctance to share his family treasure by recounting the shabby way the publishers of his Qingping sword manual had treated him.

THE FAMILY JEWELS

Chinese government researchers contacted old martial arts masters in the mid-1980s trying to revive traditional martial arts. After years of suppressing what they'd considered remnants of feudalism, the government acknowledged that traditional Chinese martial arts were an integral part of China's rich cultural legacy. Unfortunately, during the ten-year period of the Cultural Revolution that started in 1966, people were forbidden to practice traditional martial arts. Old masters were persecuted—their belongings, including their writings, were confiscated or burned. Master Lu's father, Lu Zhenduo, was one of them.

It wasn't surprising that when two researchers knocked on his door, Lu Junhai was not hospitable. The researchers discovered that he had inherited

---

35 Considered one of the crown jewels of Chinese swordplay, Qingping Jian was an ancient sword practice created by a Daoist monk who lived on Dragon & Tiger Mountain. He combined techniques from many martial arts styles to form a complete sword system. Journal of Asian Martial Arts, Spring 2009, Volume 18, Number 1, "Qingping Straight Sword The Last Remaining Chinese Sword System."

all six Qingping sword routines from his late father. The only publications available on the system at the time contained at most two routines, with poorly illustrated descriptions. They asked Master Lu to collaborate on a book. He refused. They returned again and again, telling him he had a responsibility to preserve his father's legacy by sharing his knowledge. He finally relented after a year of pressure and allowed them to photograph and videotape him performing each routine, resulting in the publication of a 518-page illustrated manual with detailed explanations of the movements. It was the most complete description of this rare art form ever published. In 1985 the Chinese government awarded him a certificate of merit to recognize his outstanding contribution.

Prior to printing his manuscript, however, the publishers had wanted to delete his name from the book. It was only after he raised havoc that they reinserted his name and a forward dedicated to his father. When the publishers wanted to sell copies of the video to the public, Master Lu reminded them that they had promised to use the photos and videos only to make pen-and-ink drawings of the movements. They agreed not to sell the video without his consent only after he threatened to take them to court. He never received any royalties from the book and said that didn't bother him because his reason for cooperating with the researchers had not been motivated by money. Unfortunately, as he would learn later, bootleg copies of the video had made their way to Taiwan and were being sold on the Internet. His one consolation was that no one could possibly learn the intricacies of Qingping swordsmanship just by watching a video. It takes one-on-one instruction.

DISCIPLESHIP

When Master Lu learned of my trip, he invited me to take the vows of discipleship. A master-disciple relationship in Chinese martial arts is like a father-son relationship. The master is supposed to guide the disciple and pass on his wisdom. The disciple, as lineage heir, is expected to show filial piety and promote the master's martial arts style. The ceremony took place the next evening in the room we trained in, now transformed into a sacred ancestral hall. A table, serving as an altar, held a candle, an incense holder, and a wooden plaque inscribed with the Chinese character for ancestors in the middle. Scrolls of Master Lu's calligraphy decorated the walls. Mr. Tay, acting as translator, addressed the students and families invited to the ceremony.

"Welcome! You've been invited to witness a traditional Chinese martial arts ceremony rarely seen by outsiders. Tonight, Master Lu will accept Hon Lee as his disciple in a ritual called Bai Shi, which means 'paying respect to the master.' Master Lu has taught thousands of students, but only a small number have been selected to be disciples. Hon will be the seventieth."

Master Lu lit three incense sticks, kneeled before the table, and bowed three times. Summoning the spirit of his ancestors, he asked their permission to accept me as a new disciple. I followed Master Lu's sequence, and then pulled out a red envelope that contained my pledge to carry out my responsibilities as a disciple. I savored what it meant to join the ranks of Lu Junyi, a Shaolin monk who, according to legend, created the Mizong system during the Sung Dynasty (circa 960–1270 AD), one of the 108 heroes immortalized in the epic novel Outlaws of the Marsh about a Chinese Robin Hood who fought against government injustice.

I recalled Master Lu's father, Lu Zhenduo, a modern-day hero who collected intelligence against the enemy during the Sino-Japanese War, dispatching, with his bare hands, three armed Japanese soldiers who were bullying civilians. Known as "Lightning Hands Lu" because he could knock out opponents with a single palm strike, he was head of a caravan guard service, a Chinese medicine practitioner, and a bodyguard for the Manchurian warlord Zhang Xueliang.[36]

Humbled that my name would be listed under these warriors in the official Shaolin Mizong archives, trying to keep anyone from noticing the tremor in my voice, I read my pledge aloud:

---

36 (From Wikipedia, http://en.wikipedia.org/wiki/Zhang_Xueliang, accessed January 25, 2014) On April 6, 1936, Zhang Xueliang met with Zhou Enlai to plan the end of the Chinese Civil War. In the Xi'an incident (December 12, 1936), Zhang and another general, Yang Hucheng, kidnapped Chiang Kai-shek and imprisoned the head of the Kuomintang government until he agreed to form a united front with the Communists against the Japanese invasion.

"Master Lu, I'm extremely grateful you're willing to accept me as your disciple. I began studying Chinese martial arts as a youngster, and it continues to be a lifelong passion. I never dreamed I'd be so honored when we first met so many years ago. Even though my level of skill is not up to your high standards, I pledge to promote the Shaolin Mizong system, to remain loyal to you as my teacher, and to treat you with the respect that a son should show his father."

Left to right: me, Madam Lu, Master Lu

I slipped the pledge back into the red envelope, bowed three times and presented it to Master Lu. Inside was a monetary offering, just enough to show my gratitude but not so much that it would seem as if I were buying my way in. Master Lu presented me with a shiny new sword and a hand-written certificate that Mr. Tay translated for the audience:

"Hon Kwong Lee, my student from the United States, has been conscientious in learning Chinese martial arts and has reached a high level of skill. He is of good moral character. Therefore, I officially accept him as my disciple, making him a seventh-generation successor of Shaolin Mizong Chinese martial arts. Signed: Lu Junhai, Sixth-Generation Shaolin Mizong Successor."

After the ceremony, Master Lu wowed the audience by performing a routine with a six-foot-long steel chain. On one end was a handle, at the other a metal spike. Attached to the spike end were two six-inch red silk streamers. Master Lu literally made the whip sing as he whirled and spun the chain around his back and neck, over his head, and under his arms and legs. A false move and the spike would take out a chunk of flesh or an eye.

LIFE LESSON

Addressing the guests, Master Lu explained the meaning of the four-character verses hanging on the left and right sides of the altar.

"Respect the ancestors, respect the teacher, respect the teachings. It means we have to treasure what has been handed down from generation to generation, from master to disciple. We must honor those who have come before us.

"Learn kindness, learn justice, learn kung fu. This means our first priority is to be kind. Treat people fairly. Be just in your actions. Learn kung fu only after you've learned the first two. Kung fu is the least important. Many people have good kung fu skills, but unless you have good relationships with others, and unless you are a good person, kung fu will be useless. What's worse, you'll shame yourself, your teacher, and your ancestors."

I realized then what I liked most about Master Lu. He was more than just an outstanding martial artist; he was an outstanding human being.

Master Lu Junhai

GRAND OPENING

April 26, 2003, marked the grand opening of our Jow Ga Shaolin Institute in Herndon, Virginia. It had taken months to prepare for this milestone, one we wouldn't have been able to achieve without the loyal support of our students. Allie, a graphic artist, designed our logos. Danielle, Wil, Chris and other assistants painted furniture, hung pictures and decorated the place. A must-have item for any traditional kung fu school is an ancestral shrine, but where do we get one? Definitely not on Amazon.com. Fortunately, assistant instructor Mike, handyman extraordinaire, custom-built a three-tiered shrine, with a statue of Guan Gong, patron saint of Chinese martial arts, on the top altar; pictures of the system founders, the Five Tigers of Jow Ga, in the center; and a tablet to the kitchen god on the bottom. On each side of the altar we hung scrolls with Chinese characters that translates as: "Leverage your opponent's strengths to your advantage. Look for opportunities to exploit your opponent's weaknesses."

Ray and I were happy to have our own space after searching over a year for a location within our budget but large enough to allow our students to swing long weapons around without poking holes in the ceiling. Hard to believe three-plus decades had passed since my first lesson in Jow Ga Kung Fu with Hoy Lee and Kung Fu Joe. Now they were our guests of honor taking part in a traditional ceremony to celebrate our new location.

Bowing before the ancestral shrine

DOTTING THE EYES

After the chief of police and a councilwoman presented a letter from the mayor welcoming us to the Town of Herndon, we kicked things off with a ceremony to honor our teacher, the late Jow Ga Master Dean Chin. We burned incense and paper money and placed food and wine on the altar as offerings before "dotting the eye" of our new lion.

In the middle of the room, hidden by a human curtain of students, sat a mythical lion with a basket-sized head made of bamboo and papier-mâché and a six-foot-long body of silk-cloth. Its head was painted bright gold, with white fur trim and a white beard; its eyes resembled those of an eagle; a single horn jutted from its crown; and a mirror was glued to its forehead to scare away evil spirits upon seeing their own reflection. Two of our students, one under the head and the other under the tail, waited to bring the creature to life, ready to perform a lion dance. This dance is part of southern kung fu tradition and done on holidays plus on special occasions to exorcise demons and summon good fortune.

Hoy Lee, the most senior Jow Ga kung fu instructor in the United States, was invited to bless the lion in a ritual called "dotting the eyes." He dipped a calligraphy brush into ink made from red cinnabar and wine— the color red symbolizing lifeblood, good fortune, and prosperity. Next he dotted the mirror to give the lion life, then the eyes to give it vision; then he brushed the nose, tongue, ears, horn, back, spine, and tail before finally tying a red ribbon around the horn to give it courage and honor.

Lion dancers

With a gentle tap on the forehead, the lion stirred from slumber, blinked its eyes, flapped its ears, batted its eyelids, stretched, and yawned. The sound of drum, gong, and cymbals accompanied the lion's movements, picking up tempo as the lion stumbled around to get its footing before bowing to the shrine. Two older lions pranced in and joined the new one, dancing and jumping over each other in search of food. The climax of the performance was the eating of the greens—a head of lettuce—which the lions chewed up and "spat" at the audience to shower our guests with wealth and good fortune.

MASTERFUL PERFORMANCES

Masters from each of the kung fu schools we invited, as well as our own students, performed routines both barehanded and with weapons. Many who couldn't attend sent warm messages of congratulations. I was overwhelmed by the generosity of our teachers and mentors. Jow Ga Master Chan Man Cheung in Hong Kong sent two giant red-and-gold banners; Mizong Master Lu Junhai in London sent beautiful calligraphy; our kung fu uncle in Florida, Wah Lum Praying Mantis Master Pui Chan, sent a saber with five tigers hand-engraved on the blade. Master Hoy Lee, our guest from Virginia Beach, gave us a beautiful ceremonial sword with a hand-carved scabbard to bring us good luck.

MOVING SENTIMENTS

At the close of the ceremony, Ray described his twenty-five-year martial arts journey. With his voice quivering with heartfelt emotions, he said there were two things he considered the most important in his life as a martial artist. The first was being chosen as a disciple, because it meant that his teacher approved of his martial skills and moral character—so it represented a personal achievement. The second was to open one's own martial arts school. But opening a school, Ray explained, is recognition not of yourself but of your teacher because it represents the chance to carry on your teacher's legacy. Reinforcing Ray's sentiments, I concluded by saying that I hoped the school would provide a venue to pass on to future generations not simply martial skills but the martial ethics that can make us better people, better citizens, and more productive members of society.

THE GOOD OLD DAYS

The ceremony was followed by dinner, giving me a chance to chat with Sifu Hoy Lee and Kung Fu Joe, my kung fu mentors in 1971 when I first arrived in Washington, DC. Now they had grown children who were national kung fu champions. We reminisced about the days when people thought kung fu was something you ate at a Chinese restaurant and the reactions we got performing at karate tournaments in front of crowds unfamiliar with the fluidity of our Chinese-style martial arts. Since I'd just started kung fu then, my performance was less stellar than those of my kung fu brothers, but their high-level skills and the cheers from appreciative audiences motivated me to continue training.

My childhood pal, Sifu Norman Chin, a Praying Mantis kung fu master, came from New York to our grand opening. As teenagers we traded karate chops on each other's arms to see who'd yield first. Neither of us wanted to quit, but we called a cease-fire after paralysis set in. I was black and blue afterward and couldn't move my arm for days.

THE BLACK GHOST

The one person I really missed was Paul Adkins, my training partner at the old Chinatown school. Sadly, an unsuccessful hip surgery had left him paralyzed. We were part of a team that did kung fu demonstrations around the city. Paul, well known for his charismatic style and "iron palm" techniques, was able to smash through a foot-high stack of cinderblocks with a single palm strike. I always liked to train with people better than me, and Paul was not only an exceptional martial artist but also one of the best fighters in the area. And he kept my dentist busy: during one of our sparring sessions, his spinning back kick caught me on the jaw and cracked a molar.

Me and Paul, 1974

He was faster than me, more powerful than me, and usually got the best of me, except on one occasion when I threw a sidekick to counter one of his punches. I meant to stop just short of his forehead, but he moved in too quickly. *THUD!* Paul crumpled to the floor, a knot welling up on his forehead. He was out cold. Dean Chin, our teacher, splashed water on his face to revive him. I was relieved when he regained consciousness. "What happened?" he asked as he sat up, head still dizzy. "You ran into my foot!" I said, trying to look concerned on the outside while stifling a grin on the inside, knowing that for once—just once—I'd gotten the best of the great Paul Adkins.

MARTIAL ARTS ROOTS

When I first met him, I told Lu Junhai how lucky I felt to have found a true martial arts master to be my teacher, but he said, "To find a good teacher is hard, but to find a good student is even harder." I knew what he meant. Out of hundreds who walked through the doors of our martial arts school, only a handful had been willing to devote the time and effort to learn what we had to offer.

Would a trip to China with our students help them appreciate the richness of our heritage? To find out, in the fall of 2005, Ray and I took eighteen of them to Beijing, the Shaolin temple, Shanghai, Jow Ga village, and Hong Kong. Many had never travelled out of the United States, so while our primary focus was martial arts, we allotted enough time for sightseeing. We visited the usual tourist attractions in Beijing, our first stop, which was more crowded than usual since it was during China's National Day celebrations. The Shaolin temple, the mecca of Chinese martial arts, was a must-see destination. The abbot, strolling through the grounds, did a double take when he saw our T-shirts with the Jow Ga Shaolin logo. He had apparently tried in vain to trademark "Shaolin," so I hoped he wouldn't report us for copyright infringement.

Jow Ga Shaolin Institute, 2005

We stood among fifty well-worn footprints on the stone floor of a training hall, imprints made by generations of monks stomping on the floor as
they practiced martial arts over the Shaolin temple's one-thousand-five-
hundred-year history—a reminder that kung fu takes time and effort. We
watched performers coached by a Shaolin temple monk put on a kung fu
show. Upon learning we practiced kung fu ourselves, the monk invited us
to perform. We begged off, saying we couldn't match their skills, but the
monk said it was OK since they were professional martial artists and we
weren't. With that, three of our students performed to hearty applause from
the Chinese side.

Posing in the Shaolin temple courtyard

We visited a group of Master Lu Junhai's students at Fuxing Park in
Shanghai, the same place where his father taught him Mizong Quan and
where I first learned the art decades earlier, a place that would later be designated an historic landmark. We walked past old men taking their caged
birds for a stroll, couples doing the latest disco steps, and groups practicing taijiquan, qigong, or kung fu. Every inch of ground in the park was

occupied by sunrise with people trying to get in their morning exercise before the heat of summer made it too uncomfortable.

Lao Chen

We joined the group in warm-up exercises. You can tell if someone has good martial arts skills just by how well he or she does jiben gong (fundamentals): punches, kicks, leaps, and spins. Even Lao Chen, at age eighty, put us to shame. Chinese and Americans took turns performing routines. We marveled at their graceful-yet-powerful demonstrations.

Mizong group

Master Lu had told his Chinese students to take care of us and wired money so they could treat us to a sumptuous brunch that included shark fin soup. One of them, noted for his brush calligraphy, presented us with the words "Jow Ga Shaolin Institute" in beautiful Chinese characters.

Beautiful calligraphy

We spent an afternoon training in another Shanghai park with Chen Enyi, whose two passions in life are martial arts and music. He was a disciple of the legendary Master Ma Jinbo, who was from a Moslem ethnic minority (Hui) known for their tough fighters. Master Chen, a walking martial arts encyclopedia, was expert in many styles, including Cha style boxing. He also studied Shaolin Mizong and Qingping sword with Lu Junhai's father.

He taught us "spear versus double sticks," a flashy Cha style routine that takes good reflexes, timing, and hand-eye coordination, so I was glad to see that our seasoned students picked it up without much difficulty. We presented him with an engraved plaque as well as some goodies for his wife in appreciation for spending time with us.

JOW GA VILLAGE

Our next stop, the Jow Ga village school, was an hour by bus from the capital of Guangdong province. Because she liked kung fu, a local guide with the bus company asked to tag along in exchange for allowing us free use of the bus during our stay at the village.

Jow Biu, one of the "Five Tigers of Jow Ga Kung Fu," opened this school, where Chan Man Cheung, our grandmaster, was a student. Master Chan, having come from Hong Kong that morning, welcomed us warmly. At age seventy-six, he still had enough energy to demonstrate the lion dance techniques that had earned him the title "Lion King." His movements, still quick and agile, showed the benefits of martial arts training. After lunch we visited a hilltop cemetery for a Bai Shan ceremony to pay respects to the departed soul of Master Chan's father. It was festive rather than somber, with lion dancing and the burning of incense, paper money, and firecrackers—not what Americans would expect at a gravesite. After dinner we headed for the old village school, passing rice paddies and farmhouses along with way.

The sounds of drums, cymbals, and gongs greeted us as we got off the bus. *DUK, DONG, CHANG; DUK, DONG, CHANG!* Lion dancers led the way to an illuminated courtyard filled with local students, friends, and families cheering and clapping as we entered. A TV crew covering our visit made us feel like rock stars.

Drum concert at Jow Ga village

After enjoying a concert of drums, cymbals, and gongs, Americans and Chinese took turns doing kung fu forms. Master Chan took over the drum as I got up to perform one of his favorite routines with the Guan Dao, a blade mounted on a six-foot rusted metal shaft. Energized by Master Chan's drumming, I got carried away, trying to keep up with the tempo, moving too fast too soon. In the muggy heat, with my hands sweaty and the weapon growing heavier by the second, I hoped I wouldn't drop it and embarrass my teacher. I spun the shaft over my head, around my back, rolled it off my neck, and barely managed to catch it in my hand.

Me posing with the Guan Dao

The evening concluded with the village's award-winning lion dance team doing gravity-defying leaps, jumping in unison from one tiny platform to another with perfect timing. Each platform, no bigger than a square foot, was mounted on top of steel poles that were ten, fifteen and twenty feet above the ground. One slip could mean broken bones or worse. This style of lion dancing was far different and more thrilling than what we did back home.

The next morning we hiked to the Five Tigers Memorial on a hillside overlooking the town—a stone pavilion and granite tablet memorializing the Jow brothers. Our students joined in the lion dancing and took part in the Bai Shan ceremony. Following custom, we ate roast pig, washed it down with maotai (Chinese white lightning), and threw firecrackers in the air, nearly igniting someone's hair. At a farewell lunch, some had too much to drink in a game that required losers to do "bottom's up," necessitating frequent, unscheduled restroom stops on our way to catch the train to Hong Kong. As our tour guide waved good-bye, she gushed that in her five years of traveling around China, she'd never seen anything like her two days with us.

Jow Ga Five Tigers Memorial

At our last stop in Hong Kong, we continued to eat, shop, and visit more Jow Ga schools. Upon returning home, I thanked my teachers in London and Hong Kong for making the journey a success, sending them a copy of our newsletter in which one of our students summarized what the trip meant to him:

Hong Kong farewell dinner

"The fellowship with our Chinese kung fu brothers and sisters allowed us entry into aspects of life in China that are accessible to few outsiders. I believe that the fundamental lesson to be learned is the sense of transmitted tradition that was brought home by these experiences. Seeing our Chinese friends practice the same Jow Ga, Mizong, and taijiquan forms that we have been taught was deeply inspiring."

MY TEACHER'S TEACHER

Four years after the trip, I had a chance to see Master Chan again, this time to celebrate his eightieth birthday. I arrived at the Golden Dragon Restaurant in Hong Kong, where the party took place. His sons kept the birthday dinner small because he didn't like big social events. Now diabetic, he seemed less robust, but his voice was still strong and his handshake firm. He always called himself the "Big-Bellied Buddha." Indeed, he reminded me of a laughing Buddha, except on the rare occasion when he got mad.

Me presenting a birthday gift to Chan Man Cheung

After Dean passed away, Sigung (my teacher's master) accepted me as his own disciple, a great honor for me. Although he had many students, he only anointed five disciples. When I presented him with a photo of our students in Virginia wishing him a happy birthday, he gave me a big hug and thanked me for coming all the way from the United States. I reminded him that our first meal together had been in the same Hong Kong locale over three decades earlier.

YUM CHA WITH SIGUNG

During an extended stay in Hong Kong in the 1970s, I met Sigung at the entrance to a department store in the middle of Causeway Bay, a crowded shopping area. (Think of Times Square on New Year's Eve and you have a picture of how crowded it was.) Out of a sea of people, I picked him out of the crowd based on photos I'd seen. It was hard to miss his trademark smile, balding pate, and slight paunch. We went to a nearby restaurant to *yum cha* (drink tea), a Chinese style brunch that consists of having tea with dim sum, light snacks such as steamed buns stuffed with roast pork, meat and vegetable dumplings, different types of noodles, and other culinary treats. The restaurant was filled with noisy kids running around and elderly patrons leisurely sipping tea and reading their newspapers. You had to shout into the ear of the person sitting next to you to be heard. Southern Chinese are known to be loud; perhaps it's because they live in a loud environment. I handed Sigung a letter from Dean Chin, asking his master to teach me kung fu. It was another example of Dean's openness in allowing me to learn from other masters, including his own teacher.

FROM CHINESE VILLAGE TO HONG KONG HUSTLE

By the time we met, Sigung was no longer teaching, occupied with supporting a wife and three young sons and making a living selling fresh fish and meat. When he first opened his market stall, he'd swim out to fishing trawlers before dawn to ensure he got the freshest catch of the day. Hard work and kung fu training added layers of muscle to a strong physique, making him look like a Chinese Charles Atlas.

He started learning kung fu at age four with his father, a student of Jow Biu—one of five brothers known as the "Five Tigers of Jow Ga" (or the Jow Family). Jow Lung, the eldest brother, founded the system and gained fame in 1914 by beating all comers in a no-holds-barred contest to select the chief martial arts instructor for the deputy military commander of Guangdong Province. Contestants faced off on a raised platform to slug it out. After winning, his four brothers joined Jow Lung as army trainers. When Jow Lung passed away, Jow Biu continued to promote his martial arts system.

When he was six years old, Sigung pleaded with his father to allow him to learn from this famous master. He practiced after school every day without complaint, even if he had to stand motionless for hours in a low squat called a horse stance. In his early teens, he became an assistant instructor. When Jow Biu moved to Hong Kong in the late 1940s, he moved too. By age twenty-four, he opened his own school. One of his students, a movie starlet, got him a job as an extra and martial arts coordinator in two feature films.

MIDNIGHT RENDEZVOUS

A few months after our first meeting, Sigung called me late at night. He spoke in such a low whisper that I could barely hear him over the phone.

"Can you come pick me up? I need to get away and would like to stay with you."

"Yes, of course, I would be honored."

"Some people are after me. There's no time to explain now. Please hurry!"

"I'll catch a taxi and be there within a half hour."

"OK, you have my address right? I'm on the top floor. Have the taxi park a half block away. When you get to my door, knock softly three times."

I got dressed, selecting a heavy pair of hard-soled shoes, the kind I could use to break a kneecap. I flagged a taxi and gave the driver directions. As we drove through the streets of Hong Kong I wondered what I was getting into. It was almost midnight, and I was being asked to come to the aid of a martial arts master who was in some sort of danger. Who could possibly be after him, and why?

In Hong Kong some in the martial arts world have links to the infamous 14K Triad—the Chinese mafia—involved in drugs, racketeering, gambling, and prostitution. I knew Sigung was not involved in anything nefarious but wasn't as positive about some of his pals, including a night-club bouncer who took us to visit a couple of underground clubs one evening. Could Sigung, who didn't smoke, drink, or gamble, have gotten into trouble at one of these places?

As the taxi neared his building, I told the driver to pull over and wait. Because it was late, I saw few people out on the streets as I looked around to make sure no one was watching. I climbed six flights of creaky wooden stairs to the top-floor apartment, one with a metal accordion padlocked gate, and knocked as instructed. Sigung opened the door, unlocked the gate and handed me a red overnight bag. He wasted no time closing the door behind him, instructing his wife to lock it. "Don't let anyone in, no matter what!" he said. We hurried to the waiting taxi and headed straight to my place.

I settled Sigung into a spare bedroom, agreeing to wait till morning to discuss what had led to his urgent call. By the time I got out of bed at six, he was already up. After breakfast, he told me what happened. It all started the previous morning, when he and other vendors were setting up shop. Out of the corner of his eye he noticed three men in their early twenties shoving their way through the crowd of shoppers.

Others had warned him of a new gang extorting protection money from neighborhood merchants. He had reached a modus vivendi with the former crime boss who controlled the area, but Sigung didn't know the new leader who had taken over. The old boss, recognizing that Sigung was well regarded in the community, had treated him with respect. But as the young thugs muscled their way toward him, it was obvious they were trying to make sure people knew they were there for only one purpose: to intimidate them and collect payment. Anyone who didn't pay would be roughed up, either then or later. As they came closer, Sigung remained calm.

"Uncle, we're from the New On Lok Protection Association of North Point. Have you paid your dues yet?"

"I've never paid protection money. I don't know you and have never heard of your organization, so please leave me alone!"

"Listen up, Uncle! If you don't pay up, my friends and I are going to stop being so polite. Don't make me pull out a weapon!"

The young thug stood facing Sigung with his left hand and left foot forward, his right hand behind his back, much like a pitcher at the mound winding up to throw a fastball. He jabbed his index finger within inches of Sigung's face. Could he have been reaching for a concealed weapon with his other hand? Sigung wondered. As they exchanged verbal insults, the youth's face got redder and his voice louder, apparently angry he couldn't intimidate Sigung as he had the other merchants. A small crowd gathered around them.

Suddenly, the thug lunged forward, grabbing Sigung's shirt with his left hand while swinging his right hand toward Sigung's head. The youth had rushed in so quickly that Sigung couldn't see if his assailant had a knife in his other hand or not. But he reacted instinctively, using a self-defense technique perfected through decades of practice, raising both his hands overhead to block the assailant's attack, then sinking his body weight forward and smashing the hard edge of his hand into the assailant's ribs. The youth groaned and buckled in agony. His two friends rushed in and tried to corner Sigung. Not waiting to find out if they were armed or not, Sigung leaped past them and made a zigzag retreat across back alleys to his apartment.

After a few phone calls to his friends, he learned the thugs were part of a Triad gang. Fortunately, the one he hit wasn't seriously injured—just a few broken ribs and a bruised ego. But they wanted to settle the score. After questioning others in the market, they learned Sigung's identity and wanted to make an example out of him. Sigung's friends urged him to stay out of sight. That's when he called me.

Master Chan Man Cheung at age 78

TRUCE DINNER

A few weeks after the incident Sigung's friends arranged a truce dinner. The young thugs came with their boss and sat at a round table with Sigung and his supporters. The Triad boss scolded his subordinates for insulting Sigung and said he would honor whatever arrangements were made with his predecessor. The thugs apologized for their rude behavior, claiming they had no idea that Sigung was such a respected kung fu master. Sigung accepted their apology and said he was sorry if he'd hurt anyone. Both sides agreed to shake hands and be friends.

While he was staying with me before the truce dinner, I had worried about Sigung's plight, but at the same time I was also thrilled with a chance to tap his expertise. Imagine how a high school basketball player would feel if Michael Jordan showed up in his living room to give him one-on-one instruction. Sigung seemed to enjoy teaching me his favorite moves and sharing his insights about the martial arts, and showed me fighting techniques perfected from his personal experience. Although a big man by Chinese standards, he moved with the effortless grace and power of a tiger in the wild. Before I left Hong Kong, Sigung gave me an eight-foot-long pole of dark hardwood and taught me one of his favorite weapon routines, the Bagua staff, a treasured reminder of his generosity in sharing his art with me.

SEEKING RESPECT

I had looked foward to partnering with Ray, my good friend and kung fu brother, to do what we both loved. But I should have paid more attention to early warning signs about nurturing our budding relationship. Tensions surfaced when we took a picture with our students for our website. Posing for a kung fu group photo follows a time-honored protocol of placing the senior person at the center. Since I was his sihing (older kung fu brother, having joined the system before him), I moved toward the middle seat, but Ray beat me to it. After a couple of photos, I let my ego get the best of me and asked to switch seats. Big mistake. That evening he sent me a blistering e-mail reminding me that we were supposed to be equals, saying he wouldn't take a subordinate role after working so hard to get where he was. He was right.

I should've been more sensitive about hurting his feelings, especially since Ray had once told me how offended he'd gotten when someone in the kung fu community hadn't accorded him the respect he deserved. The next day, when we met, I apologized and offered to let him take over the Institute rather than jeopardize our friendship. He said he felt the same. We shook hands and hoped to put the incident behind us.

Ray and me: friendly gesture or middle finger?

But simmering resentments continued to bubble up whenever he felt I did something to diminish his status and vice versa, with minor irritations, such as disagreements over how to do certain martial arts techniques, becoming thorns threatening to rupture our partnership. Ray often complained that I was too focused on my acupuncture clinic and not spending enough time on school activities, saying that he was doing all the work without getting any of the credit. It got to the point that I dreaded opening his e-mails, which, more often than not, criticized something I did or should have done. He had sufficient reason to complain, but pride prevented me from acknowledging my own flaws.

Normally a Chinese martial arts school has only one sifu or master; our students had two. Because Ray and I had different teaching styles, learned from different people, and had different ways of doing the same techniques, these differences often caused confusion, especially for our beginning students. However, when we put our egos on hold, we accomplished things together that neither of us could have done as well alone, including passing on our knowledge and developing a loyal cadre of students that we treated as family, which had been one of our initial goals when we first established the school.

WORKING TOGETHER

In March 2011 we celebrated an early tenth anniversary so that we could promote four of our senior students to instructor rank, with each receiving framed certificates after passing a three-day comprehensive exam that tested their knowledge and skills. As instructors they earned the right to be addressed as "Sifu" if they started their own schools. I was gratified when they gave us wooden plaques engraved in gold to thank us for our teaching. But, in all honesty, it was I who had them to thank, because I learned as much from them as they did from me. Take Mehran as one of many examples; he inspired me with his indomitable spirit every time he sparred against men half his age or when he performed a sword routine despite a permanently injured right hand.

Left to right: Kiyoshi, Mehran, me, John, Ray, Danielle, and Mike

Ray and I were lucky to have John Chin, our kung fu brother, take over one of our branch locations. His humble attitude and willingness to coach the next generation without expecting anything in return set an example for all of us. During our school's ten-year history, our students had competed in annual traditional Chinese martial arts competitions against participants who came from all over the East Coast and beyond. Thanks to their consistent efforts, year after year our school placed in the top ten among over forty schools.

"I always dreamed there'd be a kung fu school like this!" one of our students remarked. He'd been studying with different instructors for many years until he found us. Comments like his made me realize that despite all the time and energy devoted to making the school successful, it had all been worth the effort.

Since we didn't do any formal advertising, having a good reputation helped attract prospective students. I even joked with Ray that we should advertise as a good place to meet a future soul mate. Among the four couples that met, fell in love, and got married while taking kung fu classes were Brian and Angie. Brian is the son of Wilkin, a childhood friend from Chinatown I hadn't seen for over thirty years until we bumped into each other at a Chinatown reunion. When I learned that his son was living in Virginia and was looking for a kung fu school, I asked Wilkin to make sure Brian contacted me. A week later Brian showed up for class, and four years later he married Angie, one of our top students. At their wedding reception, the newlyweds entertained their guests by performing a two-person taijiquan routine. Picture a martial arts waltz: as one partner advances, the other yields, demonstrating the harmony of yin and yang.

Brian & Angie

LETTING GO

Among the many positive things that came out of the partnership that Ray and I started was being able to host Master Lu Junhai and his wife on visits to the US. On their first visit in 2002, they brought students from England to compete in an international martial arts tournament. They won over 20 medals, impressing the judges with their high level of martial arts even though most had been practicing for less that two years. In the years that followed, we've exchanged visits several times, each time deepening our relationship not only with our teacher but also with our Mizong brothers and sisters in the UK, a talented group of individuals I had the pleasure of seeing develop from novices to master-level instructors dedicated to preserving the art. I'm especially grateful to them for helping Master and Mrs. Lu adjust to life outside China, helping them qualify for immigrant status, and helping them find subsidized housing. They even learned Mandarin since the couple still can't communicate in English. And on one of Master Lu's trips, I was proud to witness Ray's induction into the ranks of Mizong disciples, as happy for him as he had been for me when I was inducted a few years earlier.

Master Lu (center), flanked by me and Ray, with UK and US medal winners

In early October 2012, Master Lu returned to the US to conduct a Qingping sword seminar, timing his visit so we could celebrate his, Ray's, and my birthday together since we were all born the same month. Seeing our students learning this ancient art directly from the grandmaster, and seeing their appreciation for his awe-inspiring skill, made me happy, glad that the school Ray and I cofounded had made it possible. I was hopeful our partnership could continue for a few more years before I faded into the background. But that was before Ray gave me a surprise gift, one I had to return.

A day after our triple birthday, Ray announced he was handing over the school to me because he felt our students should only have one sifu. As much as I appreciated his offer, I sensed that he was doing this because he was fed up with shouldering the burden without getting the credit. Weighing what was best for everyone in the long term, I knew the school could get along without me, but not without him. I couldn't let him just walk away because he'd done the lion's share of the work in managing the school and deserved to reap the rewards, including the recognition he deserved.

So as much as I loved the school, loved bringing out the best in our students, I knew I had to let go. And with four of our senior students promoted to the level of instructor, and with more ready to achieve this status soon, I could retire from teaching knowing that they would do their best to preserve and promote the martial arts that we'd inherited. Moreover, having studied and taught martial arts for over half a century, I felt it was well past time to let Ray get out from under my shadow and allow the younger generation of students to blossom under his leadership. Plus I had to admit he was a far better teacher than I; he was more patient, especially with beginners and kids, and had a knack for explaining complex techniques by dissecting them into easier to learn pieces.

Although Ray tried to talk me out of it, I decided to hand him the reigns instead of the other way around, telling our students that he had my full support in carrying out his vision, confident that the school would continue to thrive in his capable hands. Although I'd no longer be teaching regular classes, I assured them I wouldn't disappear, promising to conduct periodic seminars during the year.

Just as a son never wants to disappoint his father, I had a hard time breaking the news to my teachers, Chan Man Cheung and Lu Junhai. Although surprised since they knew how passionate I still was about the martial arts, both said they understood my rationale and supported my decision. But was there a hint of sadness in their responses that I detected, or was it just a reflection of my own? In any case, I expressed profound gratitude for their guidance and for transmitting their knowledge to me, adding that with my obligations fulfilled as a teacher and disciple of the martial arts, I hoped to devote more time and energy to the healing arts.

FOURTH PATH

HEALER

CHAPTER 17

HOOKED ON CHINESE MEDICINE

The art of medicine consists of amusing the patient while nature cures the disease.

—VOLTAIRE

Before retiring from the CIA, I took advantage of the Agency's ninety-day career-transition program, which included a two-week course to help prepare for post-Agency life and talks on everything from financial planning to résumé preparation. Business representatives offered postretirement employment opportunities. Many case officers returned to the Agency as consultants for those companies or as independent contractors. And who could blame them? Having spent a lifetime with the Agency, it was difficult to give up the intoxicating world of espionage. But I chose another direction, hoping I'd have enough steam left to launch a new career in Chinese medicine.

My fascination with medicine started when I was a kid. Whenever I got sick, Mama would take me to see Susie, the neighborhood pharmacist and self-chosen matriarch of Chinatown. Her over-the-counter remedies seemed able to cure any ailment, so I knew she had a magic potion that could turn me from a scrawny wimp into Superman, but I happily settled instead for malted milk balls, which Susie said would "fatten you up [with] lots of vitamins." If Susie couldn't help, Mama called Dr. Krahulic, a lanky man, with silver-rimmed glasses that matched his hair, who smelled like disinfectant. "Are we friends today?" he'd ask as he pulled out a hypodermic needle and gripped my elbow so I couldn't run.

Dr. K helped save my life when I was in ninth grade. I was feverish, losing weight, and lethargic. He came up with various diagnoses, including mononucleosis, but never pinpointed the exact cause. He tried different medications, but nothing worked. After a month of lab tests, a spinal tap, and hospital confinement, I got tired of being pricked and prodded. "Enough!" I said to myself, reciting the 23rd Psalm over and over like a mantra, praying for God's help, willing myself to get stronger.

Amazed when I recovered much faster than he'd anticipated, Dr. K brought me to the hospital auditorium, which was filled with interns and residents. It was a teaching hospital, and I was their guinea pig. He asked me to extend my arms in front of me as he addressed his students: "You can see that his hands are steady. No tremors compared with a week ago, and blood pressure and other vital signs are all normal again!" Although I'm sure Dr. K had helped, I was convinced my recovery was due to forces more powerful. I would realize years later that our thoughts influence our physiology, either positively or negatively; I came to understand that the root of my illness was as much emotional as it was physical. It coincided with a stressful period in my life, with my mind distressed over my father's bankruptcy, and my body going through adolescent hormonal changes.

After I got out of the hospital, because I was still weak, Mama dragged me to see Master Hung. He looked like Fu Manchu, with thinning hair and a scraggly goatee. He sat on a stool in front of a wooden cabinet with rows of tiny drawers, each etched with Chinese writing. I stared in fascination at a display case filled with dried lizards, tiny seahorses, scorpions, and other critters. "Stick out your tongue!" he said, examining it closely. The old man took my pulse, looked at my tongue, and questioned Mama about my bowel movements, urination, appetite, and sleep. Master Hung opened one drawer, and then another, selecting a few pinches of dark-brown twigs from one, a handful of leaves from the next. The scent of sandalwood from the incense burning on the counter barely masked the mix of strange odors emanating from the cabinet. Soon a dozen ingredients were on the counter-top, which he divided into equal portions on pieces of paper, folding each piece into packets for us to take home.

Mama boiled the ingredients into a kind of tea. "Drink the whole thing down!" she instructed, handing me a bowl of murky liquid with bits of leaves, twigs, and bark floating around. Holding my nose, I gulped the foul-tasting stuff down. Three times a day for a week. I started to feel stronger. Was this the magic potion that I'd been seeking?

Chinese herbs came to my rescue time and again when I'd come home black-and-blue from schoolyard fights. Uncle Henry's herbal liniment miraculously made my pain and bruises go away. When I studied kung fu, Master Chan Man Cheung presented me with a book of "secret" Dit Da Jow formulas created by our system founder, who specialized in traumatology. Carrying on this tradition of practicing the healing arts started by our martial arts ancestors was another factor fueling my desire to study Chinese medicine, not to mention acquiring enough knowledge to use the formulas without poisoning anyone.

MITCM

During my ninety-day Agency transition, I enrolled in a master's-level program at the Maryland Institute of Traditional Chinese Medicine (MITCM). After my stressful ordeal with the polygraph fiasco, I yearned for the inner harmony and balance promised by those Daoist principles at the heart of Chinese medicine.

As we carpooled to class, my MITCM classmate Alec and I were chatting and listening to a song on the radio. A newscaster interrupted the broadcast to report a plane hitting the World Trade Center tower and, minutes later, reported on the second plane. I knew immediately Osama bin Laden was behind it and went to the Counterterrorism Center to see if they could use an extra hand. They welcomed my help, but after learning I'd only be available one or two days a week, they said they'd need officers who could deploy on temporary assignments overseas, but for at least a month or longer. It was the only time since retiring from the Agency that I regretted not being there.

I wish I could have done more to help out at the Agency, but I was already enrolled full-time in coursework that required stuffing my brain with the theories and principles of a five-thousand-year-old medicine. According to the ancients, the body is a microcosm of the universe, with a network of pathways connecting the body's organs and structures that, when blocked, cause the body's ecosystem to become unbalanced and can lead to disease. The flow of qi through this energy network can be manipulated via acupoints near the body's surface to restore balance and promote the body's innate ability to heal itself. This is the theory behind acupuncture.

I learned to locate over 365 acupoints to treat problems from acne to stroke. I practiced needling, first on pads of paper, fruit, slabs of meat, and then on other students before doing it on real patients. The needles, sterile filaments not much wider than a hair, have lengths from a half inch to five inches or longer. Some acupoints are difficult to access, such as the one on the bottom of the torso between the anus and genitals used to treat genito-urinary and reproductive problems. We didn't get any classroom practice on this one since none of us volunteered to needle or be needled there. Silvia, a schoolmate, practiced on her husband and became so adept at it that a male patient with erectile dysfunction, after getting needled by her, refused to be treated by anyone else. A faculty supervisor, suspecting the patient was getting too attached to Silvia, intervened by telling him she was no longer available but offered to let him see a male practitioner. The patient never returned.

I learned the potency of Traditional Chinese Medicine (TCM) when his daughter wheeled John, a sixty-five-year-old stroke patient, into our student clinic. He had been paralyzed from the waist down for over a year, was unable to talk, and had only partial feeling in one hand. His doctors said there was nothing they could do. When his daughter begged our teacher, Dr. Li, for help, he responded that acupuncture might not work unless it's done within weeks of a stroke—six months afterward at most—but he agreed to try anyway. After four months of twice-weekly acupuncture, John was able to speak. After a year he was able to walk with a cane. Watching his miraculous recovery, I was determined to learn this ancient healing system.

Then, without warning the faculty quit in protest against Dr. Chang, the school president, disagreeing with her policies and wanting a greater voice in running the school. She tried to disrupt a meeting between the faculty and the students, calling in the police, barricading the school, and taking photos of the "trouble makers." Most of us sided with our teachers since we didn't have much contact with her and didn't know her side of the story.

"Let's duct tape Dr. Chang and throw her down the stairs!" Phil shouted. Usually mild-mannered, he was steaming and blamed Dr. Chang for the faculty walkout. Phil's outburst expressed the anger that my classmates and I felt.

By then Phil and I were in the second year of our three-year course. When most of our teachers quit, we felt abandoned and wondered if we'd ever graduate. Some students transferred to another school while others, turned off by the experience, gave up on Chinese medicine entirely. To have studied so hard only to have our aspirations suddenly smashed left us feeling utterly depressed.

The Accreditation Commission for Acupuncture and Oriental Medicine was inspecting the school when it imploded, jeopardizing the accreditation we needed in order to take the national board exam required by most states for licensure. Perhaps the faculty had staged their protest thinking Dr. Chang would cave in rather than risk losing accreditation. Most of our teachers were from Shanghai; Dr. Chang was from Taiwan. It was like a cross-straits standoff between Mainland China and the island of Taiwan. She didn't blink. Within a month of the faculty strike, she had lured back old faculty, hired new teachers, and negotiated with the Tai Sophia Institute[37], an acupuncture school in Laurel, Maryland, to administer a "teach-out" so that we could complete our program.

---

37 Tai Sophia is now the Maryland University of Integrative Health

With that behind us, we started our third year treating live patients in the student clinic, needing to see a minimum of one hundred people to graduate. Finding patients, even at a discounted price of forty-five dollars per treatment, wasn't easy since the school didn't have funds for advertising. Phil stood on a street corner distributing flyers. I had somewhat better luck placing brochures at a local diner but wouldn't have met my quota had it not been for friends, colleagues, and students who trusted me enough to let me needle them. Vicki and my daughters, however, ran at the sight of needles, initially refusing to come to the clinic. Jenjen, after a great deal of coaxing, finally agree to come in but remains acupuncture-phobic. Marisa, hesitant at first, became a convert after getting acupuncture to resolve a health issue. Vicki never came; it wasn't until years later that she allowed me to treat her after injuring her back. She's now a firm believer in TCM.

SHANGHAI CLINICAL TRIALS

When I graduated from MITCM and passed the national certification board exam, it felt as if I'd survived a near-fatal plane crash. As a graduation present to ourselves, five classmates and I went to the Shanghai University of Traditional Chinese Medicine for clinical training with Dr. Grant Zhang, one of our favorite teachers who had guided us through a mentally and emotionally exhausting three years.

As we landed in Shanghai, happy to have a chance to compare what we learned with how things are done in China, I stared wide-eyed at a city transformed into a gleaming megalopolis of glass and steel. Unfortunately, Long Hua Hospital, where we did our first week of clinical training, hadn't been part of the transformation. A 1940s building with a grimy exterior, the inside looked even worse, with peeling paint, dark linoleum floors, and dim hallways. Its medical staff, however, was outstanding.

With my immune system down from jet lag, feeling feverish, my nose stuffed up, and my throat sore, I needed a good night's sleep to recover. However, our hotel's denizens of the night prevented this, waking me up at odd hours. Just as I was falling asleep, the phone would ring, and a female voice would ask if I wanted a massage. I finally had to get the hotel desk to block all calls to my room. This was no longer Mao's puritanical China.

I asked Dr. Chen, one of the doctors we were observing, to give me an acupuncture treatment, wanting relief from my symptoms but also to see if he was as good as people said.

"Stop moving your arm," Alec, my classmate, admonished, wanting me to remain still so I'd get the full benefit of the treatment.

"Alec, I'm not moving. The needle is vibrating all by itself!" I told him.

My other classmates turned to look as I sat in a hardback chair in the hospital treatment room after Dr. Chen had inserted a one-and-a-half-inch stainless steel needle a fraction of an inch into the crease of my right elbow. With that single needle, my sore throat and nasal congestion eased.

Some acupuncturists can manipulate the body's vital energy, qi, and direct it to any area within the patient's body. Whereas ordinary doctors might use a dozen needles, the best use just a few to treat many health problems. Dr. Chen was one of them, accounting for why the shaft of the needle in my arm continued pulsating minutes after he had inserted it. The needle vibrated from the powerful qi that Dr. Chen had transmitted through the needle and into my body. I was inspired yet daunted, knowing I still had so much to learn and so little time to learn it. Dr. Chen was in great demand, as evidenced by the fifteen patients sitting on wooden chairs, shoulder to shoulder, along the walls of his treatment room, plus another dozen lying on padded tables. Forget about privacy. When one patient got up, another immediately would sit or lie down. Other patients lined the hallway outside waiting their turn. He saw over eighty patients a day. Even with interns taking out needles and hooking up electrical stimulation devices, it was a heavy load for one man.

But Dr. Chen's pace seemed unhurried, moving from patient to patient in a manner that was efficient but also engaged, chatting casually, remembering names and recalling details about people's families. "How's your son doing in school?" he'd ask one patient before attending to another. Unlike some other doctors we observed, Dr. Chen's needling method was gentle and fluid and almost elegant—inserting needles not in the typical point locations we had learned in school. What I needed to do was follow this masterful practitioner around for another year, I told myself.

But I had to return for fall classes at Tai Sophia, with another year left of a two-and-a-half-year postgraduate course in Chinese herbs. I was also anxious to start my own acupuncture practice, having already set aside funds to partition off two treatment rooms at our kung fu school. I wanted to emulate the founders of our kung fu systems, who made their living teaching martial arts and healing the sick. Because they specialized in treating traumatic injuries, I picked the name Sports Edge Acupuncture for my future clinic, wishing to pay homage to the martial arts tradition I'd inherited as a lineage successor, and one I wanted to carry forward. Having a clinic and martial arts studio collocated was part of that tradition. By day I would stick people with needles; by night I would teach people how to avoid getting stuck with sharp objects.

Within a four-month span, from May to September of 2004, I'd graduated from MITCM, passed the national board exam, gone to China for clinical training, received a Virginia Medical Board acupuncture license, obtained a business permit to open a clinic, carved out space to treat patients in our martial arts studio, and completed my first year of herbal studies. Phew! I was tired but felt the exhilaration of a runner sprinting toward the finish despite stumbling over a few hurdles.

But I had one more lap to go to reach the finish line: completing the Chinese herb program at Tai Sophia run by Cara Frank, a respected Chinese herbalist and owner of the China Herb Company, whose passion for herbs was infectious. Our classes met for three-day weekends about once a month over two and a half years.

LEARNING MAGIC

In our first year we had to identify over three hundred herbs, memorize their properties (taste, smell, thermal nature, etc.), and know what organs they affected. In our second year, we learned how to combine them into over two hundred formulas to treat specific conditions. Under the guidance of a clinical supervisor, we'd prescribe formulas for real patients, carefully selecting ingredients from our dispensary, stocked with the most commonly used medicinals in the Chinese materia medica, which was among the world's oldest and most sophisticated pharmacopeias. Although formulas are commercially available in the form of pills, tablets, tinctures, capsules, and powders, we chose raw herbs that patients had to cook and take as a tea. According to traditionalists these self-prepared decoctions are the most effective. Pulling together herbs to make a formula is like a chef putting together a food recipe.

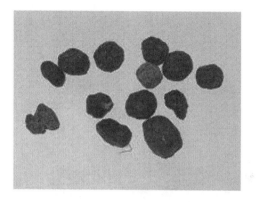

Flying squirrel poop

Although mostly parts of plants (leaves, stems, flowers, roots), herb ingredients also include mineral and animal products, such as scorpions, centipedes, sea horses and earthworms. One of the more exotic, Excrementum Trogopterori seu Pteromi (flying squirrel poop), promotes blood circulation, stops bleeding, reduces pain, and, among other things, treats abdominal pain and uterine bleeding. Our instructor encouraged us to feel, smell, and taste the herbs we handled, but I chose to skip this last task and instead accepted the textbook categorization that squirrel poop "has a bittersweet flavor."

THE SUPPORT OF FAMILY AND FRIENDS

I was lucky that Vicki and our kids didn't mind seeing my nose being buried in a textbook or me cooking up weird-looking stuff that smelled up the house. I was also grateful that despite his occasional grumbling, Ray took over the daily management of our martial arts school to enable me to pursue my studies. With his grudging approval, I constructed two small treatment rooms inside our martial arts studio, opening for business in September 2004, and offering to contribute a fixed percentage of my clinic's monthly income to the school as rent. I saw it as a win-win situation, but I think Ray viewed the clinic as a distraction, if not an encroachment, on our joint venture.

For the first few months, when I didn't have patients scheduled, I apprenticed with a former MITCM teacher to observe not only his treatment protocols but also to learn his business practices. At a marketing event I met Yu Yu, a licensed acupuncturist and graduate of one of China's best medical schools, who specialized in Chinese medical massage (or tuina). From a medical family (his mother is a senior TCM doctor in China, and his father is a Western-trained medical doctor who also practices Chinese medicine), Yu Yu came to the United States on a student visa, graduated with a degree in computer science, and works for a nearby software firm. I invited him to join my new clinic on a part-time basis so that he could help out during his lunch hour, after work, and when I was on vacation.

But even with his part-time assistance, I was essentially on my own without a clinical supervisor to double-check whether or not I was needling the right point or prescribing the right formula. It would take several years of experience and continuing education for me to feel comfortable handling the complex problems that would come my way. Many of my patients were trying acupuncture only after exhausting other remedies. Some disliked the side effects of pharmaceuticals. Others had seen Oprah getting acupuncture on television. Most thought their problems would vanish after one or two treatments, so one of the first things I had to learn was how to manage their unrealistic expectations. As a rule of thumb, it takes about one month of twice-weekly acupuncture treatments to get results for every year you've had a health problem. The effects of acupuncture are cumulative, I told my patients, provided the treatments are reinforced with timely follow-up visits.

IS IT GOING TO HURT?

A high percentage of the patients I treat come in because of a pain condition. People have a misperception that acupuncture is only used to treat pain. Marsha, a typical patient, called to make an appointment.

"Can acupuncture help with neck and shoulder pain?"

"Yes, it can be quite effective."

"What's it cost?"

"An initial visit averages $175, and follow-ups are about $90."

"How long does a session last?"

"Your first visit may last ninety minutes, follow-ups about 30 to 45 minutes."

"How many visits before I get relief?"

"Patients generally see results after five to ten visits. Each person responds differently, and much depends on the root cause of the problem."

Marsha, in her midthirties, had been suffering from neck and shoulder pain for over three years. Her pain was sharp and stabbing; she indicated it was an eight out of a possible ten on the level of intensity, radiating down the length of her arm. Steroid shots provided only temporary relief, and pain medications didn't do much except upset her stomach. In Chinese medicine we say, "Where there is pain, there is a lack of free flow of qi. When there is free flow, there is no pain."

She relaxed when I reassured her that acupuncture is safe and relatively painless. Using a technique I learned from Dr. Richard Tan called the "balanced method," I inserted a total of twelve needles to a depth of no more than a fraction of an inch. They went into areas mostly below her knees and elbows, not in her neck or shoulders as she had expected. Dr. Tan said the effects should be instantaneous, using the phrase *li gan jian ying* to describe what should happen (translated as: "when you erect a pole, you should see its shadow"). After inserting the needles, I had her rotate her neck and shoulders. She smiled, saying that her pain had gone down by more than 90 percent.

"Wow, I didn't know it would work this fast!" Marsha's response was one I never get tired of hearing. "How does this work?" I pointed to the charts hanging on the wall.

"See the lines running up and down the body?" I said. "They're similar to electrical circuits. Think of your body as a giant circuit board. The needles act as switches that connect the circuits." Dr. Tan said to avoid using TCM jargon, at least initially, so as not to confuse patients with esoteric terminology.

"How long have you been doing acupuncture?" she asked, no doubt thinking that I must have been an experienced practitioner based on my age, weathered face, and white hair. A look of incredulity replaced her smile when I told her I was newly licensed, having been in practice less than a year. "Oh, so where are you from originally?" she asked, perhaps expecting me to say China or Taiwan—perhaps from a long line of Chinese doctors— and noticeably gulping when I told her I was born in Brooklyn. Would she have come had she known I was a New York-born neophyte? I chuckled at the thought of her suppressing the urge to jump off the treatment table and run out the door. But by the time she might have considered going to the acupuncturist down the street, it was too late. She couldn't move, at least not easily, and not with the dozen needles I'd already stuck in her.

Fortunately, Marsha responded well to the first treatment, returning for five more until her pain vanished. Then she returned a month later, this time for help with weight loss, infertility, and other concerns. On her first visit, she'd skipped several sections of my questionnaire about appetite, digestion, bowel movements, menstrual cycle, urination, and sleep, assuming they were irrelevant to her neck and shoulder pain. But I told her that her answers would help me treat the root causes of her problems and not merely the branch symptoms, explaining that Chinese medical diagnosis can detect potential illnesses before they become serious.

I knew her pain, weight, and infertility problems were linked and more than physical in origin. The taut quality of her pulses and the stiff way she carried herself signaled physical tension from emotional stress. Her tongue looked swollen and pale, with a greasy white coating, indicating weak digestion, not only due to poor food choices but also due to stress. She wondered how I knew without asking that she had brittle nails, abdominal bloating, insomnia, and loose stools. After giving her acupuncture and a

Chinese herbal formula, I sent her home with two sheets of self-care information—one for nutrition, the other on qigong.

I told her to think of her body as a car and her digestive system as the engine that converts fuel into useable energy; when the system isn't efficient, leftover fuel turns into system-clogging sludge. In Marsha's case, the sludge showed up as excess body fat, nasal mucus, and high cholesterol. While her doctor's lab tests didn't indicate anemia, according to Chinese medicine, her poor digestion caused a blood deficiency that led to brittle nails, dry skin, and insomnia.

I explained that when she's "uptight," her body constricts the flow of energy and vital nutrients. Our digestive systems work best when relaxed, I pointed out, but she seldom made time to enjoy a carefree meal. Breakfast was coffee and a bagel consumed as she negotiated rush-hour traffic; lunch was either skipped or eaten during a business meeting or working at her computer—typically a salad washed downed with an ice-cold diet soda. Cold and raw foods, according to Chinese medicine, overtax the digestive system, which churns what you consume into a soup like mixture so the body can transform it efficiently. Salads, ice cream, iced drinks, and most fruits are thermally cold. The spleen/pancreas likes dryness and warmth. "So that's why I have stomachaches and diarrhea!" she said.

She felt guilty about giving in to her craving for cookies and ice cream, which also reflected her weak digestion. The weaker it was, the more she craved. And the more stressed she was, the weaker her digestion became, I explained. Dinners, although better balanced, were not tension-free because she used the dinner hour to complain about work or argue with her husband, thus diverting energy from processing her meal. Consuming it an hour or so before bed, not allowing the four hours needed for complete digestion and letting it ferment in her stomach, caused bloating and gastric upset.

EMOTIONAL HEALTH

Marsha, who worked as an executive assistant for a demanding boss, pulled twelve-hour days. I said her symptoms were her body's way of telling her to pay attention to how she treated herself—not just physically, but emotionally. If she didn't pay attention, her health would get worse until she did. But just telling patients to "chill out" doesn't work because most don't know how. So I introduced her to the five-thousand-year-old practice of qigong as a way to de-stress and, more importantly, to activate her body's self-healing abilities. "Think of it as Chinese yoga," I said, explaining that qigong means "energy cultivation." Warriors practiced it to strengthen their bodies. Daoist priests used it to attain longevity. Buddhist monks practiced it to reach spiritual enlightenment. And Confucian scholars believed it would build moral character.

Ancient figures doing qigong movements

There are thousands of qigong styles. Although they differ in focus, all can help harmonize the mind, body, and spirit. Most involve physical movement, body postures, mental focus, and breathing techniques. I've learned several styles for martial arts and found practicing qigong gave me more power, stamina, and the ability to recover faster. However, I didn't pay attention to qigong's healing benefits until I took a required class in acupuncture school, discovering that qigong therapy was the focus of many Chinese medical classics, including one of the oldest medical texts completed in 500 AD, that included 213 qigong movements. Qigong and Chinese medicine share the same concept, that health is maintained as long as there is an abundant supply of blood, energy, and vital substances flowing unobstructed through the body.

I began teaching patients simple qigong techniques to enhance what I was doing for them clinically, which was especially beneficial for those who can't afford acupuncture treatments as often as they need. Qigong helped clear their energy pathways between visits and at least doubled the effectiveness of my acupuncture and herbal treatments. However, as my practice grew, I had less time to teach qigong during clinic hours. When I suggested taijiquan classes that included meditation training at our martial arts school, most patients claimed they didn't have time to attend regular classes. That motivated me to look for self-study material they could learn and practice at home. I found three high-quality programs that were easy to follow and based on authentic Chinese medicine principles. They had instructional DVDs and CDs to facilitate home study. (I personally went through each program for at least three months before recommending them to anyone.)

I asked Marsha to try the one I thought would help her most, but I didn't hear from her until six months later when she called for a tune-up acupuncture treatment. She said her daily practice of the qigong program I'd recommended turned her life around. She no longer needed sleeping pills, was off antidepressants, had lost twenty pounds, improved her marriage, and was pregnant. "This is the best I've felt in years!" she said. I was happy to get Marsha's positive feedback about a specific program I'd learned about seemingly by accident via a mail advertisement.

CHAPTER 18

EVERYTHING IS ENERGY!

When the student is ready, the master appears.

—BUDDHIST PROVERB

Standing before the more than three hundred people seated in a Minneapolis hotel ballroom, the organizer began, "OK, when I move my hand in your direction, shout out where you're from!"

As he slowly swept his arm across the room from left to right, people called out: "Ireland! Australia! Sweden! England! New Jersey! Denmark! Mexico! Singapore! Honolulu! South Africa! California! New York! Texas!"

"Virginia!" I yelled.

Housewives, yoga teachers, carpenters, artists, musicians—people with varied interests, backgrounds, and occupations, some traveling from across the world—came to attend a weeklong Spring Forest Qigong (SFQ) retreat. Those with debilitating illnesses came to be healed. Physicians, having heard how SFQ had helped their patients, came to see for themselves. "I come year after year because Master Lin continues to evolve and bring fresh perspectives each time," said a doctor from Singapore.

I came to see if SFQ creator Chunyi Lin was for real, never having heard of him until an envelope from the Learning Strategies Corporation came in the mail, not even addressed to me but to Vicki. To make sure it wasn't just junk mail before tossing it, I read the enclosed letter which said you don't have to spend years learning qigong to be able to heal people. Intrigued by this bold statement, and by testimonials about this purported qigong master's ability to make cancerous tumors shrink, I sent for his self-study materials.

I was surprised that after only a few months, I was able to attain better results compared with other programs I'd tried for much longer. For example, I'd been doing a meditation called the microscopic orbit for years but had trouble feeling the energy move around the two main pathways that run along the centerline of the body; I'd get distracted after a few minutes. However, the first time I tried Chunyi Lin's method, I felt a warm, tingling current flow around the entire circuit. Wow!

Wanting to know more, I bought Chunyi Lin's Amazon bestseller *Born a Healer*, an inspiring story of his transformation from a tragic victim of the Cultural Revolution to an international qigong master who has helped thousands of people. As a teenager he saw his uncle buried alive, his father arrested, and his family hunted like criminals. Classmates beat him up and neighbors betrayed him. Wracked by physical and emotional pain, he was on the verge of suicide when a friend suggested he see a qigong master visiting his hometown. It was a pivotal encounter, one that relieved his pain and changed his life.

As I sat in the ballroom waiting for Master Lin to appear, I wondered if the research reports about his work with the Mayo Clinic were true. Did he really make cancerous tumors disappear? I was open-minded but skeptical, having met too many self-proclaimed "healers" with a messiah complex. I didn't want to recommend his program to my patients unless I was absolutely sure that he was who he claimed to be.

Thin, about five foot-nine, blessed with fine facial features, a smooth complexion, and appearing younger that his actual age, Master Lin got up to speak. Projecting a casual confidence—the kind that comes with knowledge of what he wanted to say—he greeted the crowd with a hearty "How ya doin' today?" in his rendition of a Minnesotan twang. Since he'd been head of an English department at a college in China, his command of the language was excellent despite his unmistakable Chinese accent. When asked how he wound up in Minneapolis, he said he came to the Twin Cities on an exchange program for visiting scholars. He loved the place and returned to carry out his vision: "A healer in every family and a world without pain."

Seemingly devoid of ego, he asked everyone to call him by his first name, which was unusual for a Chinese master. His senior students in America ribbed him about his "Chinglish." His followers in China would have treated him with extreme deference. Chunyi, as if reading my mind, said he liked placing himself below others and treating everyone as his teacher, not the other way around. "I didn't call myself 'master'; my students gave me that title," he said.

Realizing you don't have to apprentice for a lifetime or marry into the master's family to be able to heal others—because everyone is born with this gift—Chunyi Lin created a system of healing, one built on a solid, five-thousand-year-old foundation of classical Chinese philosophical thought and medical theory. Having expertise in acupuncture, massage, Chinese herbs, nutrition, feng sui, martial arts, and qigong, having studied with many of China's most renowned masters, and having extensively researched the ancient Daoist, Buddhist, and Confucian classics, Master Lin, I concluded, was no snake oil salesman.

With an amazing ability to identify someone's specific health problem long-distance, without ever having met the person, he demonstrated this skill during lunch when a woman from Australia, concerned about her father's failing health, asked for advice. Master Lin, never having met her or her father before, sat silent for a minute before saying, "There's a growth in your father's abdomen." He pinpointed the exact spot where her father had a tumor, which was confirmed by a scan only a week earlier. The woman said she hadn't told anyone about it before and thanked Master Lin for offering to send her father healing energy.

Having heard more testimonies of what some might describe as miracles, there was now no doubt, at least in my mind, that he was a gifted healer. But I still had one or two nagging questions: could I learn the things that he could do? And, more importantly, could I teach others how to do it? For answers I looked to his top students. You can tell the level of the martial arts master by the caliber of his or her disciples, so I applied the same yardstick to assess whether or not to dive deeper into SFQ, which had, at the time, four levels of instruction.

I found the core group of senior students and instructors around him generous in sharing their knowledge and skills, well-grounded people who walked the talk of "love, kindness, and forgiveness." One of them told me, "Chunyi doesn't want us to follow him blindly or put him on a pedestal." Then there was also the personal connection I felt with a man who practiced Chinese martial arts in his youth, still did taijiquan an hour a day, loved playing basketball (my favorite team sport), enjoyed watching kung fu movies, and spoke my native Chinese dialect. Frankly, if I'd won a free trip to anyplace in the world, Minneapolis probably wouldn't have come to mind as a first-choice destination—maybe not a second or even a third choice. But there I was, booking reservations for another visit even before I got home. I would, over the next five years, return many more times to complete all four levels of SFQ.

THE TWIN CITIES (THREE YEARS LATER)

I tried not to panic as I looked for my attaché case. I'd just arrived at the Ramada Inn when I realized it was gone, and with it my laptop, cell phone, house and car keys, and appointments calendar. Did I leave it on the shuttle? The desk clerk called the driver, who said it wasn't in the van. My heart sank. I was sure it was with me on landing at Minneapolis-St. Paul International. Did I leave it at the shuttle lounge?

OK, calm down, I told myself as I waited for the next shuttle back to the airport. I was in the Twin Cities again, this time for my SFQ instructor certification so that I could teach my patients this simple-yet-powerful way to enhance physical, emotional, and spiritual health.

As I boarded the van, I remembered Master Lin said my spiritual journey requires letting go of attachments, but couldn't this have waited till I got home? As I tried to quiet my thoughts, a white-haired couple climbed aboard the van. The man had on a blue baseball cap that had "WWII Veteran" in gold lettering and pinned with miniature campaign ribbons. He wore an oversized replica of a Purple Heart attached to a corded string necktie

"Excuse me, sir, I see that you're a veteran," I said as we headed for the airport. He turned, smiled warmly, and said, "Yes, sir, I'm Ruben Montoya." When I asked about the Purple Heart, he said he was wounded in Europe after only three weeks in combat and went on to describe his war experience without bravado. After hospitalization and months of rehabilitation, he attended college on the GI Bill, became an engineer, and later retired in Santa Fe. He visits VA hospitals to give veterans his hand-carved wooden figures. His creations, inspired by the desert landscapes of New Mexico, have a healing quality, according to his wife. I pictured Ruben carving a piece of wood at sunset, silhouetted against a clear sky, a shimmering sun descending behind a turquoise plateau.

When I told them I'd lost my attaché case, Ruben said, "Let's all think positive. You know, whenever I pray for something, I erase all doubt."

We sat in silent meditation as the shuttle pulled into the airport. The driver then told me, "You don't have much time because I have to get these folks over to the next terminal." I ran into the lounge, barely giving the automatic doors a chance to open, trying to ignore a message over the loudspeaker warning passengers against leaving bags unattended. I blocked out the noise and replaced it with Ruben's message: "Erase all doubt!" People moved aside as I strode toward the bench. And there my case sat, just as I'd visualized it.

Ruben and his wife cheered as I climbed back into the van, holding my attaché case with both hands raised over my head like a trophy. We bid each other farewell as we continued our separate journeys. That evening, I Googled him on the Internet and found this: "Ruben O. Montoya is the son of Dolores Ortiz Kozlowski and is a World War II Purple Heart and

Bronze Medal recipient. He retired from Los Alamos National Laboratory in 1973 and since then had devoted his life to religious art. His work is featured in museums in Berlin, Moscow, Oklahoma, Missouri, Arkansas, and South Carolina."

A MESSAGE FROM MONTOYA

To be an SFQ instructor requires not only completing four levels of training but also attaining certification as a level 1 "master healer," a credential that I hoped would help me promote qigong. But as a novice in SFQ compared to others far more advanced in their practice—and despite Chunyi Lin's assurances that each of us had the requisite knowledge, skills and ability to be master healers—doubts persisted in my mind well before I arrived in Minnesota. *Could I live up to the lofty-sounding title?* I wondered. Little did I know the answer would show up in the form of a message from Montoya: "Erase all doubt!"

During the days that followed, I listened to Master Lin review the principles of SFQ. He emphasized that healing is not about technique; it's about practicing love, kindness, and forgiveness. "If you want to be a good healer, you must really love people from the bottom of your heart," he said. Master Lin defined compassion as passion plus action, i.e., doing something you love in the service of others. He said that through our daily thoughts, words, and deeds we would have the chance to purify ourselves so that we could become radiators of love, the most powerful form of healing energy. In so doing we could influence, in a positive way, everything and everyone around us.

As we broke into discussion groups to review these concepts, I shared my story about Ruben, citing him as someone who exemplified compassion: using his love for woodcarving to make gifts for wounded veterans to help them heal. It would motivate me to offer free acupuncture treatments and qigong classes to wounded warriors.

During the conference I recalled a few things that made me think that my brief encounter with Ruben was not an accident. Perhaps it was our hotel, formerly called the Thunderbird, with its southwestern motif; or the walls of our conference room, with paintings of ancient healers, including an Indian medicine man who bore a striking resemblance to Ruben; or the painting next to it of a Chinese imperial court physician wearing a gold tunic embroidered with white cranes—and Crane Mountain in China being my ancestral home. Or maybe it was just my imagination, my wish for some divine inspiration. In the final analysis, it didn't matter because the outcome was the same: I was open to the possibility that Ruben and I were destined to meet.

Thanks to Master Lin, my mind had opened to a world that I hadn't been fully conscious of before, a world beyond so-called scientific proof, a world beyond physical form, a world of infinite possibilities. This would eventually lead me to complete a three-year program of study in medical qigong, first with Dr. Lisa Vanostrand, then with Dr. Bernard Shannon, both gifted healers who had trained under Dr. Jerry Johnson[38]

INFINITE POTENTIAL

One day after kung fu class, I overheard Kiyoshi telling others: "I want to learn the Yuen Method!" Kiyoshi, a massage therapist, reiki practitioner, and one of my best students, remarked that his friend had seen a demonstration of a wellness system created by Kam Yuen and had been impressed with its effectiveness in treating pain and other problems.

My ears perked up at the mention of a name from my boyhood past. "I know Kam Yuen!" I chimed in. Since there aren't many people with that name, I guessed they were talking about my old friend from New York's Chinatown. As teenagers, we'd played on the same basketball team, the Courtiers. Whenever anyone passed him the ball he'd invariably charge toward the basket and take a shot, even with two or three people guarding him.

"When was the last time you saw him?" Kiyoshi asked.

---

38 Dr. Johnson authored a comprehensive set of textbooks on Chinese medical qigong therapy and designed a curriculum modeled after one used by the Medical Qigong College at the Hai Dian University of Traditional Chinese Medicine in Beijing.

"Must have been well over thirty years ago," I said. "Ran into him strolling along Grant Avenue in San Francisco. He'd been working as an aerospace engineer in Silicon Valley and was on his way to Los Angeles," I recalled.

We'd lost contact, but mutual friends (including Tony, my fellow Marine and CIA ops officer) told me that after moving to L.A. Kam landed a job in Hollywood as the martial arts consultant and stunt coordinator for the *Kung Fu* television series starring David Carradine. I enjoyed watching Kam's appearances as a bald-headed Shaolin monk but found it strange that they dubbed his voice. Maybe it was his Hong Kong accent, but I thought it would have added authenticity to the character he was playing.

Kam opened a Chinese martial arts school in Los Angeles and attracted celebrity students, including the Jackson Five. Two of my martial arts friends who'd studied with Kam attested to his high level of skill. The World Black Belt Organization had called him a "living legend." He eventually went back to school to become a chiropractic doctor. His career trajectory, from engineer to martial artist to medical professional, inspired mine.

Our shared interests in martial arts and alternative medicine helped us reconnect. Kam read an article about me and Ray in an *Inside Kung-Fu* magazine article written by Stephan Berwick, my Chen style taijiquan teacher, who I would later discover knew Kam's cousin in Boston. Kam e-mailed to say he was proud of what I was doing and, in answer to my question about what he'd been doing, mentioned creating a new system of wellness that got fantastic results. He said he was traveling around the world teaching his method and attracting a large international following.

Curious, I Googled to learn more. His website described how Kam had synthesized Daoist practices, his martial arts experience, and chiropractic studies to successfully treat thousands of patients suffering from acute or chronic health conditions. According to his website: "Dr. Yuen has taken wellness and everyday living to new levels." It listed many Hollywood personalities that he had helped and three books he had authored: *Instant Rejuvenation*, *Instant Healing*, and *Instant Pain Relief*.

YouTube clips showed Kam getting rid of pain without touching people physically. He claimed he could do it long-distance. How could that be possible? Just the titles of his books seemed like marketing hype. I had known Kam as a star athlete and great martial artist, but I thought his claims were exaggerated at best. As an engineer by training, my mind demanded scientific proof.

But that was before taking a qigong healing class in acupuncture school, before using energy to treat illness without needles, before learning Spring Forest Qigong, and before my mind opened to a world that Western science was only just beginning to acknowledge. So six years later, when Kiyoshi mentioned his name seemingly out of the blue, I took it as a sign to recontact Kam and find out what his method was all about.

I invited Kam to a biannual reunion in Las Vegas for people who had grown up in New York's Chinatown. I told Chinatown buddies he'd be there. They remembered Kam from the old days and knew about his previous work on *Kung Fu*, but when I tried to describe what he'd been doing lately, they were even more skeptical than I had been initially.

Except for a few gray hairs, Kam hadn't changed much physically. Despite being close to seventy, he looked vibrant—living proof that whatever he was doing was working, at least for him. While it's not a requirement for a physician to look healthy to help others, I've always been a bit leery of getting treated by anyone who seemed like they needed more help than I did. I visited a dentist once with bad breath and never went back.

While Kam and I were standing around chatting and catching up on old times, one of the reunion committee members, perhaps thinking I could stick him with a few needles, came up to me complaining of excruciating lower-back pain. Instead I introduced him to Kam, who, within a few minutes, made the man's pain completely vanish. Impressed, I asked if he'd be willing to demonstrate his method again on others.

When we gathered for a buffet dinner, I asked the organizer to introduce Kam to the audience. She agreed that the crowd would enjoy seeing what he could do. When I broached the idea with Kam, he was a bit reluctant at first, sensing people might not be receptive. I realized it was a bad idea when the organizer introduced Kam as a chiropractor, because chiropractic adjustment wasn't what he'd be demonstrating. She invited Kam to come up on stage, thanking him for having helped her get over a recent illness but not explaining what he'd done exactly, and probably not understanding it herself.

He asked for volunteers to come up, for anyone with any kind of pain or health concern that he could help resolve. I thought this would be the moment when Kam would amaze people with how quickly he could make pain go away, the moment when people would see why their hometown boy had such a huge international following, the moment when they would realize he was more than just a chiropractor. But no one stirred: out of an audience of more than three hundred people, not one person got up. Perhaps they thought he was going to wrench their necks. (Alas, a man is never a prophet in his own country.) Undaunted, Kam told the audience he'd developed a system based on knowledge that had been kept secret for thousands of years, explaining that people usually paid hundreds of dollars to get his treatments or to attend his workshops, but he was going to do it gratis. After an interminably long pause, only three people were brave enough to step forward. To make matters worse, just as Kam was getting started, someone interrupted his demonstration by jumping on stage unannounced to make an award presentation to the organizer.

I was embarrassed and later apologized to him for having put him on the spot. I should have gone up and introduced him properly, realizing too late that most people had no idea who he was or what he wanted to do. Kam, however, being supremely self-confident (some might mistake it as arrogant), said the crowd's tepid response didn't faze him.

I persuaded him to come to Washington, DC, to do one of his seminars. He graciously invited Vicki and me to attend. After the seminar, Vicki became more open to energy work and started practicing qigong exercises and meditation regularly despite being reluctant initially. It was an even more mind-opening experience for me, one that would lead me not only to learn the Yuen Method and deepen my study of other facets of energy medicine,[39] but also to return to the study of science—not the older science of Isaac Newton and René Descartes, but the newer theories of Werner Heisenberg and David Bohm, theories very much in line with the ones that the Chinese ancients introduced five thousand years earlier.

The language of quantum physics sounds more and more like metaphysics. Or, as Gary Zukav[40] so aptly stated, "The new physics sounds very much like old Eastern mysticism." To put it more bluntly, quantum physics is now showing us that the theories that underlie Chinese medicine and qigong are not New Age mumbo jumbo.

PROFESSOR LEE

Chinese astrologers map a person's destiny in ten-year cycles to help individuals and businesses make important decisions. I started formal training in Chinese medicine in 2001. Exactly ten years later, my friend and fellow acupuncturist Hee Jung called to ask if I'd be interested in teaching at the Virginia University of Oriental Medicine (VUOM). She'd been the administrative officer for our alma mater, the Maryland Institute of Traditional Chinese Medicine. She said Dr. Lixing Lao, formerly the clinic director at the Institute and now the newly appointed president of VUOM, had been recruited to spearhead efforts to make VUOM a leading academic center for Oriental Medicine. Dr. Lao, in turn, had recruited Hee Jung to be the academic dean. To beef up the faculty, she was contacting former Institute teachers and graduates, including me. Although flattered by her invitation, I wanted to see what I was getting into, so I looked up the university's program description:

{The University's} primary academic program is the Master of Science in Oriental Medicine degree, which includes the extensive study of diagnostics, methods

---

39 Kam would differentiate his method from others by studiously avoiding the use of such terms as "energy medicine" or "healing" or "healer."

40 Gary Zukav, author of *The Dancing Wu Li Masters: An Overview of the New Physics*

of treatment, and acupuncture and Chinese herbology. The program is also designed to prepare students to sit for licensure examination. University students are NOT currently eligible to qualify for NCCAOM and state licensure examinations.

The last sentence made it clear that the first thing the new administration and faculty had to do was help the university gain accreditation. Without accreditation, students couldn't take the national board exams required by most states for licensure. I contacted Bill Reddy, a friend and fellow Maryland Institute graduate who was teaching at VUOM. I valued his judgment as a leader within the US acupuncture community and knew he'd give me a candid assessment. The students, he observed, were mainly from Korea, and classes had been taught in Korean. However, one of the requirements for accreditation was that classes had to be conducted in English. Many of the students, he said, had difficulty understanding his lectures because of their poor English comprehension.

Bill also warned me not to expect much in terms of compensation; it would be much less than what I'd earn for the same amount of time spent treating patients at my own clinic. He said the Korean woman who owned the university had appealed to his sense of community to accept a lower salary for now, claiming they were just getting started and couldn't afford higher salaries. On the positive side, Bill said the owner seemed serious about the school's future, and she had signed up board members with strong business and academic credentials to help develop it into a first-class academic institution.

I met with Hee Jung the next day at VUOM's suburban campus in Fairfax, Virginia. It occupied the entire ground floor, with classrooms on the upper floors of a three-story building (shared with a bible college). Hee Jung showed me the extensive renovations completed as a first step toward meeting certification standards: classrooms with the latest audio-visual devices, clinic treatment rooms that were well furnished, and a student dispensary stocked with a complete line of raw, powdered, and patent herbs.

Hee Jung asked if I could handle twice-weekly classes, saying I could choose whatever I felt comfortable teaching, from basic theory to advanced courses in acupuncture and herbs. Knowing my Chinese martial arts and qigong background, she wanted me to consider those subjects as well. "Here's a course catalogue. Let me know what you're willing to do," she said.

Treating patients five days a week, teaching martial arts classes three nights a week (I was still at the martial arts school then), and traveling to New York for medical qigong classes one weekend a month, I wondered if I'd have enough time and energy to squeeze in a teaching load. After mulling it over and discussing it with Vicki, I decided to join the faculty for several reasons.

First, the university had the potential to fill a great void. To me it was inconceivable that there wasn't a single institution in the greater Washington metropolitan area offering an accredited graduate program in acupuncture and Traditional Chinese Medicine. In the face of our nation's healthcare crisis, the demand for alternative and complementary care to serve the needs of the community had never been greater. Second, I had confidence in Dr. Lao, one of the most respected clinicians in the country, and in Hee Jung, a capable administrator, knowing they wouldn't commit to something they didn't believe in. Last but not least, it would force me to review what I'd learned—or should have learned—by teaching it.

I told Hee Jung I'd only have time for one evening a week at the university. To get my feet wet, I started as a clinical supervisor mentoring interns at the student clinic. I kept in mind my own struggles as a student trying to figure out how to locate acupuncture points. I was happy to share what I knew with mostly bright interns eager to learn, including one named Don. A structural engineer during the day, and having a wife and two kids to support, he couldn't afford giving up his regular job, but he loved studying acupuncture and Chinese medicine.

The next quarter I taught a class in taijiquan, a required subject. For a text, I used a book I'd edited and coauthored: *Yang Style Tai Ji Quan: A Beginner's Guide*. It came with an instructional DVD demonstrating the forty movements of the routine. Some of the students were able to learn the entire routine, but others had difficulty remembering the moves. Weary from their eight-hour day jobs, they couldn't focus. A class once a week just didn't give them enough time to practice. I had unrealistically expected them to catch on much faster than they were capable of doing.

Even though some students didn't seem interested in really learning the material, I was especially grateful for those who were conscientious about studying. The more enthusiastic they were, the more effective I was; the more they wanted to learn, the more I wanted to teach them.

For the following quarter, I taught a medical qigong class using instructional material from Spring Forest Qigong. The ten-week course provided just enough time for students to learn level one (how to heal yourself) and level two (how to heal others). I hoped they'd be able to grasp key qigong concepts better than they had taijiquan since Chinese medicine and qigong share the same theories and principles. During the course, they learned how to detect energy blockages and treat each other by moving and transmitting energy with just their hands and intentions. For homework, they were required to practice on friends and family.

"Remember, whether you're treating patients with needles or your hands, your technique is less important than your intention," I reminded them. "Your patients heal themselves. You're just catalysts, so get your egos out of the way, and don't focus on the outcome."

Because one or two of the students in the class had shown a lack of interest in the material, treating it as a required course to be endured instead of a chance to increase knowledge, I was unsure how well I was doing as a teacher. The final exam, in which students would have to diagnose and treat real patients, would tell me whether or not I was getting through to the rest of the class.

I brought Kristen into the classroom, a real patient whom they'd never met, and assigned two of the students to diagnose what was ailing her without asking what was bothering her. Using their hands like metal detectors to scan her body, they located blockages that pointed to physiological dysfunction. Then, visualizing laser beams shooting out from their fingers, they cut away the obstructions before using their palms to activate the smooth flow of qi and restore harmony to Kristen's body.

After the treatment I asked the students what they'd found. "I felt a blockage around her head area," said one. "I detected a problem in her lower abdomen," said the other. Kristen surprised the class by confirming the accuracy of their diagnosis, saying that she'd come to the clinic with a splitting headache and that she'd been having premenstrual cramps earlier that day. Kristen, who sat relaxed in a chair with her eyes closed during the whole treatment, remarked, "I don't know what you did, but my headache's gone and I feel so much better now. Thank you so much!"

That was the moment I knew that joining the VUOM faculty had been the right decision, one reaffirmed two years later when the Commission for the Accreditation of Acupuncture and Oriental Medicine granted VUOM and its master's degree program candidacy status, meaning that our graduates could sit for national board exams.

ANOTHER DOOR OPENS

When I retired from teaching regular martial arts classes, it also meant that I had to look for a new home for my clinic. It had been located inside the school, and Ray wanted to convert my two clinic treatment rooms to store supplies and to expand the martial arts training area. I asked a fellow acupuncturist whether I should buy or rent a place. "Hon, at your age how many more years are you going to practice? It's easier if you just rent."

I saw his logic. I was, after all, almost seventy years old, and buying property at this stage in my life, when most people have already retired, would be a big investment, one that I might not recoup. On the other hand, I wanted to practice medicine for as long as I could and to do it with maximum flexibility, setting office hours according to my own schedule and not someone else's. So I purchased an office condo with enough space for three treatment rooms, located just ten minutes from home.

New clinic front entrance

I've arrived at a happy place now, doing what I love, doing it even if I were to win the Mega Millions lottery, doing it even if I were told I'd never have to work another day in my life. I don't view it as work but as a chance to satisfy my desire to make a positive difference in the lives of others. And one way to do that is by helping my patients get better and stronger via Chinese medicine and qigong— patients who are often unable to get the results they need from Western medicine. Don't get me wrong, I believe in Western medicine. It's fantastic, especially for treating acute conditions. I'd be the first in line at the emergency room if I had a serious, life-threatening injury. But for chronic conditions, the holistic methodologies first developed by the Chinese in ancient times, refined over thousands of years of scholarly research and clinical experience, offer much-needed, time-tested solutions to modern health problems.

Afterword

I don't know what your destiny will be, but one thing I know: the only ones among you who will be really happy are those who will have sought and found how to serve.

—Albert Schweitzer

I chose *Paths Less Travelled* as the title for my book because I wanted to explain why I selected one path over another when facing two often equally attractive life choices. For example, should I go for a draft-deferred engineering job or join the Marines and go to Vietnam? Should I accept a high-salary job with Ross Perot or become a spy with the CIA? Should I work as a government contractor with guaranteed benefits or fulfill my dream of practicing Chinese medicine without any financial assurances? Where the paths diverged, I followed my heart, and that has made all the difference.

Actually, all the paths I've travelled have intersected, all have been interrelated and mutually supporting—like yin and yang—and all have been well worn by others since time immemorial. The tales about the knights of ancient China and their daring exploits compelled me to follow my own variation of what was actually a singular path—a fourfold one of Scholar Warrior Teacher Healer.

THE SCHOLAR WARRIOR

In ancient China there was a warrior class known as "shi.[41]" This Chinese archetype dates back centuries, according to Ming Dao Deng, author of *Scholar Warrior.*

Such a person strives to develop a wide variety of talents…. Poet and boxer. Doctor and swordsman. Musician and knight…uses each part of his or her overall ability to keep the whole in balance and to attain the equilibrium for following the Tao. Lao Tzu was a renowned swordsman, and Confucius held the title of Leader of Knights.

As a Marine, I felt part of an elite brotherhood of warriors. Having gone to battle in Vietnam against an enemy we didn't understand, I realized, even as an expendable second lieutenant, the value of good intelligence. To "know your enemy," to paraphrase Sun Tzu, was half the key to winning a hundred battles. The other half of Sun Tzu's admonition was to "know yourself." As a CIA officer I believed the critical intelligence I tried to provide to US policymakers would help them "to subdue the enemy without fighting," which Sun Tzu described as "the acme of skill." My passion for Chinese martial arts and the healing arts led to a quest for greater self-knowledge.

In studying role models I could emulate, I observed that the most effective leaders, whether on the battlefield, playing field or boardroom, have presence of mind and clarity of spirit. Those I admired most exhibited "grace under fire" no matter what was happening around them or to them. But how might I acquire these attributes? For answers I looked to China's ancient warriors. They practiced some form of meditation and self-awareness. Studying qigong sprang from my desire to "still the mind and calm the spirit" so that I too could maintain equanimity in the face of adversity.

---

41 From Wikipedia: The Four ocupations, http://en.wikipedia.org/wiki/Four_occupations, accessed January 25, 2014. The shi (±): During the ancient Shang and Zhou dynasties, the *shi* were regarded as a knightly social order…distinguished by the weaponry they used, the double-edged sword, or *jian*…the *shi* eventually became renowned not for their warrior's skills, but for their scholarship, abilities in administration, and sound ethics and morality supported by competing philosophical schools.

THE TEACHER

I've had the privilege of leading Marines in combat and CIA officers in the field, and mentoring students of martial arts, medicine, and qigong. More rewarding than any form of external accolades received or rank attained has been the chance to help others reach their full potential. Whenever someone comes up to me, often decades later, to thank me for sharing my experience, knowledge, or skills with them, I'm always grateful to them for having given me the opportunity to do so.

As a Chinese martial arts teacher I've tried to honor those who have come before me, and I am thankful for the chance pass on the rich heritage of the Mizong and Jow Ga kung fu systems to my students. As a teacher of qigong and Chinese medicine I hope to follow the examples set by my mentors, especially those who are well-versed in the Daoist, Buddhist and Chinese medicine classics, to continue learning and growing. As someone once said, "I'm sometimes a teacher but always a student."

THE HEALER

Among my reasons for studying Chinese medicine was a desire to uphold the moral code of traditional Chinese martial arts, which considers it unethical to be able to hurt people without knowing how to heal them. Although I have a general practice and treat a variety of problems, I named my clinic Sports Edge Acupuncture to pay homage to martial arts medicine's focus on treating sprains, strains, and musculoskeletal and traumatic injuries.

Chinese martial arts and the healing arts enjoyed a synergistic relationship until the Cultural Revolution, when traditional martial arts and medicine were suppressed. This relationship, preserved within the overseas Chinese kung fu communities around the world, is only now being reestablished in China.

Martial arts medicine was a closely guarded secret within the Shaolin Temple. Valuable manuscripts on secret herbal formulas and Chinese boxing were destroyed during the Cultural Revolution; those that were not are now being rediscovered. For example, in 2011 the Temple unveiled a 101-volume collection including two-thousand-year-old documents on

Buddhist medicine. "We use medicines to cure people's physical illnesses and Buddhism to solve their mental problems; the combination of the two is aimed to restore the balance and harmony of man's body and spirit," said Shi Yongxin, Abbot of Shaolin and one of the principal compilers.[42]

In striving to become a better healer, one of the key lessons I learned was that "healers in all major traditions recognize that the power of love is the most potent healing force available to all human beings." [43] It's the same lesson that great healers, spiritual teachers, and religious leaders have been trying to convey throughout the ages.

...AND KNOW THE PLACE FOR THE FIRST TIME.[44]

After travelling my own version of the fourfold path, I realize the truth in the homily that the "journey, destination, and traveller are one," having come full-circle to discover that my mission in life is to be of service, a mission I hope to fulfill by using the healing arts to help others.

And as I aspire to become not only a better healer, but also a better person by following the Dao, perhaps it would help if I developed a more enlightened-appearing persona. First, I'll have to get rid of my New York accent. Next I'll need to order a silk gown with long, flowing sleeves. Then I'll have to grow a long, wispy white beard, one that I can stroke ever so slowly while uttering wise-sounding fortune cookie-type aphorisms.

"Aaah yes, grasshopper, you must become one with the donut hole."

---

42 Xinhua News Agency, 2011

43 Angeles Arrien. *The Fourfold Way*, New York: HarperOne, 1992, page 49.

44 "We shall not cease from exploration, and the end of all our exploring will be to arrive where we started and know the place for the first time." T. S. Eliot, *Four Quartets*, Section V.

ABOUT THE AUTHOR

Hon K. Lee, a retired Lieutenant Colonel in the United States Marine Corps Reserves, was an artillery forward observer and platoon commander in Vietnam. After leaving active duty, he became a CIA clandestine operations officer, serving undercover in seven field assignments and in three of the Agency's four directorates. Studying Chinese medicine after a 30 year CIA career, he is now a nationally certified and Virginia Medical Board licensed acupuncturist. When not practicing medicine, Lee practices martial arts, having co-founded a school that teaches kung fu, taijiquan and qigong. He's married, has two daughters, and enjoys living and working in Northern Virginia.

Made in the USA
San Bernardino, CA
28 February 2017